LITURGY IN

LITURGY IN DIALOGUE

ESSAYS IN MEMORY
OF
RONALD JASPER

Edited by

Paul Bradshaw and Bryan Spinks

First published in Great Britain 1993
Society for Promoting Christian Knowledge
Holy Trinity Church
Marylebone Road
London NW1 4DU

British Library Cataloguing-in-Publication Data

A catalogue record for this book is available from the British Library

ISBN 0-281-04734-0

Phototypeset by Paul Bradshaw
Printed in Great Britain at the University Press, Cambridge

Contents

The Contributors

Paul Bradshaw, an Anglican priest, formerly Vice-Principal of Ripon College, Cuddesdon, Oxford, is Professor of Liturgy at the University of Notre Dame, Indiana.

Raymond George is a distinguished British Methodist scholar who worked with Ronald Jasper in the Joint Liturgical Group. Now retired, he is President of the Society for Liturgical Study.

David Glover, an Anglican priest, is Chaplain of Hatfield College in the University of Durham. He has an M.Phil. in doctrine and liturgy from the University of Cambridge.

Gordon Jeanes, an Anglican priest, is the Cuming Fellow in Liturgy and Chaplain of St Chad's College in the University of Durham.

Maxwell Johnson, a Lutheran pastor, has a Ph.D. in liturgical studies from the University of Notre Dame, and is Assistant Professor of Liturgy at St John's University, Collegeville, Minnesota.

Ruth Meyers, a priest of the Episcopal Church, has a Ph.D. in liturgical studies from the University of Notre Dame, and is a member of the steering committee of the International Anglican Liturgical Consultation.

L. Edward Phillips, a Methodist minister, has a Ph.D. in liturgical studies from the University of Notre Dame, and is Head of the Department of Religion and Philosophy, Union College, Barbourville, Kentucky.

Catherine Pickstock, a graduate in English and Theology, is completing a Ph.D. on language and liturgy at the University of Cambridge.

Grant Sperry-White, a Methodist, has a Ph.D. in liturgical studies from the University of Notre Dame, and is Assistant Professor of Church History at St Paul School of Theology, Kansas City, Missouri.

Bryan Spinks, an Anglican priest, is Chaplain to the Chapel of Churchill College in the University of Cambridge, and a member of the Church of England Liturgical Commission.

Phillip Tovey, an Anglican priest, has taught liturgy in Africa and is currently serving within a Local Ecumenical Project church in Banbury, Oxfordshire.

Susan White, an Episcopalian, has a Ph.D. in liturgical studies from the University of Notre Dame, and is Lecturer and Tutor in Liturgy and Worship at Westcott House, Cambridge, England.

Preface

This volume is intended to be different in at least two ways from typical collections of essays, memorial volumes, and *Festschriften* within the field of liturgical studies. First, it is not exclusively about liturgy nor directed solely towards an audience interested in liturgical matters. Rather, it seeks to demonstrate that liturgy is not an isolated and self-contained subject, but on the contrary has a wide range of connections with other academic disciplines and other areas of religious and human concern—a dimension which was of considerable interest to Ronald Jasper himself. Questions raised by liturgical study and practice have ramifications for those interested in other areas, of which they need to be aware, and conversely liturgical scholars need to be attentive to the impact that advances and changes in other disciplines should have on their own work. Clearly in a volume of this size it has been impossible to cover everything which has some relation to liturgy. Nothing is said here, for example, about the unquestionably crucial subjects of architecture and music. All that we have been able to do is to begin to explore some obvious and some less obvious areas of connectedness, and perhaps suggest a fruitful dimension that others many want to take up in future publications.

The second major difference is that the contributors are for the most part not the well-established scholars in the field or close contemporaries of the person being honoured, but rather their more junior colleagues, the next generation of scholars, who are drawn from several Christian denominations on both sides of the Atlantic. The two editors chose to take this somewhat unusual course as a means of repaying in a small way the debt of gratitude which each of them owes for the great encouragement and support given by Ronald Jasper when they themselves were mere beginners in the field.

Paul Bradshaw was given his start in the pursuit of serious liturgical scholarship when Ronald enabled him to gain admittance as a Ph.D. student at King's College in the University of London in 1967, suggested the topic of the Anglican Ordinal as his dissertation there, and supervised his research work. Paul's subsequent first steps into publication and teaching were also due in large measure to invitations and opportunities provided by Ronald, and later in life the two of them collaborated on *A Companion to the Alternative Service Book* (SPCK, London 1986).

Bryan Spinks first encountered Ronald when the latter came to speak on the topic of liturgical revision to the ordinands of St Chad's College, Durham, and he went on to study under him for the M.Th. degree at King's College, London. As part of the work required for the degree, Bryan was encouraged by Ronald to write on the impact of the liturgical movement on the English Congregational Church, and this heralded the way for his B.D. thesis at the University of Durham on the eucharistic liturgy in the English Independent tradition from 1550 to 1975, completed in 1978. Although no formal supervision is provided for the work for this degree, Ronald kindly agreed to look at it as it progressed and offer advice. Ronald was again involved in Bryan's academic progress at a later date when he acted as one of the examiners for the D.D. degree awarded to Bryan by the University of Durham.

A bibliography of Ronald's works has not been included in this volume, since one will appear in the biography by Donald Gray, to be published by SPCK in 1995. In the meantime his entry in the *Dictionary of National Biography, 1986–1990*, edited by C. S. Nicholls (Oxford University Press), gives an outline of his life and achievements.

Paul Bradshaw
Bryan Spinks

August 1993

Ronald Jasper: An Appreciation

RAYMOND GEORGE

Ronald Claud Dudley Jasper, C.B.E., D.D., bore his honours and his learning lightly, but this must not disguise the fact that he was the chief architect not only of the *Alternative Service Book 1980* (hereafter *ASB*), but also of ecumenical co-operation in liturgical matters in the English-speaking world. In the Introduction to his invaluable book *The Development of the Anglican Liturgy 1662–1980* (hereafter *Development*)[1] he records that he had been a foundation member of the Liturgical Commission of the Church of England and the only one to remain until the appearance of the *ASB* in 1980, serving as its chairman for the last fifteen years. The last seven chapters of the book are thus autobiographical, and are essential reading for anyone interested in the history of liturgical revision. If they are compared with a somewhat similar account of the Roman Catholic process of revision found in Annibale Bugnini's *The Reform of the Liturgy 1948–1975*,[2] it can be seen that both processes were extremely intricate, though in different ways and for different reasons. Someone has remarked that this comparison reminds us that the Anglican work was done on a shoe-string, though indeed the supporting resources of the Church of England, though much smaller than those of Rome, were much greater than of the Free Churches. All the time Ronald Jasper held other academic or ecclesiastical offices, culminating in his being a Canon of Westminster and then Dean of York, and indeed in these capacities gave gracious hospitality in church and in his home to colleagues whom he had met in liturgical pursuits. He was also engaged in other literary work such as his biographies of Bishop Headlam and Bishop Bell as well as numerous writings on various aspects of liturgical history.

The Introduction to *Development* also records: 'Furthermore I had a large part in creating and running two other associated

[1] SPCK, London 1989.
[2] Liturgical Press, Collegeville 1990.

bodies, the Joint Liturgical Group and the International Consultation on English Texts.' It is primarily of these two bodies that I write, because I too was a foundation member of both of them and also because as a Methodist I necessarily observed his Anglican activities from without, and in any case they are fully recorded in *Development*.

The idea of the Joint Liturgical Group began in a conversation between Ronald Jasper and John Lamb of the Church of Scotland. Ronald took this up privately with Archbishop Donald Coggan, then the Chairman of the Church of England Liturgical Commission, who gave his permission to take soundings, and as a result a 'hand-picked' group met in March 1963. We agreed to form a Joint Liturgical Group, and the Archbishop of Canterbury (Michael Ramsey) was asked to write to the heads of other churches asking them to agree to the setting up of the Group, and inviting them to appoint two members each. This he gladly did, and he also produced a statement to the effect that the work of the Group would have no authority greater than that which its own members gave to it by their own weight, but that particular churches might make use of the results if they were willing to do so. The heads of the other churches willingly agreed to the formation of the Group and, almost or perhaps entirely without exception, appointed the members of the 'hand-picked' group.

This whole operation was a good example of Ronald working quietly behind the scenes to achieve a result which in the end was acclaimed and made official. It was possible only because those who knew him came immediately to trust him. It also showed the care with which he had conducted the soundings which had led to the choice of the members. So began JLG, as it is familiarly known; Douglas Harrison, Dean of Bristol, was elected Chairman, and Ronald records that 'it seemed to be assumed that I would be secretary and generally responsible for running the group'.[3] This he did till he retired from the active liturgical scene. JLG soon acquired an observer and later full members from the Roman Catholic Church; originally this representation was for England and Scotland, but recently it has also included Wales. In the course of the years some churches

[3] *Development*, p. 229.

have arranged for periodic changes in their members, largely to make sure that their own liturgical committees are represented; other churches have let their representatives stay on until they died or left the group for other reasons.

JLG's most influential publication was *The Calendar and Lectionary*;[4] this lectionary for Sundays and other special days, which involves also some changes in the calendar, was adopted, with some modifications, by all or almost all the churches in England and Scotland which use lectionaries, except the Roman Catholic Church, and is still in widespread use, as for example in *ASB*. It has been criticized, unfairly in my opinion, as being didactic and thematic. A recent revision of it, *A Four Year Lectionary: JLG 2*,[5] has attempted to meet this criticism by not publishing themes. Easily the best-seller of JLG's publications was *The Daily Office*,[6] which ran through numerous impressions. It was timed to influence the Lambeth Conference of 1968. Certainly some of its features have been seen in recent Anglican offices, such as those in *ASB*, for example the greater choice of canticles, though such ideas were in the air in any case. It contained a set of collects for Sundays and other principal days which fitted *The Calendar and Lectionary*. Many of these found their way into *ASB* and into the books of other churches. The Church of England Liturgical Commission and other churches were working on collects in the same period, and such was the exchange to and fro, chiefly through Ronald, that it is difficult to indicate all the original sources in every case.[7] *The Daily Office* came out in an amended form as *The Daily Office Revised*.[8]

Down the years JLG produced a considerable number of other books, mostly collections of essays on various aspects of worship, all expertly edited by Ronald. This is perhaps the best place to describe some of his qualities, for it was in JLG that I knew him most intimately. He was well-organized; his papers

[4] Oxford University Press 1967.

[5] Canterbury Press, Norwich 1990.

[6] SPCK/Epworth, London 1968.

[7] As is stated in the authoritative work by Ronald C. D. Jasper and Paul F. Bradshaw, *A Companion to the Alternative Service Book* (SPCK, London 1986), p. 267.

[8] SPCK, London 1978.

were always in perfect order, and he was master of the situation. This was obviously achieved by hard work, but he never seemed hurried. I recall him saying that after a certain hour in the evening (I forget which) he always stopped work and relaxed, and no crisis, however great, would induce him to work on. He was essentially Anglican in his general style and ethos, but he was appreciative of other traditions, and was quietly friendly to everyone, always approachable and courteous. He usually got his way in JLG without much difficulty, and I suspect that he found JLG a more tractable body than the General Synod of the Church of England. He referred over and over again to 'our Commission', by which he meant of course the Liturgical Commission of the Church of England, and I sometimes wondered whether he was equally insistent on bringing the views of JLG to the notice of his Commission. An incident related in *Development*, pp. 242–3, shows that he did so when necessary. Soon after he had taken over as Chairman of the Church of England Liturgical Commission, he discovered that plans were already afoot for a further revision of the lectionary. 'I was furious', he relates, and he reminded Michael Ramsey that he (Ramsey) had expressed his warm approval of JLG undertaking the very same thing. The Archbishop admitted that that had slipped his mind and he changed his view accordingly. No doubt Ronald always did his best to keep the two bodies in harmony, but in fact they have diverged not infrequently.

Meanwhile, however, developments had recurred on a wider front. The Second Vatican Council's Constitution on the Sacred Liturgy was being put into operation by the *Consilium ad exsequenda Constitutionem de Sacra Liturgia*. This body in 1965 obtained the Pope's permission to invite observers, and the Anglican Communion appointed Ronald and the American scholar Massey Shepherd. I represented the World Council of Churches, and Ronald and I travelled to Rome twice a year for some years. I well remember the first such journey in 1966. We had as a companion on the plane a veteran Roman Catholic liturgiologist, Canon R. Pilkington, who was a *peritus* at the *Consilium*. As the plane approached Rome he was plainly excited, partly at the sight of the city and partly at the prospect of the reform of the liturgy, which he said would soon be so changed as to be almost entirely acceptable to us all. I think he was envisaging a vernacular version in the style of Cranmer. Ronald was not one to betray much emotion, but I think we all had a sense of making history.

The *Consilium* was a large and impressive body, consisting almost entirely of cardinals and bishops, but with many *periti* in attendance, who could be called to speak but could not vote. There were six of us observers, and Archbishop Bugnini's book defends our role against malicious insinuations that we had unduly influenced the proceedings, especially the composition of the third eucharistic prayer. We took no part in the discussions, but Archbishop Bugnini records: 'They were the first to arrive at the meetings, the last to leave the hall. They were always affable, polite, sparing of words, and ready to engage in a friendly way in any conversation that might be requested.'[9] That certainly describes Ronald's style very well.

Once we were consulted officially. A conservative group was opposed to the composition of a new three-year Sunday Mass lectionary on the ground that this would diminish Roman Catholic links with some Lutheran churches and to some extent with the Anglicans. We had a meeting with the relevant *periti*, subsequently reported to the *Consilium*. We confirmed what the *periti* had already ascertained, that other churches were already effecting revisions — indeed the JLG two-year lectionary was approaching publication; and we were able to correct a misapprehension that JLG was a purely Anglican body. We therefore assured them that ecumenical considerations need not deter them. We also suggested that the new Roman lectionary should be used experimentally for a certain period and that in the meantime an attempt should be made by the Roman Catholic and other churches to agree on a lectionary. The Common Lectionary used by many churches in North America and elsewhere is in a sense the fruit of this, as it is based on the Roman lectionary, but the Roman Catholic authorities will not allow the use of it even experimentally in a few churches. The JLG lectionary, both in its original form and in its recent revised form (*JLG 2*), cannot be reconciled with either the Roman lectionary or the

[9] *The Reform of the Liturgy*, pp. 199–202 (see also pp. 415–17).

Common Lectionary; so in a sense the hopes of the observers remain unfulfilled. Unfortunately the impulse to revise was, as it were, just ahead of the impulse to co-operate. We said the JLG office for the first time at a JLG meeting, and less than a week later a revised Roman office was said for the first time at the *Consilium*.

Though our official part was small, the *Consilium* brought us, of course, into easy contact with the leading Roman Catholic liturgical scholars, and we made a number of suggestions in private conversations. Moreover, the Roman Catholics had formed the International Commission on English in the Liturgy (ICEL). Ronald says[10] that the observers attended the meetings of its Advisory Committee, which coincided with the meetings of the *Consilium*; but I was not involved in this, and I think he refers only to the Anglican observers. The result of their contacts, however, was soon the formation of the International Consultation on English Texts (ICET). This started in 1969. The secretarial work was done by ICEL. The choice of members was a bit haphazard. To have invited all the world's English-speaking churches to send representatives would have sounded simple, but in fact would have raised enormous ecclesiological and practical problems. There was probably a certain amount of hand-picking; the location of the meetings, which was always London, influenced the matter and made it easy for JLG to be strongly represented.

The Roman Catholic Harold Winstone and Ronald were elected joint chairmen; they worked harmoniously together, and Ronald displayed the same calm persuasive style which we already knew in JLG, though in one case he was secretary and in the other co-chairman. We produced *Prayers We Have in Common*,[11] which contained translations, with brief commentaries, of the Lord's Prayer, the Creeds, the *Gloria in excelsis* and other similar parts of the eucharistic liturgy, and the familiar canticles. Most of these were widely adopted, except for the Lord's Prayer, which has caused continuous difficulty. After we had produced

[10] *Development*, p. 290.
[11] Geoffrey Chapman, London; Fortress Press, Philadelphia 1970, revised and enlarged in 1971.

the second revised edition,[12] we thought the work was done, and no arrangements were made for the continuance of the organization. We did not foresee the problem of inclusive language. Later, after Ronald had ceased to be active in such matters, the work had to be taken up again by a fresh but somewhat similar group, the English Language Liturgical Consultation (ELLC), which began at Boston, Massachusetts, in 1985 and has produced *Praying Together*.[13] ELLC has also taken up other matters, including the question of the two types of lectionary, but with no real hope of reconciling them.

I was also to see something of Ronald's work in the totally unofficial learned societies which liturgical scholars form. The international body is Societas Liturgica, which meets every two years. Ronald's vigorous part in this led to his being President for 1969–71, chosen by lot after a tied vote. His address on 'Christian Initiation: The Anglican Position' at its Canterbury Congress in 1977 was printed in *Studia Liturgica*.[14] On this international occasion his essential Englishness was shown in that he confined his account to the Church of England, 'for it can be regarded in its very comprehensiveness as representative of many—if not all—views to be found in other parts of the Anglican Communion'.[15] Ronald was also prominent in the affairs of the Alcuin Club, a largely though not entirely Anglican organization, and for some years was its Editorial Secretary, responsible for the preparation of all its manuscripts for publication.

No doubt there were other activities of which I was not aware, but enough has been said to show that Ronald led a very busy life and was a very hard worker. *ASB* will probably be replaced by another book in AD 2000; ICET has been replaced by ELLC; JLG might modify its role. This is what Ronald would have wished, for he knew that liturgy must never again enter into a sort of ice-age. It changes with the culture. Indeed after his retirement from the official liturgical scene, he continued to be

[12] SPCK, London; Fortress Press, Philadelphia 1975.
[13] Canterbury Press, Norwich 1990.
[14] Vol. 12 (1977), pp. 116–25.
[15] ibid., p. 116.

active in this sphere, editing jointly with his son David a volume of essays on *Language and the Worship of the Church*.[16] He virtually presided over the thaw in the Church of England and created the new style of ecumenical co-operation. Only a person as friendly as Ronald could have achieved it. His place in liturgical history is assured.

[16] Macmillan, London 1990.

1

Liturgy and Ceremonial

GORDON JEANES

Behind the drama of words is the drama of action, the timbre of voice and voice, the uplifted hand or tense muscle, and the particular emotion. The spoken play, the words which we read, are symbols, a shorthand and often, as in the best of Shakespeare, a very abbreviated shorthand indeed, for the actual and felt play, which is always the real thing. The phrase, beautiful as it may be, stands for a greater beauty still.[1]

Such a passage from T. S. Eliot might seem a strange introduction to ceremonial in worship, when in much liturgical study it is relegated to a more technical role:

According to strict ecclesiastical usage, ceremonial refers to the prescribed and formal actions that constitute worship. It is therefore to be distinguished from ritual, which refers to the prescribed form of words. . . . If this strict sense of ceremonial is adhered to, it includes such actions as the kiss of peace, the fraction, elevation, the pouring of water in baptism, the laying on of hands in ordination, etc.[2]

A correct definition indeed, but its clinical precision perhaps brings out the wariness with which ceremonial has often been regarded. 'Liturgy is the science of the black print, rubrics that of the red print', said Adrian Fortescue.[3] Ceremonial was not meant to be worthy of serious study.

Eliot was writing about Greek drama, but what he says is a far better description of liturgical ceremonial than the liturgists' own. Liturgy does not exist in a book. It is not a written text. People worshipping together, and the way in which they worship, the liturgy, is something of which the book is a mere skeleton.

[1] T. S. Eliot, 'Seneca in Elizabethan Translations', in *Selected Essays*, 3rd edn (Faber & Faber, London 1951), p. 68.
[2] 'Ceremonial', in J. G. Davies (ed.), *A New Dictionary of Liturgy and Worship* (SCM, London 1986).
[3] Quoted in C. Jones, G. Wainwright, E. Yarnold SJ, and P. Bradshaw (eds), *The Study of Liturgy*, revised edn (SPCK, London; Oxford University Press, New York 1992), p. 543.

The relegation of ceremonial to an ancillary role was a complex process which would take an essay in itself to describe.[4] Let us simply note the following features. First came the scholarly distinction between the words and the ceremonial. Once that distinction was observed as more than a mode of analysis, it became easier to claim some kind of priority for one aspect over the other. Discussion of ceremonial then tended to concentrate on the less important features of a service, failing to recognize that the central feature of each of the two great sacraments is an action. Furthermore, in Christian history, liturgy has often been seen as a touchstone of theological orthodoxy, and in particular from the Reformation period to the present day the concern of authorities has been to ensure orthodoxy primarily in the small print of the written text. The end result of all this is that in worship the action is of less interest: the central actions are effectively subordinate to the word, and details dismissed as trivia while the small print of the text assumes all-consuming importance.

It was Dom Gregory Dix's great study, *The Shape of the Liturgy*, which marked the sea-change in liturgy and put the ceremonial action at the heart of worship.

> All eucharistic worship is of necessity, and by intention, a *corporate action*—'Do this' (*poieite*, plural). The blessed Bread is broken that it may be *shared*, and 'we being many' made 'one Body'; the blessed Cup is delivered that it may be a '*partaking* of the Blood of Christ'. . . . It is the sequence of the rite—the Shape of the Liturgy—which chiefly performs the eucharistic action itself, and so carries out the human obedience to the divine command 'Do this'. It is the phrasing of the prayers which chiefly expresses the *meaning* attached to that action by the theological tradition of the church. Both are essential parts of eucharistic worship.[5]

Ceremonial could no longer be regarded either as secondary to the text or as of only pedantic interest, but was now portrayed

---

[4] Aidan Kavanagh, *On Liturgical Theology* (Pueblo, New York 1984), pp. 103–5, links it with the rise of printing and a 'slide into textual absorption'. However, a move away from action to the written text can be detected, albeit in the matter of drama rather than liturgy, with Aristotle and Seneca. See Eliot, 'Seneca in Elizabethan Translations'; O. Taplin, *Greek Tragedy in Action* (Methuen, London 1978), p. 2. Perhaps it is more a question of the prejudice of the intellectual.

[5] *The Shape of the Liturgy* (Dacre, Westminster 1945), pp. 1–2.

as the core around which the liturgy developed over the centuries. Whatever the historical accuracy of Dix's work,[6] its influence on modern eucharistic composition has been immense, and the notion of the 'fourfold shape' of taking the bread and wine, giving thanks, breaking the bread, and sharing the bread and wine in communion has become the cornerstone of contemporary eucharistic rites in virtually every denomination. Although it would be a wild exaggeration to give Dix all the credit, his role must be acknowledged in turning the tide which, at least from the sixteenth century up to the beginning of this century, viewed the written and spoken word as supreme over the action.

This essay will examine ceremonial very much on its own terms. We shall be less concerned with the incidentals of ceremony and more with the significant ceremonial action, the central sacramental act in baptism and eucharist, and those acts which are integral to a liturgy. Most of the discussion will be based on a detailed examination of particular baptismal liturgies which are selected to demonstrate the points to be considered. After a brief look at the ceremonial action first as central to a rite and then in its ancillary role, we shall proceed by looking at what one may call the dynamics of ceremonial: how ceremonial communicates relationships within a congregation or community; how ceremonial is interpreted by other ceremonial; how ceremonial is interpreted by written liturgy; and how ceremonial may reinterpret a liturgy. In all this it will be seen that the importance of ceremonial often lies not just in the action in itself, which is generally clear in its purpose though it may be inexplicable or trivial, but also in how it relates to other features or how it establishes a relationship between people. Context, subject, object, count as much as the detail of the activity. It is in this as much as in itself that a ceremonial action is symbolic, because it points beyond itself. And, as with a symbol, the meaning of a ceremonial action is open and undefined. The individual occasion of an action is always open to improvisation.

[6] cf. Paul Bradshaw, *The Search for the Origins of Christian Worship* (SPCK, London; Oxford University Press, New York 1992), pp. 140ff.

Ceremonial: The Heart of the Rite

Ceremonial is central to the liturgical performance of the sacraments. We have already seen Dix's treatment of the eucharist as a corporate action. With regard to baptism, the core of the liturgy is immersion of someone in water, or the pouring of water over them. While the details of how the baptism is performed can always vary, so can the words said. Baptism in New Testament times might have been in the name of Jesus (Acts 2.38; 8.16; 10.48; 19.5; Rom. 10.9; 1 Cor. 6.11) or using the trinitarian formula of Matthew 28.19; either form could have been declared by the baptizer or have been in the form of questions answered by the candidate, or the action might have been done in silence and the name of Jesus or the trinitarian notion formed some other feature. There might be a minister who baptized the candidate, or perhaps the candidate baptized him or herself, as in Jewish proselyte baptism.[7] However it happened, and now happens, the act of baptism carries an emphasis and an interpretation by the very manner in which it is done. Immersion speaks more of burial. Pouring speaks of cleansing. It cannot be said that one way is more normal or definitive than another.

Ceremonial in an Ancillary Role

At the beginning of this century W. H. Frere in *The Principles of Religious Ceremonial* set out to present ceremonial as something natural, and therefore innocuous. For many Anglicans, wearied by the ritual disputes of the time, this book must have come as a breath of fresh air, tempering factional shibboleths with a sound Anglo-Saxon common sense. Frere discusses ceremonial under three headings: 'utilitarian' ceremonial, which is simply the way of doing somehow something which has to be done (e.g., an entrance procession gets clergy into their seats at the beginning of the service); 'interpretative' ceremonial (e.g., kneeling for a confession, standing to hear the gospel read) marks something already a part of the service as important or represents the appropriate response of the worshippers; and 'symbolical' ceremonial, an action which does not so much comment on something already present but rather introduces a new motif

---

[7] See *The Study of Liturgy*, p. 117.

(e.g., the handing of a lighted candle to the newly baptized, which brings into the service the theme of illumination).

Frere's book makes fascinating reading, and he has a fine judgement in the use of his material, being aware of the problems of generalization and also of the chance-laden conditions of historical development: how something which once was purely utilitarian may take on symbolism and significance, for example when at the burial service the casting of earth on the coffin is performed ceremonially; and when forms of service have a long history, ceremonial may accumulate, and the meaning and purpose of individual actions be changed or lost altogether.

> Interpretative ceremonial may . . . acquire a new and valuable significance in addition to, or in place of, its original significance. Or it may also lose its significance altogether, and so become what is called in the preface to the Prayer Book a dark and dumb ceremony. In such cases even the most conservative mind must be content to forgo it. But an old ceremony must be well, patiently and tenderly tested before it is condemned as dumb or dark; and due disregard must be paid to those who only think it dumb and dark because they are constitutionally deaf to the appeal of such things and blind to their beauties.[8]

Frere makes ceremonial seem natural, innocuous, and reasonable, safely framed within liturgies which are essentially written texts with more or less definable meanings. We may speculate how Frere might have written the same book in the light of Dix's *Shape of the Liturgy*, which did not perhaps overturn the idea of definable meaning, but certainly placed the action at the heart of the liturgy.

Ceremonial as communicating relationship

Context helps give a ceremonial action meaning, and part of context is the question of personal relationships. This is particularly clear in initiation rites, where part of the purpose of the rite is to integrate a person into the group. The ceremonial intricacies of many baptismal rites are about integration into the congregation, so that the initiand is brought into relationship with the various significant individuals through the course of

[8] *The Principles of Religious Ceremonial* (Longmans, Green & Co., London 1906), p. 143.

initiation. Let us take as examples the *Apostolic Tradition* of Hippolytus and the modern Roman Catholic *Rite of Christian Initiation of Adults*.

Hippolytus' *Apostolic Tradition* probably dates from about AD 215. The surviving versions date from later periods and differing situations, which have led to confusing changes in the text. But while it is impossible to tell with certainty all the details of the original initiatory scheme, it is clear on reading the work that it set out with care a (somewhat over-theoretical?) system in which the baptismal candidate was initiated by a lengthy procedure involving interaction with members of the church hierarchy. The enquirers and catechumens under instruction were placed under teachers, and not allowed to pray with the baptized faithful or to share the kiss of peace. Only when they applied for baptism did they relate liturgically with the bishop, and then only shortly before the day of baptism.

It was the same during the actual baptismal ceremonies. The bishop presided over the whole; that is made clear from the fact that he blesses the oils used for anointing the candidates. But the candidates meet and interact with presbyters and deacons (the details are now confused) until they have been baptized; only at the end do they come before the bishop for a final prayer. He then gives each candidate the kiss of peace. And this is the concluding act of their initiation, after which they can join the congregation for the prayers, the kiss of peace, and the eucharist.[9]

A somewhat different rationale underlies the modern Roman Catholic *Rite of Christian Initiation of Adults*, which otherwise might seem to be archaeological in its use of initiatory ceremonies. Here the significant persons who meet and interact with the candidate are the congregation, the local priest, and the candidate's sponsor, who plays a special pastoral role. The Rite of Acceptance into the Order of Catechumens is one in which the candidate is integrated into the congregation. The service begins outside the church building, and is concluded with entry

[9] Sections xvi–xxiii, in Gregory Dix (ed.), *The Treatise on the Apostolic Tradition of St Hippolytus of Rome*, revised Henry Chadwick (SPCK, London 1968), pp. 23–43.

into the church, in every sense. The catechumen counts as a Christian, and can be married in church or receive a Christian funeral.[10]

Likewise in the baptismal ceremonies, important features bear witness to the role of the significant persons. After the immersion, the candidate is handed a lighted candle by the sponsor. The person is as important here as the object. And Confirmation is now normally administered by the minister of baptism (bishop or priest), instead of being limited to the bishop. This maintains the unity of the rite rather than splitting off Confirmation, but also means that the whole initiation happens within that congregation, and in many cases the significant minister is the local priest.[11] However similar the ceremonial actions, the meaning given by the significant persons could hardly be more different from the pattern of Hippolytus. If we look at the ceremonial actions in the light of their context, the new rites are very different and far from being archaeological reconstructions of their ancient and medieval models.

Ceremonial Interpreted by Ceremonial
The baptismal rites of the early Church amassed ceremonial additions with, as far as we can tell, freedom and spontaneity. Slow as that development itself was, yet regional variation was considerable, adaptation was evident, and controversy virtually non-existent. By the late fourth century a complex structure of initiation was widely in place, in which the adult convert was brought into full membership of the Church in a process which could take years. Linked together with a full catechetical programme, every step was taken with some ritual action. One became a catechumen in a rite in which one received the sign of the cross. One might remain in the catechumenate for years, but then application for baptism involved the next step into a period of intense preparation (in the West the origins of our Lent), including teaching, exorcisms, and purificatory rites. The baptism itself was surrounded by numerous ceremonies, one scheme

[10] Sections 47, 48, 60; cf. section 80.
[11] Sections 230, 232. Cf. Aidan Kavanagh, *The Shape of Baptism* (Pueblo, New York 1978), pp. 138–40.

of which we shall follow in detail through Ambrose's *De Sacramentis*.[12]

But as we read Ambrose's rite, as with all the variations from congregation to congregation around the Mediterranean, we must look not so much at the details of the ceremonial actions in themselves as at the general pattern of the relationship of the details to the central action of baptism. The ceremonies before the immersion were essentially preparatory: they speak of enabling, purification, and communicate the 'negative' aspects of baptism—forgiveness of sins, death to sin, the world, and the devil; and the ceremonies after the immersion likewise affirm what has taken place by communicating the 'positive' aspects—incorporation into Christ, priesthood and royalty, sanctification, the purity of the Christian life. The ceremonies need to be seen in their relation to the immersion rather than independently of it; they function as a commentary on and extension of the immersion. Using this kind of analysis, let us follow the full progress of a candidate through the final baptismal ceremonies as described by St Ambrose.

The normal occasion for baptism is during the Easter celebrations, during the Saturday night or towards dawn on Easter day. Presumably children are being baptized as well as adults, but Ambrose considers and addresses only the latter in his explanation given afterwards. On the Saturday morning the candidates assemble in the church for a rite called the Opening (*Apertio*), when the ears and nostrils are touched so that the candidate is rendered capable of receiving the meaning and grace of the coming rites. The ceremony is based around the gospel passage of Jesus healing the deaf and dumb man, and the Lord's word *Effeta* (Mark 7.34) evidently plays a significant part.[13] The ceremony is preparatory. It speaks of human inadequacy and of God's enabling grace.

The candidates are dismissed and return to the church that evening for the vigil service. Towards the end of that service, shortly before the Easter eucharist, they enter the baptistery

[12] English translation in E. J. Yarnold, *The Awe-Inspiring Rites of Initiation* (St Paul Publications, Slough 1972), pp. 99f.

[13] *De Sacramentis* I.2–3 (Yarnold, p. 100).

complex and are anointed with olive oil 'like an athlete . . . for an earthly wrestling match'. (Athletes were covered in oil, so the candidates must by now have stripped off their clothes. The somewhat prudish Ambrose makes no mention of the undressing, though other contemporary commentators draw obvious symbolism from the practical action.) But the opponent in the wrestling match is the devil, and the confrontation is in the renunciations: 'Do you renounce the devil and his works?' The ceremony of anointing marks and heightens the significance of the renunciation: Frere might have described it as interpretative. The renunciation is thus seen to be no empty words, but a battle for the soul as in baptism the candidate is taken from sin into the kingdom of God.[14]

Other ceremonial details might be used to emphasize this important moment. Ambrose himself in his other explanatory work, *De Mysteriis*, mentions that the candidates face west, commonly regarded as the direction of darkness in a society where it was common to face east to pray, and they renounce the devil 'to his face' and then turn to the east.[15] Although Ambrose mentions the move, its explanation is unnecessary. The action speaks for itself and for the liturgy it interprets.

Only then does one go into the baptistery.[16] Access is carefully staged, and the candidates have entered the holy of holies (Ambrose calls it that) only after the most careful and lengthy preparation. And when they step down into the water, they do so as ones who have been purged of all that opposes God, whose senses have been opened to his grace, and who have confronted and renounced the devil. Immersion in the font (probably under a fountain or stream of water, as ancient fonts were not made for adults to be submerged in a pool) is threefold. Each immersion corresponds to a person of the Trinity. Ambrose links it to sharing in the death and resurrection of Christ, though, apart from the resurrection being on the third day, this is somewhat weak, and also he says that it is 'so that the threefold confession might absolve the manifold lapses of the past'.[17] One might wonder here whether there are shades of Peter's confession. . . .

[14] ibid., I.4–5 (Yarnold, p. 101).
[15] *De Mysteriis* 7 (see Yarnold, p. 17).
[16] *De Sacramentis* I.9 (Yarnold, p. 103).
[17] ibid., II.20 (Yarnold, p. 117).

Then follow a series of ceremonies which serve to affirm the immersion. The candidates are anointed 'into eternal life', with a formula affirming the immersion which has just taken place.[18] Secondly, the candidates' feet are washed in imitation of Jesus' washing of the disciples' feet at the Last Supper. Ambrose denies that the ceremony is performed as an example of humility, as some others explained it who evidently made it an image of the Christian community that the newly baptized were joining. But Ambrose says it is 'a mystery and sanctification', protecting the new Christian against being tripped and poisoned by the devil as Adam was.[19] Thirdly, a further ceremony, either of anointing or handlaying, is described both as a sealing and as imparting the Holy Spirit.[20] This is the final ceremony of initiation. The candidates then dress in white garments, their symbolism clear enough, and enter the church to share in the eucharist for the first time with their Christian brothers and sisters.

In all this, to concentrate on the ceremonial detail would be to lose sight of the wood for the trees. It is by its relation to the central act of immersion that the ceremonial both derives its own meaning and lends emphasis and understanding to that central act. So it is that in the varying patterns of initiation around the Mediterranean, features which appear to be very similar can in fact fulfil very different roles. For example, both Ambrose and Cyril of Jerusalem describe an anointing of the senses. But while, as we have seen, Ambrose has it as one of the preparatory rites, Cyril's church has it after the immersion. The descriptions of the ceremonial actions and their symbolism *in themselves* are very similar. However, the purpose of the rites, their context, is very different. Ambrose's anointing is the 'Opening', to be understood as preparing the candidate for the initiation. Cyril presents his anointing as a sanctification of the senses, an endowment with the Holy Spirit, affirming the immersion which has taken place.[21]

---

[18] ibid., II.24 (Yarnold, p. 119).
[19] ibid., III.4–7 (Yarnold, pp. 121–4).
[20] ibid., III.8 (Yarnold, pp. 124–5).
[21] *Mystagogic Catecheses* 3 (Yarnold, pp. 79–83).

We have a situation, then, in which the central ceremony, immersion in water accompanied by a trinitarian formula, is interpreted by other dependent ceremonies. Their meaning is never precise, but all the same richly communicates to the candidate the manifold meaning and grace of baptism.[22] One feature of such a language of ceremonial and symbol is that the dependent actions not only interpret the central sacramental act but are portrayed as actually communicating its benefits. Thus, in an extreme case, the final anointing which spoke of the giving of the Holy Spirit actually became separated in the Western Church from baptism and became the distinct sacrament of Confirmation. But others remained within the sequence of the rite. The language of the accompanying prayers and formulae was of the rite performing the effect and not simply illustrating it.

To entertain such a notion of extending the effect of the sacrament might seem strange. However, there is nothing eccentric in such an idea. In ordinary life many things are effected by a symbolic act, the authentication of which may yet be required by a further act. For example, an agreement may be made by a handshake (and perhaps sealed by a meal). A written contract will normally follow, without which the original agreement may not stand, with considerable pain at the disruption. In human society we take it for granted that things of this nature are made in stages, usually with one definitive act which authenticates the whole. The ancient process of initiation described above fits fully with this understanding: the immersion authenticates the entire pilgrimage made by the candidate into communion with God and the Church. Each step is valid, and validated by baptism.

Ceremonial Interpreted by the Written Text

The Reformers' concentration on the written and spoken word and their generally negative attitude to ceremonies were the

---

[22] This interpretation of 'negative before, positive after' applies only to the more richly developed rites described here, and to their descendants. Other, much simpler rites, e.g., the early Syrian rites where a single anointing preceded the immersion, did not have the division into 'positive and negative'. See G. Winkler, 'The Original Meaning of the Prebaptismal Anointing and its Implications', *Worship* 52 (1978), pp. 24–45; *The Study of Liturgy*, pp. 127–9.

opposite of the attitude of Ambrose and Cyril. As the inheritors of a medieval liturgy, the meaning of which they believed to be 'dumb', or wrong, the more moderate among them sought to explain, the more radical set out to abolish, the ceremonies not found in scripture. Cranmer set out the problem and his solution in an appendix to the 1549 Prayer Book:

> This our excessive multitude of ceremonies was so great and many of them so dark, that they did more confound and darken, than declare and set forth Christ's benefits unto us. . . . As those be taken away which were most abused, and did burden men's consciences without any cause; so the other that remain are retained for a discipline and order. . . . And moreover they be neither dark nor dumb ceremonies, but are so set forth that every man may understand what they do mean, and to what use they do serve.[23]

As he says, Cranmer both reduced the number of ceremonies and made their meaning clear. Now they were carefully portrayed as tokens without any sacramental effect of their own; the old ceremonies are re-presented simply as didactic aids. Thus in his somewhat provisional 1549 rite those ceremonies which are retained have their verbal formulae changed. The giving of the white garment to the newly baptized is accompanied by the following words:

> Take this white vesture *for a token of the innocency* which by God's grace in this holy sacrament of baptism is given unto thee, and *for a sign whereby thou art admonished*, so long as thou livest, to give thyself to innocency of living, that, after this transitory life, thou mayest be partaker of the life everlasting. Amen.[24]

This may be contrasted with the Sarum version:

> N, receive a white robe, holy and unstained, *which thou must bring* before the tribunal of our Lord Jesus Christ, that thou mayest have eternal life and live for ever and ever. Amen.[25]

By the 1552 revision, only the sign of the cross is left as a ceremonial action in addition to the baptismal immersion itself,

---

[23] 'Of Ceremonies', *The First and Second Prayer Books of Edward VI* (Everyman edition, London 1910), pp. 287–8 (spelling modernized).

[24] ibid., p. 241 (emphasis added).

[25] English translation from J. D. C. Fisher, *Christian Initiation: Baptism in the Medieval West* (SPCK, London 1965), p. 174 (emphasis added).

and whereas in the medieval rite the sign of the cross was associated with the imparting of God's grace, in 1552 it is simply a token that the child will not be ashamed to confess the faith of Christ and to follow him. The baptismal immersion now stands out with almost solitary splendour. As far as the reformers were concerned, the minimalism by no means detracted from the solemnity of the rite: rather it enhanced its power and meaning. Ceremonial minimalism is not an attempt to eschew ceremony but a style of ceremony in its own right. When left alone in the middle of the stage, the simple action, even a small one, assumes great significance.

The baptismal immersion was a ceremonial action which exercised the full interest of the reformers. Traditionally, as in the time of Ambrose, one was baptized by a triple immersion, corresponding to the threefold nature of the Trinity. (In many parts of Europe, though not in England, the immersion was being replaced by pouring.) The reformers preferred to present the exact mode of baptism as something in itself indifferent, and Cranmer allows pouring as an alternative to immersion, though not the sprinkling which was favoured by the Swiss churches. Another feature of ceremonial minimalism is that as less significance is paid to the visible action, so the participant is enjoined to seek its significance beyond the visible. And the smaller the action is which is accorded significance, the more it is seen to point beyond itself. But in his 1552 rite Cranmer shows his preference in bringing to the fore the understanding of baptism as dying and rising with Christ, best signified by a full immersion rather than pouring, and by a single rather than triple immersion.[26]

So much for the immersion itself. While Cranmer reduces the importance of the traditional ceremonies, he by no means leaves the service simple or naked, but introduces a whole new complex of meanings centring on the baptismal immersion itself. The aim of these is to meet contemporary needs and issues, providing both a theological defence of infant baptism against

[26] See G. W. Bromiley, *Baptism and the Anglican Reformers* (Lutterworth Press, London 1953), pp. 140–1.

Anabaptist criticisms and a much needed personal warmth in the service.

The gospel reading is of Jesus blessing the children, and Cranmer chose the Markan account in preference to the Matthean version which had previously been standard in England. The difference is that Mark, but not Matthew, has Jesus say that 'whosoever doth not receive the kingdom of God, as a little child, he shall not enter therein', and, while in Matthew Jesus laid his hands on the children and departed, in Mark, 'when he had taken them up in his arms, he put his hands upon them, and blessed them'. Cranmer uses these elements in Mark as a commentary on the baptismal immersion, as Stephen Sykes describes:

> The emotionally powerful image of the child being embraced in the arms of Jesus' mercy forms the affective heart of this liturgy. The word 'receive' significantly continues to echo at regular intervals throughout the rest of the service. . . . When the priest at the height of the drama takes the child into his arms, he is doing what Christ himself did. The congregation witnesses Christ's own embrace. The sacrament is God's own act.[27]

Contrary to the use by Cranmer of the traditional ceremonies as tokens, his concentration of the notion of receiving is understood by Sykes, surely correctly, as in some way an effective sign. But for us to see how Cranmer arrived at this use of the gospel in reflecting on the immersion, we need to look to the Lutheran origins of the motif, first to Luther's own theology and then to liturgical antecedents.

As a natural course Luther would quote in favour of infant baptism the verses in the gospels about Jesus' dealing with children, and we have discussions of Matthew 19.14, when Jesus both tells the disciples to let the children come to him and declares that the kingdom of heaven belongs to children. Luther defends the literal meaning of the parable against those who would qualify it in some way, and we can see here the germs of the treatment of the story (taken from the version in Mark) that

[27] 'Baptisme doth represente unto us oure profession', in M. Johnson (ed.), *Thomas Cranmer* (Turnstone Ventures, Durham 1990), pp. 130–2.

is to be found, much developed in detail, in the Lutheran rites and in Cranmer's service.[28]

But Luther develops more fully another theme which is close to his own theology and also feeds the other picture just described, that of the meeting of Jesus and John the Baptist *in utero* in Luke 1. Luther is discussing the problem of whether infants can have faith, and he cites the example where John leaps in his mother's womb (Luke 1.41, and cf. 1.15), taking it as evidence of faith. He continues:

> What if all children in baptism not only were able to believe but believed as well as John in his mother's womb? We can hardly deny that the same Christ is present at baptism and in baptism, in fact is himself the baptizer, who in those days came in his mother's womb to John. In baptism he can speak as well through the mouth of the priest, as when he spoke through his mother. Since then he is present, speaks, and baptizes, why should not his Word and baptism call forth both spirit and faith in the child as then it produced faith in John? He is the same one who speaks and acts then and now.[29]

The validity of infant baptism depends, then, not only on the possibility that the infant may possess some kind of faith, but also on the conviction that the true minister of the sacrament is Christ, whose word and work are all-powerful. Luther extends the argument from John the Baptist to the children brought to Jesus: '[A child] comes to Christ in baptism, as John came to him, and as the children were brought to him, that his word and work might be effective in them, move them, and make them holy, because his word and work cannot be without fruit.'[30]

This principle of Jesus as the true minister of the sacrament is not restricted to baptism, but underlies much of his thinking. Vilmos Vajta describes the principle in this way:

> As a matter of fact the ministry is Christ's continued activity on earth. In the pulpit he speaks through the mouth of the preacher, at the font he himself is the Baptist, at the altar he imparts the remission of sins through the hands of the minister. There is no delegation of authority here. The minis-

---

[28] 'Concerning Rebaptism', in *Luther's Works* 40 (Fortress Press, Philadelphia 1958), pp. 242–3.

[29] ibid., pp. 242–3.

[30] ibid., p. 244.

ter is simply an instrument of the Holy Spirit, and his office a kind of stewardship.[31]

Sykes is no doubt correct, but only partly so, when he speaks of the image of the child being embraced by Jesus as 'the affective heart of this liturgy', and that 'the justification for baptising infants lies . . . in the quality of [Christ's] response to little children'.[32] This is not just sentiment. The Jesus who 'embraces with the arms of his mercy' is also, if we follow Luther, the one whose 'word and work cannot be without fruit'. The gospel passage in the liturgy then serves both to appeal to the hearts of the congregation and to give a theological defence for the practice.

So much for the gospel passage in itself and the theology that derived from the notion of Christ as the minister of the sacrament. Now we may turn to see how this idea was applied to the composition of the liturgy by means of its ceremonial. In fact the earliest form that we meet could be described as following the principle we have already seen, of ceremonial interpreted by ceremonial. However, the interpretation is as much in the wording of the rubric as in the ceremonial action itself. Both Luther's First and Second *Taufbüchlein* demonstrated the theme by a subtle adaptation of the traditional rite. The gospel reading finished with the words, 'And he embraced them and laid his hand on them and blessed them.' The following rubric reads: 'Then shall the priest lay his hand upon the child's head and pray *Our Father*, together with the godparents, kneeling.'[33] In other words, the priest's action here directly parallels that of Christ in the gospel story.

[31] *Luther on Worship* (Muhlenberg Press, Philadelphia 1958), p. 112.

[32] 'Baptisme doth represente unto us oure profession', p. 132.

[33] E. Sehling (ed.), *Die evangelischen Kirchenordnungen des xvi. Jahrhunderts*, vol 1 (Leipzig 1902), pp. 19, 22; English translation from J. D. C. Fisher, *Christian Initiation: The Reformation Period* (SPCK, London 1970), pp. 14, 24. There was a similar action in the Magdeburg rite on which Luther based his service, but the rubric there reads, 'Then the presbyter holding his hand with his stole upon the head of the infant shall say *Our Father* and *I believe in God*' (Fisher, p. 14). The practice of holding the hand on the child's head originated with the priest speaking in the child's name at this point, and had nothing to do with the gospel reading. Luther is the first to make anything of the juxtaposition of the two elements.

Luther's simple juxtaposition of gospel and action were evidently not enough for some, for in 1540 the meaning is spelled out in the revised baptism service of the Albertine-Saxony *Kirchenordnung*, where an exhortation links the gospel reading and the rubric. This exhortation is the basis of Cranmer's exposition of the gospel in 1549 and 1552.[34] Where Cranmer differs, however, is that he omits any mention of laying a hand on the child at this point. Rather, the symbolism is attached to and centred exclusively on the act of baptism proper, where the priest then takes the child into his hands for the administration of the sacrament.

This move by Cranmer has a double result. First, it resists the accumulation of new ceremonies in a rite that has just been cleared of old ones, and concentrates instead on a sophisticated theological interpretation of the sacramental act, using scripture and other written texts. Secondly, the concrete linking action has changed. In the Lutheran rites it was the laying on of the hand by the priest which echoed and communicated the action of Christ. In Cranmer the link is the action of the priest receiving the child, and the many verbal references to that effect. Here, unfortunately, one must note that Cranmer has made a disappointing slip. The word 'receive', which, as Sykes points out, is used ten times besides its occurrence in the opening rubric, has a different subject in the rite (Christ receiving the children) from that in the gospel ('whosoever doth not receive the kingdom of God, as a little child'). The gospel use of the word is suppressed and twisted round. Stylistically this is extremely awkward. From the point of view of Cranmer's theological aims, to justify the baptism of infants against Anabaptist criticisms, this clash of meaning is quite disabling and a major fault in the service.

But let us leave criticism aside and follow Cranmer in his aim. The theme of reception occurs in the 1552 wording of the signing of the infant with the cross after it is baptized:

> We receive this child into the congregation of Christ's flock, and do sign him with the sign of the cross. . . .[35]

---

[34] Sehling, *Die evangelischen Kirchenordnungen*, vol. 1, pp. 266 – 7; cf. F. E. Brightman, *The English Rite* (Rivingtons, London 1915), p. cxviii.

[35] *The First and Second Prayer Books of Edward VI*, p. 398.

The declaratory formula, 'we receive', is Christ's own embrace, not only by the priest but by the whole congregation through the godparents who receive the newly baptized child from their minister. In effect the formula fulfils the role of the post-baptismal ceremonies in Ambrose, in affirming what has taken place in the central act. The sign of the cross also would seem to fulfil much the same role, though its perception in the years after Cranmer, and indeed right up to liturgical revisions in the present day, has been dogged with controversy.

Ceremonial as Reinterpretation

In the context of the reception at the conclusion of the baptismal service, one might mention the role of ceremonial as reinterpretative of a rite. Where the written text reigns and is imposed by authority, but is disliked by some, its ceremonial performance may be altered in order to give a new emphasis or even an interpretation quite at odds with its original sense.

After Cranmer there was a reaction, particularly among the Laudians of the seventeenth century, against his emphasis on the congregation as opposed to the Church as the universal body of Christ. This found itself expressed in some of the verbal changes in the 1662 Prayer Book.[36] But it is no coincidence that the first ceremony we hear of being added to the baptismal rite—illegally—was when Puritans objected in 1641 to some ministers 'carrying children from the baptism to the altar so called, there to offer them up to God'.[37] Both the ceremonial action and the verbal emendation worked to broadly the same end: to introduce the transcendent element where the localized, immanent aspect was believed to have been over-emphasized. But the ceremonial addition occurred at a time when the verbal change was politically impossible.

A more extreme example of the same tendency is the case of the Church of England clergy of the late nineteenth and early

[36] The changes may be conveniently reviewed in Brightman, *The English Rite*, pp. 725–47.

[37] E. Cardwell, *A History of Conferences and Other Proceedings* (Oxford 1841), p. 273; G. Cuming *A History of Anglican Liturgy*, 2nd edn (Macmillan, London 1982), p. 106.

twentieth centuries who, with or without textual changes, made the eucharist of the *Book of Common Prayer* virtually indistinguishable from the Roman Catholic Mass, thereby seeking to make a theological and ecclesiological point.

Such extremes apart, there is a clear moral here. The written text may be composed by an élite or imposed by authority, but its actual performance inevitably slips into the domain of the popular and the uncontrolled and uncontrollable. A congregation or an individual will do somehow what has to be done. The 'how' inevitably interprets, and the meaning of the rite is thereby open, new, and individual for every congregation and every occasion.

'The phrase, beautiful as it may be, stands for a greater beauty still.' And when we see, not the words, but the action, as the centre of the rite, ceremonial and text blend together in a complex pattern of interpretation and reinterpretation. The words in particular are always prey to definition and intellectual precision. The action remains especially open to the spontaneous, the individual, and the indefinable. It is labile. And its immediacy brings the participant most totally into the actual and felt worship which is always the real thing.

2

Liturgy and Culture: Is Modern Western Liturgical Revision a Case of Not Seeing the Wood for the Trees?

BRYAN SPINKS

Our faith and worship are not part of the modern secular world in which we live, not part of its socially shared and confirmed reality. As believers and worshippers we step outside the dominant secular culture as social deviants.

This quotation from a paper by Charles Davis read at a World Council of Churches consultation in 1969[1] formed one of the passages for discussion in the examination for the Master of Theology in Liturgical Studies of London University in 1972. The syllabus had been newly created by Geoffrey Cuming and Ronald Jasper, and this formed part of Ronald Jasper's paper on the Liturgical Movement. Although many subsequent liturgists have judged Ronald Jasper by the somewhat pedestrian and timid rites of the *Alternative Service Book 1980* (*ASB*) of the Church of England, he was in fact well aware of where progressive liturgical thought was heading, and he knew that what the Church of England would allow him to achieve in terms of a revised liturgy would seem light-years behind.[2] Thus, believing that 'Liturgy and Culture' would be a major growth area in liturgical theology, he included the most recent writings on the subject as a topic of study in his examination syllabus. As he so rightly discerned, the topic is one which has continued to proliferate, one of the most recent examples being the 1989 Congress of Societas Liturgica held at York with the title 'The Inculturation of the Liturgy'.

The idea of the liturgy and the Christian values it articulates interacting with society was of course one of the central hopes of

[1] 'Ghetto or Desert: Liturgy in a Cultural Dilemma', *Studia Liturgica* 7.2/3 (1970), pp. 10–27; quotation from p. 17.
[2] It is becoming clear now that much of the conservative nature of the *ASB* was the result of the Archbishops' deliberate directives to the Liturgical Commission.

the Liturgical Movement as envisaged by its early exponents such as Lambert Beauduin, Virgil Michel, and Gabriel Hebert.[3] These ideas also form the basis of Brian Wicker's 1963 book *Culture and Liturgy*.[4] But the whole topic was given fresh impetus by the Constitution on the Sacred Liturgy of Vatican II, promulgated in the same year as Wicker's book. Among other things this important document envisaged the revision of the Roman rites to make them suitable for the twentieth century, but in articles 37–40 also outlined norms for 'adapting' the Roman liturgy to the culture and traditions of peoples, an approach which was reinforced by *Gaudium et Spes*, the Constitution on the Church in the Modern World, in 1965. This was a different emphasis from the early pioneers of the Liturgical Movement, for here was not just the hope that the liturgy would interact with and infect society, but the recognition that as a society changes so will the liturgy celebrated within its midst change; and since societies differ across the world, the liturgy will need to accommodate different cultures. Liturgy was no longer seen as monochrome, but as a variety of cultural colours. Since then both Catholic and Protestant scholars have penned articles, books, and reports on the subject of liturgy and culture. These tend to fall into five groups:

(a) General reflections on the context of culture and liturgy, looking at the function of worship in a society;

(b) Concern to adapt Western liturgy to the needs of Third World cultures, and for those cultures to produce their own rites;

(c) Historical studies concerned with examining how liturgies of the past have reflected the culture of their time and geographical place;

(d) A concern with the question of how to modernize or inculturate Western liturgy;

(e) Theological reflection and critique of the topic.

---

[3] See Lambert Beauduin, *Liturgy the Life of the Church* (Liturgical Press, Collegeville 1926); Paul Marx, *Virgil Michel and the Liturgical Movement* (Liturgical Press, Collegeville 1957); A. G. Hebert, *Liturgy and Society* (Faber & Faber, London 1935).

[4] Sheed and Ward, London.

Some Basic Observations on the Literature
(a) *Problems of definition*
The first problem that is encountered when reading the literature on this topic is the difficulty in precise definition of terms. The very word 'culture' heads the list. As David Power reminds us, everyone knows what it is but finds it difficult to define. Power describes it as 'whatever is expressed in traditions, beliefs, customs, institutions, art and artefacts, symbols, myths and rites; its core is the values and the meaning on which human life, individual and collective, is based'.[5] Hugh Montefiore in a recent collection of essays describes it thus:

> It forms the background of the lives of people who live in a country, and it is compounded of its dominant religion (or lack of it), its ethics and ideology, its literature and art, its science and technology, its philosophical and ethical traditions, and its ethos and way of life.[6]

Among the most important of its ingredients are the unconscious assumptions which underlie the thinking of a society and by which its members live their lives. These are the root paradigms, or set assumptions about the fundamental nature of the universe, humankind, or the way in which people behave, which are so deeply held by the members of a society as to be essentially unquestioned by them. 'Culture' thus covers so many facets of human life and thought as to become almost unmanageable. In addition, each country and ethnic group has its own distinctive culture and/or sub-cultures. 'African' culture or 'Latin American' culture consists of very different sub-cultures, as indeed does 'European' culture. The picture is made even more complex by the fact that in the 'global village' the 'modern' culture prevalent in Western Europe and North America with its stress on technology impinges on nearly all other cultures.

There is also confusion over the terminology used by liturgists. 'Indigenization' was the word preferred by many

---

[5] 'Cultural Encounter and Religious Expression', in *Worship, Culture and Theology* (Pastoral Press, Washington DC 1990), pp. 39–52; quotation from p. 40.

[6] Hugh Montefiore (ed.), *The Gospel and Contemporary Culture* (Mowbray, London 1992), p. 2.

Protestant writers on liturgy, whereas Catholics opted for 'adaptation' and then 'inculturation'. American writers tend to speak of 'contextualization' of worship. Geoffrey Wainwright once urged 'localization';[7] J. S. Pobee, looking at a specifically African setting, preferred the term *skenosis* or 'tenting' to indicate that authentic liturgy should be incarnational.[8] In his 1982 book *Cultural Adaptation of the Liturgy*, Anscar Chupungco differentiated between acculturation of liturgy, which he described as the adaptation of the Roman rite, and inculturation of the liturgy, which takes pre-Christian rites and endows them with Christian meaning.[9] In his later book, *Liturgies of the Future*, published in 1989,[10] he speaks of adaptation, or updating the liturgy; acculturation, or interacting with other cultures; inculturation, or sharing the hopes, laws, and ritual patterns of a culture; and creativity, where new liturgical texts are composed independently of the traditional structure of the (Roman) liturgy. There is thus no agreed or common terminology.

(b) The benefits of hindsight

Those studies which are concerned with liturgies and cultures of the past usually yield concrete examples of inculturation or creativity. Perhaps one of the earliest and quite unintentional ventures into this area was Edmund Bishop's celebrated paper 'The Genius of the Roman Rite', where the simplicity of the Roman prayers was contrasted with the more exuberant form of the Gallican and Mozarabic rite, illustrating 'a style, a run of thought, and a mode of expression so clearly different as to declare the two things to be the product of the mind, spirit, and genius of two different peoples'.[11] It is equally possible to pick out the 'Semitic' flavour of the East Syrian anaphora of Addai and Mari, where 'you put on our humanity', far from being

---

[7] 'The Localization of Worship', *Studia Liturgica* 8 (1971–2), pp. 26–41.

[8] 'The Skenosis of Christian Worship in Africa', *Studia Liturgica* 14 (1980–1), pp. 37–52.

[9] Paulist Press, New York.

[10] Paulist Press, New York.

[11] *Liturgica Historica* (Oxford University Press 1918), pp. 1–19; quotation from p. 14.

Nestorian as William Bright feared,[12] reflects the ancient Syriac manner of describing the incarnation.[13]

In *Cultural Adaptation of the Liturgy* one of the best chapters is the historical section, where Chupungco looks at the apostolic period with its christological qualifications of Judaism and Hellenism. Later there is the adaptation in the age of persecution, where among other features is the Church's first attempt to express the apostolic tradition in the language and rituals of a pagan culture, the Greco-Roman culture. Another division he makes is from the Edict of Milan to the seventh century, when *honor*, *dignatus*, and *gradus* creep into the ordination prayers, and the pagan cults become the storehouse for the Church's rites. Indeed, some of the sacrificial language of the canon of the Mass is taken from obsolete pagan cultic terminology, inculturated and pressed into Christian usage. Similarly in the *Te igitur*, language used to address the imperial majesty is now addressed to the Lord of Heaven. From the eighth century to the Baroque age the Roman ritual yielded to the pressure of the Franco-Germanic cultures. Medieval drama intruded, and then Baroque theatre. The Enlightenment makes its mark in the period up to the Liturgical Movement.

Slightly different paradigms or divisions were used in a recent article by German Martinez: the Judeo-Christian to the Hellenistic paradigm; from the Hellenistic to the Greco-Roman and Byzantine paradigm; from the Greco-Roman to the medieval Roman Catholic paradigm; from the medieval to the modern Evangelical Protestant paradigm; and finally the Second Vatican Council paradigm and beyond. In the second paradigm, for example, he is able to point to altars, incense, candles, garlands, litanic prayer, oaths and salutations, rank, honours and vestments of the imperial court, artistic motifs and symbols being adapted with some new meaning and symbolism.[14]

[12] For the details see Bryan D. Spinks, *Western Use and Abuse of the Eastern Liturgical Traditions: Some Cross-Sections in its History* (Centre for Indian and Inter-religious Studies, Rome; Dharmaram Publications, Bangalore 1993), ch. 7.

[13] See R. Murray, *Symbols of Church and Kingdom* (Cambridge University Press 1975), pp. 310–12.

[14] 'Cult and Culture: The Structure of the Evolution of Worship', *Worship* 64 (1990), pp. 406–33.

Again, one of the most concrete papers at the 1989 Societas Liturgica Congress was P.-M. Gy's historical paper on inculturation in the West.[15] Gy was able to illustrate how the Latin liturgy borrowed words from Greek and Hebrew, and also altered the sense of certain Latin words, giving them a completely new meaning to their hitherto common meaning. *Oratio*, meaning ordinary speech, was adopted for Christian prayer rather than the pagan religious word *preces*. The feasts of the Church, even if computed,[16] may also have been instituted in opposition to pagan feasts such as *natalis solis invicti*, and represent inculturation through conflict.

(c) Sharp focus on non-Western inculturation
The most obvious paradigms for discussing the progress and success or otherwise of inculturation of liturgy seem to be those developed in and for the Third World cultures, or at least non-European and North American cultures. In India, for example, the process of inculturation was pioneered by the (Roman Catholic) National Biblical, Catechetical and Liturgical Centre at Bangalore by D. S. Amalorpavadass and Paul Puthanangady with the new Orders of the Mass for India finalized in 1973, and published for limited use in 1974. This introduced inculturation in the form of ceremonial and texts. At the level of ceremonial, Indian-style gestures were introduced: semi-prostrations instead of genuflections; squatting instead of kneeling; oil lamps instead of candles; and floral tributes, joss sticks, and arti lamps as used at *puja* (Hindu daily worship). In terms of texts, provision was made for the reading of Hindu scriptures, and a eucharistic prayer was composed using concepts and language drawn from the ancient Hindu philosophies, but also in one particular stanza, from other Indian religious traditions, particularly Sikhism, Buddhism and Islam.

This was certainly Indian, and a brave attempt to de-westernize and Indianize the eucharistic liturgy. The texts were,

[15] 'The Inculturation of the Christian Liturgy in the West', *Studia Liturgica* 20 (1990), pp. 8–18.
[16] For the theory of computation see T. J. Talley, *The Origins of the Liturgical Year* (Pueblo, New York 1986).

however, open to some theological objections,[17] and the Sacred Congregation for Divine Worship and the Sacraments declined to give permission for non-biblical readings or for the Indian eucharistic prayer. Another criticism which has been made of this rite was its 'exclusive' ethos. Much of the language, especially of the eucharistic prayer with its echoes of Sanskrit concepts, was too elitist for the less educated and lower-caste Indians.

In the 1980s the United Theological College of Bangalore under the chairmanship of Dr Eric Lott began to develop the Indian Protestant interest in inculturation. A eucharistic liturgy for the Church of South India has been published, and it has been adapted by the Church of North India. Virginia Kennerley describes it thus:

> Specifically Indian motifs include: the chant of a *saranam* (song of refuge sought in God under various attributes) both at the lamp-lighting preceding the confession and as an alternative to the Sanctus; the use of the *Asato* in the Awakening litany preceding the readings; provision for a reading from an Indian scripture on special occasions; the idea of God as 'greater than all names and forms, our inmost self' in the newly drafted affirmation of faith at the close of the Liturgy of the Word; the *namajapa* or recital of the names of Christ in an Indian language while the table/altar is prepared before the Institution Narrative; the prayer for *darshana*, awareness of Christ's presence, before the sharing of the bread and wine.[18]

There are also fewer Sanskrit or Vedic words, and so this liturgy appears less elitist than the Catholic attempt.

In an African context various suggestions have been made for incorporating ceremonies or customs which are deep-seated in African cultures into Christian liturgy, for example the Jando ceremony (circumcision connected with puberty) as part of Christian initiation.[19] A Mass for Zaire (which the Pope

---

[17] See Bryan D. Spinks, 'The Anaphora for India: Some Theological Objections to an Attempt at Inculturation', *Ephemerides Liturgicae* 95 (1981), pp. 529–49.

[18] 'The Use of Indigenous Sacred Literature and Theological Concept in Christian Eucharistic Liturgy in India', *Studia Liturgica* 19 (1989), pp. 143–61; quotation from pp. 155–6.

[19] See David R. Holeton (ed.), *Liturgical Inculturation in the Anglican Communion*, Alcuin/GROW Liturgical Study 15 (Grove Books, Nottingham 1990), pp. 27–31.

declined to use when he visited Zaire) was completed in 1972, and attempted to combine liturgical antiquity with the religious and cultural heritage of Zaire. The result is an example of Chupungco's category of 'adaptation'. Raymond Moloney has summarized this rite thus:

> The Zairean Mass is basically the Roman rite, but it has introduced a number of changes which help to give it a character of its own. These changes are mainly four: 1) the invocation of the saints and ancestors at the beginning of the Mass; 2) the relocation of the rite of penance, together with the sign of peace, to a position after the gospel and creed and before the bidding prayers; 3) the reorganization of the presentation of gifts; 4) a modified version of the eucharistic prayer based on the second of the four in the Roman missal.[20]

The eucharistic prayer describes God as 'the sun too bright for our gaze', and thanksgiving is included for 'our river the Zaire, our forests, our rivers, our lakes'. The Anglican Church in Kenya had for many years used the 1662 *Book of Common Prayer*, but its new rite draws upon material from African traditional religion. Philip Tovey notes of this rite that in the intercessions a litany is developed that is based on a Kikuya litany, and the final blessing is also based upon a Tarkana blessing.[21]

At a more general level, J. S. Pobee suggested use not only of African music, but also of regional African association of colour for vestments (for example, gold or yellow are festive, but red is a sign of death), and that perhaps the language of the royal courts of African tribes would be worth serious study for forms of addressing God.[22]

These various examples from India and Africa can be discussed and assessed because they contrast with traditional Western forms, and the differences can be kept in sharp focus. The non-Christian religious traditions of these countries are living religions, and they form a useful identifiable conceptual background. It is possible to see where they have suggested a counterpart in an inculturated Christian rite, or where their

---

[20] 'The Zairean Mass and Inculturation', *Worship* 62 (1988), pp. 433–42; quotation from p. 435.

[21] *Inculturation: The Eucharist in Africa*, Alcuin/GROW Liturgical Study 7 (Grove Books, Nottingham 1988), pp. 38–9.

[22] In the article cited above, n. 8.

influence has crossed a threshold to verge upon syncretism. In some unofficial rites and ceremonies, especially of fringe churches, syncretism is obvious and the Christian rite has been absorbed by some local religion, such as in some African Messianism movements and Haiti Voodoo rites. The contrast and perspective allows this sharp focus.

(d) Blurred vision on Western culture and modern Western liturgy
I detect a certain impasse when liturgists turn to discuss modern culture and modern liturgical revision in the West. Usually there is considerable discussion about what constitutes Western culture as it has developed since the Enlightenment. The recent symposium edited by Hugh Montefiore provides a good analysis, but there is far from agreement among the contributors. The Enlightenment has, for example, produced a particular idea of history,

> a system closed by the parameters of data, positivist in being preoccupied with archivally substantiated fact, dominated by the rational criteria for analysis, occupied with limited problems and concerned to establish cause and effect in as concrete a fashion as is possible.[23]

It is a culture which believes in material progress, which is achieved by high technology. Science is regarded by many as autonomous, and is perceived as knowledge conceived as simply exact information about the physical world, acquired professionally by experts using experimental methods. It is frequently described as pluralistic, though Colin Gunton challenges this, suggesting that there is a levelling down achieved by the mass media and mass production.[24] The mass media is indeed a powerful influence since it expresses, circulates, and popularizes underlying cultural assumptions and attitudes. However, according to Jim McDonnell, the result of competing media allows and creates a fragmentation of corporate experience as sub-cultures proliferate.[25] It is recognized as a secular society, though not *a priori* hostile to religion. However, each religious claim is regarded on its merits and its usefulness.

[23] Montefiore, *The Gospel and Contemporary Culture*, p. 15.
[24] ibid., pp. 84ff.
[25] ibid., p. 160.

Within this post-Enlightenment culture and with the appearance of the new missal of Paul VI, Herman Schmidt was able to ask: 'Have we really succeded in giving the [new] liturgy that cultural content and structure which should make, pastorally speaking, an impact on the modern world?';[26] and Charles Davis claimed that 'the general verdict upon liturgical reform is that it has failed to solve the problem of worship in a secular age'.[27] Unlike studies of Indian or African liturgies, those dealing with Western culture and modern Western liturgical revision seem unable to discuss the new ceremonies and texts within a cultural context.

For example, the papers on Worship and Secularization published in *Studia Liturgica* in 1970 and 1971 never actually discuss concrete liturgical reforms. M. Francis Mannion in an excellent article in 1988 entitled 'Liturgy and the Present Crisis of Culture' only refers in broad terms to the liturgies of Vatican II.[28] At the 1989 Societas Liturgica Congress, William Crockett spoke on the title 'Christianity and Culture in Modern Secular Society' rather than on 'Liturgy and Culture in Modern Secular Society', and managed to avoid speaking specifically about any liturgical rite.[29] Indeed, in his presidential address to the Congress, Donald Gray urged that if it was to yield any solutions, then it was liturgy which must be considered and not religion in general. By and large, his words fell on deaf ears; and yet his address assumed that there was a problem or problems, and that solutions were needed.[30] From the literature one senses that there is an acceptance that there is a problem, that modern Western liturgies are at variance with modern Western culture, and that at the moment they are a-cultural, with inculturation a distant goal. Part of the problem is the difficulty of looking at one's own culture and liturgy from within, since it lacks perspec-

[26] 'Liturgy and Modern Society—Analysis of the Current Situation', in Herman Schmidt (ed.), *Liturgy in Transition = Concilium* 62 (1971), pp. 14–29; quotation from pp. 16–17.

[27] 'Ghetto or Desert', p. 10.

[28] *Worship* 62 (1988), pp. 98–123.

[29] *Studia Liturgica* 20 (1990), pp. 28–35.

[30] 'Bridging the Gap: Presidential Address', *Studia Liturgica* 20 (1990), pp. 1–7.

tive. The problem seems to be that we cannot see the wood for the trees.

An Attempt to See the Wood

In a final, withering paper at the 1989 Societas Liturgica Congress on the subject of inculturation, Aidan Kavanagh called in question the whole enterprise. Whatever is supposed to be conveyed by 'inculturation', so he argued, has always happened, and it continues to happen with or without conscious reflection, or conferences on the topic.[31] The inference is that liturgies are themselves a product and part of the complexity which makes up culture, including Western culture; indeed, it is difficult to see how they could be otherwise. Perhaps stating the obvious, Charles Davis also wrote:

> The individual comes to be a person only in and through the action of the social environment upon him. From infancy onwards by socialization he internalizes the social reality that surrounds him. That social reality is drawn into his consciousness and is built into him as the structure of his inner life. His thought and imagination, his emotions and activity are ordered into a pattern given by the culture in which he has been formed, and he depends upon society for the continuance of his attitudes and activity, which otherwise would disintegrate and become meaningless.[32]

Those who drew up and revised the liturgies of the latter part of the twentieth century were and are themselves products of Western culture. They were educated within it, and have absorbed its ethos, even if this is tempered and critiqued by their religious beliefs. The 'experts' of the Consilium[33] or of the Episcopal Church's Standing Liturgical Commission or of the Church of England's Liturgical Commission, are products of the culture, many of them schooled in its best universities. Methods of revision were scholarly and scientific as taught in the Academy. The first drafts were circulated for discussion, and were experimented with, and revised in the light of experience and fresh

---

[31] 'Liturgical Inculturation: Looking to the Future', *Studia Liturgica* 20 (1990), pp. 95–106. Known for not suffering fools gladly, Kavanagh in his paper indicted the whole proceedings as a fools' errand.

[32] 'Ghetto or Desert', pp. 14–15.

[33] For the names of those concerned in the Roman revisions, see A. Bugnini, *The Reform of the Liturgy 1948–1975* (Liturgical Press, Collegeville 1990).

expert advice, be it pastoral, educational, or theological agencies. They were subject to pressure groups and some financial restraint. The final products were typeset, using modern printing methods and design. Celebrations of the new liturgies have been filmed and reviewed on video. Ulrich Simon, reviewing the Church of England draft Series Three communion rite in 1971 wrote:

> The sociologist will certainly identify this work with the generation from which it springs and which it serves. Here is the liturgy of the Western middle-class, full of good intentions, decent, and just a little dull. . . . 1971 must be reckoned to be petty bourgeois to the point of nausea.[34]

Simon's concern was with what he regarded as a surrender of 'protest' and 'eschatology' in the liturgy, and is not without validity.[35] However, it would be hard for '1971' not to be identified with the generation from which it sprang, be it the decent middle-class or hippy protest, unless it really was a totally a-cultural work. But no liturgy is. Without necessarily being as negative as Simon, it is possible to observe a whole number of characteristics of modern Western liturgies which show deference to their cultural milieux.

(a) Change in political and theological thought
The Church of England liturgies of 1552/1662 have enshrined within them the Tudor concept of monarchy and government, and a particular view of God's providence, not to mention theological phraseology such as 'merit' which reflects medieval legal categories of discussion. The American Prayer Book of 1789 had to alter the political dimension to suit a republic, which in turn underwent temporary alteration at the hands of Bishop Polk in January 1861 when the State of Louisiana withdrew from the Union, and again in the February when it joined the Confederacy. Similarly, the 1980 *ASB* Rite A no longer promotes the Royal Supremacy. Her Majesty is still prayed for ('Bless and guide . . .'), but English Anglicans no longer ask that

[34] 'Alternative Services', *SPCK View Review* 22.4 (November 1971), pp. 18–19.
[35] See Bryan D. Spinks, 'Christian Worship or Cultural Incantations?', *Studia Liturgica* 12 (1977), pp. 1–19.

under her the nation may be godly and quietly governed in the Tudor understanding of those words.[36] Prayer for justice and peace replaces prayer for justice and punishment, and 'the common good' replaces 'maintain thy true [i.e., Established] religion, and virtue'. The changes befit a democratic nation and a pluralist society.

(b) God and social justice

David Holeton has drawn attention to the concern for social justice in the new Anglican Canadian liturgy. He cites the old 1662 Collect for the Holy Innocents, with its spiritualizing of the deaths of the children, as lacking any reality of the slaughter of babies or any appeal to God's righteous justice. 'It should not be surprising to find that Christians living in a post-holocaust, post-Ethiopian world have difficulty in praying this prayer.'[37] The new rite has:

> Merciful God, accept all we offer you this day. Preserve your people from cruelty and indifference to violence, that the weak may always be defended from the tyranny of the strong.

This is a theologico-cultural shift. The same could be said for the address of God. The Collect for Morning Prayer in the 1662 Anglican rite, which emphasizes God's majesty and distance, in the *ASB* is recast with language which makes God much nearer and more approachable. God is perceived as a gentle, gracious father rather than His Imperial Majesty.

(c) Social awareness

Here we may cite the concern for anti-Semitism in the toning down of the references to the Jews, for example, in the Good Friday collects in the Roman rite and the Lent, Holy Week, and Easter services of the Church of England.

---

[36] cf. Paul Avis, *The Church in the Theology of the Reformers* (Marshall, Morgan & Scott, London 1981); Marion J. Hatchett, *The Making of the First American Book of Common Prayer* (Seabury Press, New York 1982); William M. Polk, *Leonidas Polk: Bishop and General*, 2nd edn (Longmans, Green & Co., New York 1915), vol. 1, pp. 306–8.

[37] 'The Formative Character of Liturgy', in T. J. Talley (ed.), *A Kingdom of Priests*, Alcuin/GROW Liturgical Study 5 (Grove Books, Nottingham 1988), pp. 8–14; quotation from p. 11.

Another concern which emerged out of the feminist movement of the 1960s was the criticism of the male-orientated nature of the English language. Thaddaeus Schnikter in his study of the social setting of the 1979 American Episcopal Prayer Book writes:

> There is an attempt throughout the prayer book to employ what is called inclusive language: verbal expressions that are as broad as possible to include all circumstances and elements of human society. . . . By employing inclusive language the Episcopal Church has been sensitive to the complaints and demands by those groups who in traditional parlance have been all too easily left out of the recognition they deserve and have been all too often discriminated against. The struggle against injustice, which was one of the reasons for the social unrest in the 1960s and 1970s, has left its mark on the vocabulary used in the liturgy too.[38]

The marriage service of the *ASB* recognizes the mutuality of marriage in the provision for the exchange of rings—an example of the liturgy catching up with changing customs. The Exhortation in the same service also reflects the higher evaluation of sexual intercourse, and has abandoned the suspicion of sex found in the 1662 rite. The new Roman Funeral rite allows for the traditional five-stage rite where it is still practical, but assumes that, in urban areas with modern funerary customs and transport, a three-stage rite will be the norm—vigil in the home, Mass with commendation and farewell, and burial or cremation; the processions with prayers to and from the church are simply not practical in modern urban settings.

(d) Informality

'Traditional' eucharistic ceremonial reflects fourth- and fifth-century imperial court ceremonial just as much as the present Byzantine rite reflects the Byzantine Court ceremonial of Constantinople. But from the 1960s Western culture has seen a trend towards informality. In England, for example, schoolteachers abandoned academic gowns, as did the older universities for their undergraduate students' dress; BBC announcers abandoned dinner jackets or evening dress, and the

---

[38] *The Church's Worship: The 1979 American Book of Common Prayer in a Historical Perspective* (Peter Lang, Frankfurt/New York 1989), p. 160.

'BBC English' was joined by regional accents. A similar relaxation of 'presidency' of services took place in church. The ceremonial was simplified; the celebrant faced West; the language became less formal. It is perhaps no accident that many celebrants, especially in Evangelical churches, have modelled themselves loosely on the television chat-show host, greeting the audience, warming them up, and introducing and explaining various parts of the 'entertainment'.

(e) Choice
One characteristic of modern Western society is its pluralism and individual choice, with market forces determining the survival of the fittest. Not only are people offered the traditional denominational differences within Christianity, but even denominations offer different styles of worship—folk or choral music, modern English, Tudor English, Latin, as well as 'formal' and 'informal' or 'family' worship.

(e) Sub-cultures
The pluralism of modern culture means that suppliers feed the markets of sub-cultures, be it pop cults, sport, the arts, etc. Liturgy in the past has been mainly concerned with the whole Church where all are one in Christ, and theoretically without concern for wealth, status or age. A modern phenomenon has been the growth of special services for special groups. 'Family' services are particularly popular in English middle-class suburbia; there are services for children, and the Roman Catholic eucharistic prayers for children; and there are also feminist liturgies, as well as—for an even more specialized market—gay and lesbian liturgies, the latter reflecting the Western concern for individual human rights (sometimes, so it is argued, against the interests of the rights of society). Whether such concern for special groups endangers catholicity is another question.

(f) Syncretism
The old religions of Europe are dead, but the West has managed to provide its own examples of liturgies where the cultural concern for novelty, entertainment, and self-expression has become

the prime criterion. A service in an American college was described by John Killinger:

> The reader read, and Ortmayer blew up balloons and let them sail around the Chapel as the air rushed out. Helpers in the balcony sailed paper plates over the heads of the people below. Each plate had a news clipping on it with instructions for the person catching it to stand and read it aloud, whatever else was going on. Some persons were throwing paper streamers; others were wrapping themselves or their neighbours in them.[39]

Here is a Western counterpart to the vaguely Christian Voodoo rites of Haiti. Killinger's book was entitled *Leave it to the Spirit*, but the spirit in question is the *Zeitgeist* of the late 1960s.

No doubt other examples could be added, but these are sufficient to illustrate the truth of Kavanagh's assertion that inculturation happens without having to agonize over it. Western liturgists need to accept that their liturgies do reflect and engage with their Western cultural context, even if the eucharistic prayers do not specifically give thanks for the river Tiber or the Thames or the Hudson!

Looking at Two of the Trees in the Wood

In his classic work *Christ and Culture*,[40] Richard Niebuhr outlined five approaches or characteristics: Christ of culture; Christ against culture; Christ above culture; Christ and culture in paradox; and Christ and the transformation of culture. Of these, three seem to be important ingredients for assessing a balanced liturgy.

(a) Christ of culture

Central to Christianity is the belief that in Christ God took human flesh. The incarnation confirms the creation as God's deliberate act, and its intrinsic goodness. God is the God of culture, and the work of human hands is always offered to God in thanksgiving. In the incarnation God affirms human societies and cultures. Liturgy needs to affirm those things in human culture which are in harmony with the gospel—for example, law

[39] *Leave it to the Spirit* (SCM, London 1971), p. 95.
[40] Harper & Row, New York 1951; Faber & Faber, London 1952.

and order, peace and justice. By itself, however, this can lead to syncretism.

(b) Christ against culture

God in Christ also judges the world and convicts it of sin. The incarnation is inextricably bound up with the atonement and resurrection and the *eschaton*. This world is passing away; there will be a new heaven and a new earth. There are some human activities which are in contradiction to the gospel, and will be challenged and condemned in the liturgy: racism, persecution, atheism, indifference, and greed. Christ against culture is a safeguard against syncretism.

(c) Christ the transformer of culture

The gospel is to be proclaimed to the world and forgiveness declared—God's amnesty. The result is not total destruction of human culture, but transformation and redemption. For example, in Islamic countries Christian liturgy (where tolerated, since Eastern culture does not always share the West's idea of toleration!) will be seen to challenge the fatalistic predestination which Islam seems to imply.

With the conviction that modern Western liturgies do reflect interaction with modern Western culture, in the final part of this essay I want to focus on two recent liturgical compilations of the Church of England with which I have been involved—*Patterns for Worship* (hereafter *PW*), a draft report of 1989, and *The Promise of His Glory* (*PG*), services from All Saints to Candlemas published in 1991—and to look at these with the three categories selected from Niebuhr.

PW, not all of which has yet been authorized for use, was completed to meet three needs: to demonstrate the flexibility of the *ASB* by giving alternative forms for use where the rubrics allow such; to provide forms for use at the 'family service', which are often home-spun liturgies replacing the official liturgy; to provide for places designated as Urban Priority Areas (UPAs)—'working-class' urban areas where 'bookish culture' is alien. The *Daily Telegraph* standard of language of the *ASB* was not considered user-friendly for this particular social grouping.

Guidelines for the language of the new prayers included the use of concrete visual images rather than language which was conceptual and full of ideas; the avoidance of Latin-style constructions with dependent clauses; and the rejection of stark and empty language.

Two of the stated purposes of *PW* are cultural and social. The 'family service' in the Church of England has a history reaching back beyond the provision of a 'Third Service' in 1872, to be celebrated in addition to the statutory services. In some parishes it has become the main service of a Sunday, in others it is monthly. These services tend to be informal, involve children, drama, sometimes non-biblical readings, and a 'talk' (as opposed to a non user-friendly 'sermon'!). Sometimes these services are aimed exclusively at children, though many middle-class suburbians seem to cling to a childlike faith that does not make too many demands on the intellect (the cool medium of television presentation, insisting on superficial ideas which are to be communicated within a minute or so). Sometimes the home-spun prayers, although 'from the heart' and 'sincere', are neither good theology nor good English. In some of them there is a tendency to speak of wrong or faults rather than sin—a move away from theological categories to a human error. Some confessions simply say sorry rather than express repentance.

PW provides liturgical forms for this socio-economic group,[41] recognizing the need for such services, but it reins in the wilder excesses, and gives stronger and more varied confessions. Thus:

> Lord God, we have done evil in your sight. We have sinned against you alone.
> Lord our God, we have sinned and avoided your call.

There is also the tendency in *PW* to concern itself with the family of humanity and the Church rather than with the modern

[41] Those engaged upon the compilation of *PW* were always aware that it was mainly a resource book for the 'family service' of middle-class suburbia. Kieran Flanagan was informed personally by the writer of this fact, but for the purposes of his book *Sociology and Liturgy* (Macmillan, London 1991) refused to accept this information, and insisted that *PW* was essentially a response (inadequate in his view) to the need for a liturgy for the working class. It simply will not do to manipulate history in this manner for the sake of one's own sociological analysis.

nuclear family with its 2.3 children. In both these examples we have expressions of the Christ of culture and against culture —affirming, providing for, but challenging.

The collection was also intended for another socio-economic group whose drab surroundings and prospects of employment often contrast considerably with the middle-class suburban congregation. Francis Mannion has argued that given the importance of images and metaphors in shaping and orientating faith, the image of the Church as a city seems more adequate than the images of family or community of friends.[42] Perhaps this has not been exploited sufficiently, but nevertheless there is material for confession, intercession, post-communion, and proper-prefaces for the city, as well as concern for mercy and justice. God is addressed as God of Glory, God of Compassion, God of Truth, God of Power. One of the proposed eucharistic prayers prays:

> Lord God of justice and mercy
> You care for the world and for every child of your creation; we glorify your Name.
> You call us to share your life and you give us your love.
> You are our Father, kind and compassionate, always ready to forgive.
> You rejoice in our joy, listen patiently to our troubles, and comfort us in distress.

Another eucharistic prayer prays in the anamnesis: 'Father, we plead with confidence his sacrifice made once for all upon the cross.' Here is a specific example of transformation of language. This is not the pleading with fear before the local magistrate, nor the pleading of desperation and anger in front of the Social Security officials, nor the old 'plead' of Federal Theology, but like some of those Latin terms cited by Gy, it is pressed into new use: pleading with confidence in anticipation of receiving forgiveness and benefit from a caring, compassionate God.

There are other hints of cultural influence. Compared with the 1970s, there is far more confidence in religion concerning creation and science, the 'big bang' and 'cosmic ripples' being not incompatable with a *creatio ex nihilo* theology. *PW* provides thanksgivings and intercessions on the theme of creation, reflecting this confidence, as well as present Western environmental

---

[42] 'Liturgy and the Present Crisis of Culture', p. 121.

concern (which often only the West can afford). Thus
Eucharistic Prayer A prays:

> Blessed are you, Lord, God of the universe,
> you bring forth bread from the earth.
> Blessed are you, Lord, God of the universe,
> you create the fruit of the vine.
> The created universe praises you, its creator.
> Sun and rain, hills and rivers praise you.
> The fruit of the earth itself praises you:
> Wheat and grape, this bread and wine,
> are part of the riches of your earth.

And Eucharistic Prayer B, developed from the eucharistic prayer
composed by the (Roman Catholic) International Commission
on English in the Liturgy:

> From the beginning you have created all things
> and all your works echo the silent music of your praise.

There is also concern for social justice:

> You sent your Son to give his life as a ransom for the whole human family.
> Give justice, peace, and racial harmony to the world he died to save.
> We have condoned evil and dishonesty and failed to strive for justice.

What we have here is both affirmation of modern Western culture, but also some theological transformation of middle-class
and UPA perceptions.

PG was aimed at the Church as a whole, and provides a rich
fare of traditional services and ceremonies, and new ones. There
are indications of these services affirming culture (Christ of culture) and protesting against it (Christ against culture) with transformation as the goal.

Christmas and some of the ancient pre-Christian symbols
have become deeply embedded in English culture. This folk religion is reflected in the provision for the Advent wreath, the
blessing of the crib, carol services, the Jesse tree, and the candle-
lit services, as well as the popular newcomer to the English
scene, the Christingle service.

At the same time there is a deliberate compromise with the
secular Christmas, which destroys the Western four-week
Advent and ends abruptly on 26 December. Since Advent was

not always four weeks, the eschatological theme now begins six weeks before Christmas, with the two Sundays before Christmas being given over to the theme of annunciation. This restores the integrity of Advent, and at the same time gives a smoother transition from Advent to Christmas. The commentary explains:

> Much of Advent—the season of watching and waiting—has been engulfed by the anticipation of Christmas, and in recent years, it has seemed a little like a clerical killjoy, frowning at society. To make the Kingship of Christ the focus of some Sundays before Advent links the theme of his universal kingdom with the more nationalistic commemorations of Remembran-cetide, and provides for Advent a more resonant context than simply 'preparing for Christmas'. So Advent can now stand out more clearly by challenging, at the same time as valuing, the world Christ came to judge and save.

In England Epiphany is not a public holiday, and the com-memoration, following the traditional Western concern, has been about the visit of the Magi. The importance of the festival in the East, with its associations with the baptism of Christ and the Wedding at Cana of Galilee, has been the basis for a fairly lavish service celebrating Epiphany with plenty of use of sym-bols, and it includes the presentation of gold, incense, and myrrh, the paten and chalice, and water with the renewal of bap-tismal vows. The latter is patterned after the theme of covenant, emphasizing the community of the Church in relation to God. In this case we have Christ against culture, with the hope of trans-formation and the rediscovery of Epiphany as an important festi-val.

In contrast with the Church of England tradition from 1549 onwards, *PG* makes considerable provision for observing All Saints' and All Souls'. Although some naive Evangelical critics have seen this as 'creeping Romanism', it is rather to be seen as a Christian response to the growing Western fear of death and dying, and to the more fanciful concern with Halloween and a hideous malevolent afterlife. Something more imaginative for children still needs to be thought of to challenge the popular 'trick or treat' which has crossed from the USA to England.

Lastly, the increased use of symbolism in these services may also represent an unconscious response to the observation of anthropologists that Western culture is beginning to value and use symbolism which it once freely jettisoned as outdated fo modern man. The service of light for vigils, the Advent wreath, the Epiphany symbols, and candles for Candlemas come into this category.

It is my contention, therefore, that the crisis Western liturgists allege exists in the modern liturgies is more a problem of perspective than failure to interact with culture. If anything, the problem is to guard against the modern liturgies being just a religious gloss on a developing Western culture. Modern Western rites cannot but help reflect the culture from which they spring, either in affirming that culture (Christ of culture), or in challenging it (Christ against culture), and/or in working for its transformation (Christ the transformer of culture). If there is a crisis, the fault is probably not that the liturgies are not modern, but possibly because, in affirming culture, they have obscured the mystery and transcendence of God.[43] But it is possible that the fault also lies elsewhere—with preaching, mission, pastoralia, and public stance. The liturgy cannot be the whole missionary activity of the modern Western Church; nor can it be the scapegoat for all other ecclesiastical shortcomings.

[43] See W. J. Grisbrooke, 'Liturgical Reform and Liturgical Renewal', *Studia Liturgica* 21 (1991), pp. 136–54.

3

Liturgy and Doctrine: Recent Debate about Eucharistic Sacrifice in the Church of England

DAVID GLOVER

The issue of eucharistic sacrifice has been an extremely thorny one in Western churches since the Reformation. Both then and since, the debate has centred on the question of the relationship between the sacrifice that Christ himself offered and any sacrifice that the Church offers. Nearly all of the diversity and polarity of opinion that has existed on this question can be seen in the Church of England. On one side, Thomas Cranmer conceived the eucharist to be primarily a 'communion' in which the communicants participated in the benefits of Christ's once-and-for-all sacrifice. Any notion of the Church's sacrifice in the eucharist was limited to a post-communion, non-reconciliatory, sacrificial response of praise and thanksgiving, which was ontologically distinct from Christ's atoning sacrifice. The primary activity was understood to be from God towards humanity, and Cranmer therefore attempted to avoid any notion of human offering to God in the heart of the eucharistic action.

This interpretation dominated the eucharistic rite of the 1552 *Book of Common Prayer*,[1] and Cranmer's conviction that the essence of the Church's sacrifice consisted in praise and thanksgiving as an obedient response by the Church, on behalf of all creation, to God's act of creation and redemption, has been generally held within the Church of England ever since. Differences have arisen, however, concerning the relationship between this sacrifice and Christ's sacrifice on Calvary, and consequently over the place and significance that the Church's sacrifice should have within a eucharistic context. At the other extreme, for example, the medieval interpretation of eucharistic

[1] See Colin Buchanan, *What Did Cranmer Think he was Doing?*, Grove Liturgical Study 7 (Grove Books, Nottingham 1976).

sacrifice to which Cranmer was reacting was revived in the Church of England during the nineteenth century and has been held since by some of its members. This latter view considers that Christ is 'slain', albeit mystically, in each Mass, and that this immolation has a propitiatory effect. It had been rejected by the Reformers as undermining the all-sufficient efficacy of Christ's sacrifice upon Calvary.

Part of the liturgical renewal and revival which has been so prominent in the Church in the twentieth century has involved the attempt to find common ground and consensus on this issue. Since the Church of England contains such diverse opinions, consideration of how this issue has been handled in that church over the last few decades forms an ecumenical study in miniature, which both reflects and may inform the wider debate. Therefore, one of the aims of this essay is to examine recent trends on this issue within the Church of England. Its second purpose is to consider the extent to which any development on this matter has had specific influence upon liturgical rites. A number of scholars have shown how Cranmer's theology directly influenced his liturgical composition. However, during recent liturgical revision in the Church of England, there seems to have been a far less clearly defined link between theological conviction and liturgical composition. At present the climax of eucharistic liturgical reform in the Church of England has been the composition of the Rite A forms of the *Alternative Service Book 1980*. Therefore we will consider to what extent the recent thinking on eucharistic sacrifice has been reflected in the four Rite A eucharistic prayers.

'Catholic' Reconsiderations of Eucharistic Sacrifice

During the twentieth century there has been a considerable re-examination of sacrificial concepts of the eucharist in the Church of England. The impetus for this has come, perhaps not surprisingly, from 'Catholic' members who have attempted to reassert the sacrificial nature of the eucharist in a way that is more widely acceptable and avoids the sixteenth-century divisions. This has involved a reconsideration of three closely related tenets in Cranmer's theology: first, that the eucharistic pattern necessarily consists of communion and response; second,

that the entirety of Christ's sacrificial action before God consisted solely in his actual death on the cross at Calvary; third,
that any sacrifice the Church offers is necessarily ontologically
distinct from Christ's unique offering at Calvary.

In response to Cranmer's first tenet, it has been claimed that
Christians can and should make an 'offering' to God within the
heart of the eucharistic action, and not just as a response to
communion. J. L. Houlden, for example, argued that not merely
the post-communion response but the entire orientation of the
Christian life, of which the eucharist forms a liturgical focus, is
to be a sacrificial offering to God.[2] Furthermore, it has been
emphasized that there are 'Dominical' and 'Apostolic' com-
mands to offer sacrifice in the eucharist, and this primarily in
relation to the bread and the cup. Firstly, the word *kataggelete* in
1 Corinthians 11.26, which is often translated as 'you do show
forth', has been understood as having the sense of a Godward
action which incorporates the sense of 'showing forth' or offering
up to God. Secondly, it is argued that within the primitive tradition Christians regarded the eucharist as a sacrifice and claimed
that Christ commanded the Church to offer it. A. H. Couratin,
for example, cited Justin's *Dialogue* (41), which he considered
spoke of the bread of the eucharist handed down by Jesus Christ
for us to offer. Thirdly, it has been claimed by Couratin, among
others, that Christ's words at the Last Supper include a command to offer. Christ commanded us to do as he did 'in remembrance'. His first action was to take and give thanks. Couratin
suggested that this giving of thanks was understood as an 'offering' up of thanks in association with the bread and the cup.[3]

With regard to Cranmer's second tenet, that the entirety of
Christ's sacrificial action before God consisted solely in his
actual death on the cross at Calvary, there have been two distinct conceptual trends in the reconsideration of this by
'Catholic' theologians. Both can claim to have roots within historical Anglicanism, and each includes an understanding that the

[2] 'Good Liturgy or even Good Battlefield? "We offer this Bread and this
Cup": 1', *Theology* 69 (1966), p. 434. Cf. Kenneth Stevenson, *Accept this Offering* (SPCK, London; Liturgical Press, Collegeville 1989), p. 79.

[3] 'The Tradition Received: "We offer this Bread and this Cup": 2', *Theology*
69 (1966), pp. 437–42, esp. p. 439.

Church's eucharistic action is both a reflection of and in some sense an entering into the heavenly action of Christ. However, they differ on their understanding of the nature of Christ's continuing sacrificial action, and thus on the nature of the Church's eucharistic sacrificial action.

On the one hand, there has been a revival of the largely seventeenth-century notion, held by such diverse divines as Richard Baxter and Jeremy Taylor, that while the sacrifice of Christ is completed upon the cross of Calvary and that Christ is not offering his sacrifice in heaven, nevertheless he continues to 'plead' the merits of his sacrifice before his Father, and thus there is a continual memorial in heaven of the one sacrifice made by Christ. The biblical basis claimed for this understanding rests on passages such as Hebrews 7.25 ('Consequently he is able for all time to save those who draw near to God through him, since he always lives to make intercession for them'). The earthly eucharist is then regarded as a reflection of the heavenly action of Christ. Further evidence, as we have seen earlier, is the interpretation of *kataggelete* in 1 Corinthians 11.26.

Gregory Dix was one of the twentieth-century proponents of this view. He argued that, as a response to the act of remembering, the Church offers the bread and wine as a Godward action reminding God of the work of Christ.[4] The sense of this position is that having made remembrance in response to Christ's command, we now offer to God this memorial sacrifice. This is not an addition to or a re-enactment of Calvary, but a 'showing forth' before God in union with Christ's eternal 'showing forth', or eternal sacrificial memorial, of the all-sufficient sacrifice of Calvary. Therefore, this notion also challenges Cranmer's third tenet, that any sacrifice the Church offers is ontologically distinct from Christ's unique offering at Calvary. In what Houlden has called 'dependent parallelism', Christ's eternal pleading of his once-and-for-all sacrifice at the heavenly altar is understood to correspond to the Church's offering of its eucharistic worship at the earthly altar.[5]

---

[4] *The Shape of the Liturgy* (Dacre, Westminster 1945), pp. 243ff.

[5] 'Sacrifice and the Eucharist', in *Thinking about the Eucharist: Papers by Members of the Church of England Doctrine Commission* (SCM, London 1972), p. 94. Houlden himself sees an inherent weakness in this view.

The second 'Catholic' conceptual trend, on the other hand, goes beyond the notion of memorial sacrifice and claims that the eucharist can be understood as containing an offering of Christ to God in a sense that is more generally acceptable. This notion involves the related ideas that Christ's sacrificial offering has an eternal dimension and that the Church is in some sense able to enter into this eternal offering. Here we see a more systematic reconsideration of the third of Cranmer's tenets, for it asserts that the true sacrificial offering of the Church, while having numerous manifestations, is essentially and ontologically one with the essence of Christ's own sacrificial offering.

The foundation for this concept has been a re-interpretation of Christ's sacrifice, based upon the work of F. C. N. Hicks. In a book that went through many editions and reprints and figured prominently in ecumenical discussions, he had put forward the argument that the actual death of Christ, which was necessary because of human sinfulness, was only the first stage of the sacrifice. Jesus then took his blood, which was his life offered, through the veil, his flesh, into the presence of God. There he atones for us; and his life and humanity, in which our life and humanity are joined by the incarnation, are offered to the Father in eternal service.[6] The sacrifice of Christ, therefore, is not limited to the cross but continues as an eternal act of atonement before the Father. When this concept was combined with a renewed emphasis on the notion of the Church as the 'mystical body of Christ',[7] it allowed the Church to do more than merely parallel Christ's sacrifice: it could participate in it.

Added impetus was given to this interpretation by the 1958 Lambeth Conference Report on Prayer Book Revision, which adopted it in the expectation that it would prove to be decisively unitive. It followed Hicks and Louis Bouyer in suggesting that the nature of Christ's eternal offering was of the order of 'willing obedience', and claimed that the Church participated in it by its union with Christ in his body: 'we offer our praise and thanksgiv-

---

[6] *The Fullness of Sacrifice* (Macmillan, London 1930); précis in 'Anglican (c)', in P. Edwall, E. Hayman, and W. D. Maxwell (eds), *Ways of Worship* (SCM, London 1951), pp. 206ff.

[7] See for example L. S. Thornton, *The Common Life in the Body of Christ* (Dacre, London 1941), pp. 387–8, 425ff.

ing for Christ's sacrifice for us and so present it again, and ourselves in him, before the Father'.[8]

Thus the combination of the ideas of eternal sacrifice and 'mystical body' gave rise to a new understanding of the essence and nature of Christ's sacrifice in relation to the Church. Since the offering of the body mystical is, by the power of the Spirit, the offering of Christ, and since Christ's sacrifice is single and not multiple, one and eternal, the offering of the body mystical must be identical with the offering of the body personal. The Church by its offering of 'obedience' and 'thanksgiving' enters into and becomes organically one with the eternal offering of Christ before the Father. The implication here is that the Church itself, as Christ's mystical body, takes upon itself a share in Christ's high priesthood, in that it enters into the sacrificial offering of Christ for the sins of the whole world.

Not surprisingly, theologians of this camp have perceived the eucharist as being the focus of this offering, and suggested that the entire sacrificial offering of the body mystical is recapitulated in the offering of the bread and the cup. Some have stressed the interrelatedness of the body of Christ personal, or natural, the body of Christ mystical, and the body of Christ sacramental. Thus William Temple argued that each is in some sense an expression of the Son and a means for the Son's interaction and personal interrelationship in the world.[9] E. L. Mascall claimed that the bread and the wine are the place of meeting between the offering of the body mystical and the perfect offering of the risen and ascended Christ.[10]

These ideas were also combined with the results of liturgical research. Dix popularized the notion that an initial offertory is integral to the entire eucharistic action. He pointed out that in the *Apostolic Tradition* the deacons bring up the 'oblation' (*prosphora*) of the people.[11] A. G. Hebert argued that in this offertory, taken up to the altar by the deacons from the people,

[8] *The Lambeth Conference 1958: The Encyclical Letter from the Bishops Together with the Resolutions and Reports* (SPCK, London 1958), 2.84.

[9] *Christus Veritas: An Essay* (Macmillan, London 1924), pp. 292ff.

[10] *Christ, the Christian and the Church* (Longmans, Green & Co., London 1946), pp. 181–2, 198.

[11] *The Shape of the Liturgy*, p. 110.

the gifts of bread and wine represent the lives of the people, or in Temple's terms the 'body mystical'. The elements are taken by the bishop and offered as a thank-offering to the Father, and so the Church's offering of thanks both for creation and for redemption is recapitulated in the elements.[12] A. H. Couratin observed that this fulfils the Church's obligation of obedience to the command of Christ, who took bread and offered thanks.[13] The argument would seem to be that recapitulated in the elements is the whole dedicated oblation of the Church, which is united to the offering of thanks and realizes the memorial of Christ's passion before the Father, and moreover becomes an offering before the Father of the passion of Christ. Couratin claimed that this was precisely the argument which was put forward in Justin Martyr's *Dialogue* (41) and which was preserved in the prayer of the *Apostolic Tradition*. Thus Hebert and Couratin appear to have seen the basic elements of the concept we have outlined as a reassertion of primitive eucharistic theology and believed that this offered a unitive way forward in considering the doctrine of the eucharistic sacrifice.

'Evangelical' Reactions

That neither of the above 'Catholic' trends has in fact offered a unitive way forward within the Church of England has largely been due to 'Evangelical' reaction to both of them. In opposing the first, W. M. F. Scott argued that nowhere in the Acts of the Apostles or the New Testament epistles is the word *kataggelete* understood as a 'showing forth' to God. Rather, he argued that it is always used for the proclamation of the gospel before human beings. Moreover, he considered that the notion of 'heavenly intercession' in Hebrews 7.25 does not necessarily imply pleading. It does so only if we read a notion of pleading into it.[14]

'Evangelicals' were also unhappy with the second approach, which redefined the nature of Christ's sacrifice in such a way that it made it possible for the Church's sacrifice to have an

---

[12] 'The Meaning of the Epiclesis', *Theology* 27 (1933), pp. 198–210.

[13] In the article cited in n. 3 above.

[14] 'The Eucharist and the Heavenly Ministry of Our Lord', *Theology* 56 (1953), pp. 42–8.

ontological identity with it.[15] R. J. Coates argued that Hebrews emphasizes the uniqueness and perfection of Christ's sacrifice for us. His offering was in his suffering alone fulfilled and complete.[16] C. O. Buchanan and R. T. Beckwith argued that in the New Testament Jesus' sacrifice consists only in his death and in his obedience to death, not in his obedience as such.[17] Scott argued that Hebrews 9.11 – 12 asserts that Christ obtained redemption before entering the heavenly sanctuary. Further objections were raised to the implication that if the Church is thought of as sharing in the sacrifice of Christ, then this assumes that the Church shares in Christ's high priesthood. It was claimed that in the New Testament the Church only participated in Christ's sacrifice as a beneficiary, and that Hebrews considers Christ's high priesthood to be unique and not transmissible.

Therefore, though these 'Evangelical' writers essentially agree with the 'Catholic' position, that the essence of the Church's sacrifice is to offer obedience, praise, and thanksgiving, they assert that the Church's offering can only be a response to the reception of the benefits of Christ's unique sacrifice: there can be no ontological identity between the two types of sacrifice. Thus, while there is implicit agreement on the nature of the Church's sacrifice in general, there is fundamental disagreement between the two groups within the Church of England, both about the nature of Christ's sacrifice and consequently about the significance and precise relationship of the Church's sacrifice to it.

A Further Strand

It can be objected that both groups failed adequately to take into account the broader perspective of Christian reconciliation in which the notion of Christ's sacrifice has a paramount place. For example, J. I. Packer noted that the 'Evangelical' doctrine of penal substitution, though acknowledging Christ's work in deal-

[15] See J. I. Packer, 'Eucharistic Sacrifice', in idem (ed.), *Eucharistic Sacrifice: The Addresses Given at the Oxford Conference of Evangelical Churchmen* (Book Room Press, London 1962), pp. 3 – 10.

[16] 'The Doctrine of Eucharistic Sacrifice in Modern Times', in ibid., p. 150.

[17] ' "This Bread and This Cup": An Evangelical Rejoinder', *Theology* 70 (1967), p. 267.

ing with sin to be primarily substitutionary, that is, done 'in our stead', must nevertheless understand the broader concept of reconciliation to involve also an identification with the action of Christ.[18] This notion of identification, as integral to the pardon of justification, is as much an element in the process of atonement or reconciliation as the actual act of dealing with sin. There is an implication in the penal theory that humanity can only benefit from Christ's sacrifice by participating in some sense in it through an identification by faith with Christ. This begins at baptism as we share in his death, and, one might argue, is proclaimed and reasserted in the eucharist. Therefore, set in the broader picture of reconciliation, the Christian response is not simply one of thanksgiving and praise but of identification with and incorporation into the sacrificial action of Christ. On the other hand, while the 'Catholic' position has had a more adequate notion of identification, it has expressed itself in ways which appear at least to others to undermine the unique nature of Christ's own sacrificial action in reconciling humanity to God.

There is, however, a further strand discernible in eucharistic theology within the Church of England which generally holds in greater tension the broader picture of Christian reconciliation, and includes within it much of the concerns of both 'Catholics' and 'Evangelicals'. This line of thought is found in two crucial statements by the Anglican-Roman Catholic International Commission (ARCIC) about the eucharist and the sacrifice of Christ. The first is that 'Christ's death on the cross . . . was the one, perfect and sufficient sacrifice for the sins of the world. There can be no repetition of or addition to what was then accomplished once and for all by Christ'. The second affirms that in making memorial in the eucharist, the Church is making present the benefits of Christ's sacrifice for the Church to participate in, with the result that the Church enters into 'the movement of his self-offering'.[19]

A Church of England response to these statements accepts that Christ's sacrifice was his death, which was historically

---

[18] 'What Did the Cross Achieve? The Logic of Penal Substitution', *Tyndale Bulletin* 25 (1974), pp. 3–45.

[19] *The Anglican-Roman Catholic Agreement on the Eucharist* (SPCK, London 1971), section 5.

unique and 'once-and-for-all'. In this sense it is unrepeatable and complete. This appears to rule out Hicks' notion of an eternal offering by Christ. However, in reflecting upon the ARCIC notion of participation, the Church of England response seems to understand that while Christ's sacrifice is complete, what continues is the incorporation of the believers into Christ's death by baptism which is renewed and continually made manifest in the eucharist.[20]

This incorporation and renewal can and has been understood in sacrificial terms within Church of England, even by 'Evangelical' writers. W. M. F. Scott, while critical of much of the above 'Catholic' theology, was nevertheless aware that the New Testament abounded in a whole variety of sacrificial metaphors. In particular, he considered that, on the basis of Colossians 1.22 and 1 Peter 3.18, while not offering his own sacrifice in heaven, Christ does still bring before or offer to God humanity.[21] This notion finds a richer but related focus in C. F. D. Moule's appropriation of the concept of the Church as the 'mystical body of Christ'.[22] Moule's position seems to be that the Church's obedience is in response to the obedience of Christ on Calvary, and as such is ontologically distinct. Nevertheless, our obedience, praise, and thanksgiving are integrally related to Calvary, which is the historical focus for our continued obedience. Furthermore, as the Church is the body of Christ, its obedience, praise, and thanksgiving are offered by Christ and in Christ.

Out of all this, one might be able to say that in offering to the Father the sacrifice of the mystical body, in the power of the Spirit, Christ is offering his own sacrifice, and in a sense his people are offering him and his obedience, since both offerings are related as reception is related to gift. Therefore, this offering is neither an eternal pleading of the sacrifice nor an eternal offering of the sacrifice of redemption. Rather it is the offering, offered by Christ to the Father, of the Church's obedient and

[20] *A Response by the Church of England to the Agreed Statements of the Anglican-Roman Catholic International Commission: A Report by the Faith and Order Advisory Group of the Board for Mission and Unity* (Church House Publishing, London 1985), pp. 4ff.

[21] In the article cited in n. 14 above.

[22] *The Sacrifice of Christ* (Hodder & Stoughton, London 1956), pp. 30–58.

related sacrificial response to Christ's sacrifice. This notion was taken up by E. L. Mascall and Michael Green, who represent contrasting ecclesiastical traditions. In a joint essay they accepted that we must distinguish ontologically between Christ's sacrifice and the Church's, but they argued that the Church's sacrifice is only pleasing to God when presented in Christ and through his sacrifice.[23]

This approach clearly picks up much of the 'Catholic' concept, but maintains the 'Evangelical' emphasis on the ontological uniqueness of Christ's sacrifice. It may thus offer a way forward which preserves a greater sense of the richness and diversity of biblical and theological atonement metaphors. It understands the Christian response of obedience, thanksgiving, and praise in terms both of its inclusion in and relationship to Christ's sacrifice, and of its inevitable distinction from it. However, this approach has not gained universal acceptance. Although there has been a movement within the Church of England to achieve a theological consensus on the issue of eucharistic sacrifice, it has not been successful. In addition to a minority who hold to the old teaching of a 'Real Sacrifice' within the eucharist, propitiatory for the living and the dead, there remain at least four views concerning the nature of the Church's eucharistic sacrifice:

(a) that the Church's sacrifice is in response to Christ's sacrifice in which the Church has no part other than in receiving the benefits from it;

(b) that it is a memorial sacrifice parallel not to Christ's actual atoning sacrifice on Calvary but to his 'eternal pleading' of that sacrifice;

(c) that it has an ontological identity with Christ's sacrifice and is included within the one and the same offering;

(d) that it is the sacrificial offering by Christ of the Church's responsive obedience to Christ's unique atoning sacrifice and the integration of the Church into the salvific movement of that sacrifice.

---

[23] 'Eucharistic Sacrifice: Some Interim Agreement', in C. O. Buchanan, E. L. Mascall, J. I. Packer, G. D. Leonard, *Growing Into Union: Proposals for Forming a United Church in England* (SPCK, London 1970), p. 191.

Eucharistic Rites

The environment in which recent liturgical revisions have occurred is thus one still characterized by a diversity of opinions on this crucial theological point. Our aim now is to consider to what extent the notions of eucharistic sacrifice expounded above find expression within the four eucharistic prayers of Rite A of the *Alternative Service Book* of the Church of England (referred to from now on as *ASB* 1, 2, 3, and 4). We would want to argue that to at least some degree all the above notions of eucharistic sacrifice can be seen as expressed in one or other of these prayers. This is never an explicit expression, partly owing to the theological ambiguity of any liturgical text and also partly because of a conscious theological compromise.

The key section of these prayers for our purpose would seem to be the anamnesis. The contemporary understanding of the biblical concept of anamnesis, or 'remembrance', has chiefly been that that which is remembered has a dynamic and active effect in the present. Thus, the liturgical anamnesis gives expression to the idea that in some sense Christ's sacrifice, or the benefit of Christ's sacrifice, is made present in a special and focused sense to the congregation, as recapitulated in the bread and wine. If it is also the case that the Church's sacrifice has, in some sense, been recapitulated in the bread and wine, then the anamnesis section of a eucharistic prayer, as well as expressing Christ's presence to the communicants, can be also expressive of the integral relationship between Christ's sacrifice and the Church's sacrifice. What the Church now does with the bread and the wine is, therefore, expressive of the sense in which the Church's sacrifice of obedience, thanks, and praise is being offered in relation to Christ's own sacrifice.[24]

[24] However, this is not to say that consecration is necessarily complete at the point of the anamnesis. The Church of England Liturgical Commission has asserted that the whole eucharistic prayer is to be understood as consecrating and that no one 'moment' or formula of consecration is to be identified: see *The Alternative Service Book 1980: A Commentary by the Liturgical Commission* (CIO Publishing, London 1980), p. 79. And J. H. Mckenna reminds us that we can express liturgically the ritual 'moments', while acknowledging that the actual 'moments' are a mystery contained within the entire eucharistic action: see his *Eucharist and Holy Spirit*, Alcuin Club Collection 57 (Mayhew-McCrimmon, Great Wakering 1976), p. 187.

As we have seen above, there has been a division of opinion in the Church of England between those who have accepted some reconsideration of Cranmer's first tenet and the conservative 'Evangelicals' who have continued to view the eucharist as purely a movement by God towards human beings. For them, of course, the liturgical anamnesis is seen as being merely reflective of this one-way movement, and the inclusion in Rite A of a pattern following the traditional *Book of Common Prayer* order was an attempt to provide a liturgical expression of this particular theological stance, rather than a reflection of the normative place of the *Book of Common Prayer* within the Church of England. This is clearly shown by the fact that the order was inserted as part of the conservative 'Evangelical' demand in a 'deal' with 'Anglo-Catholics'.[25]

Marks of theological compromise between the two positions can be found in all four prayers in the *ASB*. For instance, *ASB* 1 can be interpreted in conservative 'Evangelical' terms. The anamnesis in this prayer runs as follows:

> we remember his offering of himself made once for all upon the cross, and proclaim his mighty resurrection and glorious ascension. As we look for his coming in glory, we celebrate with this bread and this cup his one perfect sacrifice.

It could be argued that the prayer simply contrasts Christ's eternal and all-sufficient sacrifice with the Church's appropriate response of proclamation and celebration of it, understood in an inter-human sense of proclaiming and celebrating our participation in the benefits of Christ's sacrifice. In this sense the elements are to be understood both as a recapitulation of the redemption made present and as a proclamation and celebration of it to and by the assembled Church.

However, Ronald Jasper and Paul Bradshaw have pointed out that, though the word 'celebrate' can mean no more than 'to do' or 'to perform' in the history of liturgical usage, it can also contain within it all the meaning conveyed by the expression 'to make the anamnesis of', depending on the context in which it is

[25] On this, see below p. 66.

used.[26] We would want to argue that its contextual use in *ASB* 1 makes the second of these definitions more appropriate and that the meaning given to the words 'remembrance' and 'memorial' in recent Anglican discussion suggests the presence of a theology in line with that of the writings of Moule, Scott, and ARCIC.

First, Jasper himself, who chaired the Liturgical Commission, recognized and commented upon the influence of the ARCIC statement and the essay by Mascall and Green during the drafting of Series 3, which was the experimental liturgy from which *ASB* 1 developed.[27] Second, in his apologetic on the Series 3 eucharistic prayer, R. J. Halliburton noted that 'remembrance' has to do not so much with a passive receiving of the benefits of redemption but more with an active entering into the whole mystery of redemption. Halliburton too recalled ARCIC's notion and argued that 'to make the memorial of Christ's saving work' means that we become involved in his redeeming work. Halliburton considered that the omission of an explicit offering of the elements in the anamnesis in Series 3 was unfortunate, but did not eliminate sacrificial notions.[28] Third, the phrase which follows the anamnesis in *ASB* 1, 'Accept through him, our great high priest', is strongly reminiscent of the understanding that our obedient responsive sacrifice is offered by and through Christ to the Father. This has an active Godward movement but is distinguishable from the unique movement of Christ to the Father. Furthermore, the whole movement of the prayer is one of thanksgiving, which is more than a mere response to communion.

In the light of the above, it would seem plausible to interpret the word 'celebrate' in this prayer as reflecting the notion that recapitulated in the bread and the wine is not only a movement of Christ's redemption from God to humanity but also a movement of humanity's obedient response to God, offered through

[26] *A Companion to the Alternative Service Book* (SPCK, London 1986), p. 225. See also Paul F. Bradshaw, 'Celebration', in R. C. D. Jasper (ed.), *The Eucharist Today: Studies on Series 3* (SPCK, London 1974), pp. 130–41.

[27] *The Development of the Anglican Liturgy 1662–1980* (SPCK, London 1989), pp. 308f.

[28] 'The Canon of Series 3', in Jasper (ed.), *The Eucharist Today*, pp. 110–16.

and by Christ. This, therefore, perhaps gives liturgical expression to Moule and Scott's assertion that in offering to the Father the sacrifice of the mystical body, in the power of the Spirit, Christ is offering his own sacrifice, inasmuch as our sacrifice must be reappropriated in his, and thus the Church is in a sense offering his sacrifice, since it is only through Christ's sacrifice that our responsive sacrifice can be offered to and become acceptable before God.

Ambiguity is also present in the anamnesis section of *ASB* 2:

> having in remembrance his death once for all upon the cross, his resurrection from the dead, and his ascension into heaven, and looking for the coming of his kingdom, we make with this bread and this cup the memorial of Christ your Son our Lord.

The phrase 'make . . . the memorial' is open to diverse interpretation. Jasper and Bradshaw claimed that it simply picked up on the ambiguous anamnesis phrase in Cranmer's 1549 rite.[29] But it could also be regarded as effectively preserving the 'Catholic' notion of the eucharist as a 'memorial' sacrifice. The language is suggestive of the notion that the earthly eucharist is offered in dependent parallelism to Christ's 'eternal pleading' before God of his sacrifice in heaven, and thus we are making with the bread and the cup a 'memorial' sacrifice. That this is a possible interpretation of the phrase is strengthened by the fact that it replaced the words 'we offer you this bread and this cup' in the earlier Series 2 prayer, and so possibly retains, though ambiguously, some of that meaning. However, the phrase is so 'helpfully' ambiguous that it could and has been interpreted along 'Evangelical' lines. For example, Colin Buchanan noted that when this phrase was drafted by Jasper, 'Catholic' Geoffrey Willis criticized it for excluding any possibility of regarding the eucharist as a sacrifice and confining it instead to a bare memorial of the passion, while 'Evangelical' Derek Scales criticized it for containing strong sacrificial overtones.[30]

In contrast, *ASB* 4 seems to eliminate all notions of eucharistic sacrifice. There is no explicit mention, ambiguous or

---

[29] *Companion to the Alternative Service Book*, p. 226.
[30] *Recent Liturgical Revision in the Church of England* (Grove Books, Nottingham 1973), p. 26, n. 3.

otherwise, of an oblation of the bread and the cup. The anamnesis section runs:

> in remembrance of the precious death and passion, the mighty resurrection and glorious ascension of your dear Son Jesus Christ, we offer you through him this sacrifice of praise and thanksgiving.

Furthermore, the prayer as a whole stresses the uniqueness and finality of Christ's atoning sacrifice on Calvary, and in its epiclesis section points to a memorial reception of the fruits of this sacrifice as being the high point of the action. Therefore, the prayer seems to reflect a clear 'Evangelical' stance: the eucharist is a setting forth of the benefits of Christ's sacrifice and a feasting upon them.

Nevertheless, it is still possible to interpret the anamnesis as giving liturgical articulation to the theology of Moule, Scott, and others. In association with the bread and the wine, this prayer both makes remembrance of Christ's death and passion and, dependent upon this, offers through Christ a sacrifice of praise and thanksgiving. Thus, the humanward and the Godward movements meet and are focused in the making present of Christ's redemptive action in association with the bread and wine. The implication is that our sacrifice is both derived from and enabled by Christ's sacrifice, and our sacrifice is acceptable because it is reappropriated in and offered through and in association with the fruits of Christ's sacrifice made present. Therefore, both God's movement to us, in setting forth Christ's sacrifice, and the Church's movement or offering to God are recapitulated in the bread and wine, as the latter participates in and becomes integrated with the fruits of Christ's sacrifice, which fundamentally consists of a movement by humanity in Christ to reconciliation with God.

Although the language of eucharistic offering in the anamnesis of *ASB* 3 appears to be the most explicit of all the prayers, it still remains ambiguous and open to interpretation along different lines:

> calling to mind his death on the cross, his perfect sacrifice made once for the sins of all men, rejoicing at his mighty resurrection and glorious ascension, and looking for his coming in glory, we celebrate this memorial of our

redemption; we thank you for counting us worthy to stand in your presence and serve you; we bring before you this bread and this cup; we pray you to accept this our duty and service, a spiritual sacrifice of praise and thanksgiving.

The prayer, based on that in the *Apostolic Tradition*, was originally penned in the context of a compromise between 'Anglo-Catholics' and 'Evangelicals', represented by Brian Brindley and Roger Beckwith respectively.[31] In return for the inclusion in the *ASB* of a prayer along the lines of the *Book of Common Prayer* order, Beckwith was willing to accept a 'Catholic' prayer, as long as a certain fundamental safeguard was assured. Essentially this seems to have been Beckwith's insistence that the medieval understanding of the offering of Christ's sacrifice and any notion of a repetition of Christ's sacrifice must be avoided and repudiated. The prayer does just this in the expression 'calling to mind his death on the cross, his perfect sacrifice made once for the sins of all men'. However, the 'Catholic' position was equally keen to avoid such an interpretation of Christ's sacrifice, and so it seems that Beckwith imposed a 'No go' area into which, ironically, the 'Catholics' had no need to tread.

Beckwith also insisted that as part of the compromise each should be able to use the prayer without strain to conscience. This is possible because its language, especially in its finally revised form in the *ASB*, is ambiguous. The fact that, as in *ASB* 1 and 2, the language of celebration and memorial is set in contrast to the language of Christ's once-and-for-all death could be seen as strongly expressive of the 'Evangelical' position, and thus the words 'we bring before you this bread and this cup' could mean no more than a setting of the elements at God's disposal. An 'Evangelical' could, it seems, use the prayer without strain of conscience. However, there is also scope to accommodate the second of the 'Catholic' concepts expounded earlier. In remembering Christ's offering on the cross, the Church celebrates the memorial of it, since Christ has fulfilled a unique function towards God which human beings were incapable of fulfilling,

[31] See R. T. Beckwith, *The Revised Series 3: A Way Forward* (Latimer Studies, Oxford 1979), p. 33.

but 'we bring before you this bread and this cup' can be seen as pointing to an offering of the Church which is identical to the offering of Christ, and thus in effect an offering of Christ's sacrifice.

Conclusion

Three points can be made by way of summary. First, it is clear there has been within the Church of England a determined attempt to reconsider the eucharist in sacrificial terms without reasserting sixteenth-century divisions. Secondly, because consensus has not yet been possible on this issue, the eucharistic liturgies of Rite A of the *Alternative Service Book 1980* reflect and implicitly accept the reality of diversity. Some might argue that this is so simply because diverse theological notions have been read into the prayers, but it does seem that the liturgies were deliberately framed to encourage this to happen.[32] Thus, despite there being few formal links between the Church of England Doctrine and Liturgical Commissions, the Rite A prayers do reflect, albeit ambiguously, recent Anglican theological positions, even if the links are not as clear as they were between Cranmer's theology and the *Book of Common Prayer*. Finally, it can be argued that the theological strand found in the ARCIC statement offers the most realistic way of uniting 'Catholics' and 'Evangelicals' in the Church of England, and also at the same time reflects best the growing consensus between the Reformation churches and the Roman Catholic Church.[33]

[32] Two pieces of evidence may be cited in support of this. First, Jasper has written that the only doctrines which the eucharist must safeguard are the fundamental essentials (though what these are is not made clear); apart from this there should be a 'studied ambiguity' such as will accommodate every school of thought about the eucharist: see Jasper, 'Gore on Liturgical Revision', *Church Quarterly Review* 166 (1965), p. 27. Secondly, Beckwith and John Tiller have pointed out that a similar principle is stated in the introduction to the Series 2 experimental rite: 'We have also, where matters of eucharistic doctrine are concerned, tried to produce forms of words which are capable of various interpretations.' See R. T. Beckwith and J. E. Tiller (eds), *The Service of Holy Communion and its Revision* (Marcham Manor Press, Abingdon 1972), p. 28.

[33] Not only does the ARCIC connection imply this, but it would seem that the notion of eucharistic sacrifice in Roman Catholic liturgy is being interpreted in similar ways. See for example Enrico Mazza, *The Eucharistic Prayers of the Roman Rite* (Pueblo, New York 1986), p. 241.

4

Liturgy and Ecumenism:
Three Models of Development

PHILLIP TOVEY

Two great movements have had a profound impact on the churches in the twentieth century, the Ecumenical Movement and the Liturgical Movement. It is common to trace the origin of the former to the Edinburgh Missionary Conference of 1910, and the latter to the Malines Conference of 1909. It is impossible in a short essay to analyse fully these two great currents in the Church, and so only a few examples will be discussed to illustrate the interaction of these movements. This is not exhaustive, and to some extent it will concentrate on where Ronald Jasper has been of influence, drawing on some of his reflections on the process. Three models will be considered: united churches, inter-church bodies, and individual initiatives.

United Churches

Churches have united with one another before the Ecumenical Movement began, but this century has seen many schemes for church unity, some of which have failed, but others of which have produced united churches. To begin with the Church of South India (CSI) is to acknowledge that this scheme had great influence throughout the world, not least in its worship, 'one of the most interesting and influential of the new wave of liturgies'.[1]

CSI was a union in 1948 of Anglicans, Methodists, Congregationalists, and Presbyterians. The first liturgy that it produced was an Ordinal, necessary for the consecration of its bishops. This was based on the Church of England *Book of Common Prayer*. Leslie Brown reports that 'when the Church was

[1] D. Forrester, J. H. I. McDonald, and G. Tellini, *Encounter with God* (T. & T. Clark, Edinburgh 1983), p. 124.

inaugurated . . . it had no intention to compile a liturgy of its own', but it 'very rapidly became conscious of itself as a united body and wished some form of expression in its worship of the unity which was transcending the differences of tradition within it'.[2] He sees three factors which forced the Church to re-examine its liturgy: the evangelistic motive, the movement towards Christian unity, and biblical theology. Indeed, he says, 'the Liturgical Movement is one of the great means which the Holy Spirit is using to bring renewal to the Church and to promote its unity'.[3]

Liturgical production began with the eucharist in 1950 and the lectionary in 1953. Over thirteen years, ten different services were produced in a series of 'flimsy booklets',[4] coming together in *The Book of Common Worship* in 1963. The Ordinal was one of the last services to be looked at, and entailed a revision of the original services produced at the union. With regard to the production of the CSI liturgy, T. S. Garrett says:

> although there has been no bargaining about it, each order of worship has turned out to be a happy blend of contributions from the different heritages. At the same time these varying contributions have been transcended, and a mere miscellany of existing practices avoided, by our aim of reappropriating the great classical tradition of Christian worship, as found in the ancient liturgies, while subjecting it to the critical insights of the Reformation.[5]

These last phrases read like a manifesto for the Liturgical Movement in the churches of the Reformation. It is to the credit of those involved with the CSI that they so skilfully fulfilled their objectives. Clearly in this united church, worship was not reduced to the lowest common denominator. Rather, a liturgy was produced that received great acclamation from representatives of many churches and had considerable influence on liturgical revision elsewhere.

[2] 'The Making of a Liturgy', *Scottish Journal of Theology* 4 (1951), pp. 55–63; quotation from p. 55.

[3] *Relevant Liturgy* (SPCK, London 1965), pp. 28–30; quotation from p. 30.

[4] J. R. MacPhail, 'Worship in the Church of South India', *Scottish Journal of Theology* 17 (1964), pp. 25–42; quotation from p. 25.

[5] *Worship in the Church of South India* (Lutterworth Press, London 1958), p. 8.

Various elements of the CSI eucharistic rite are now taken for granted and common in many churches: the president facing west, an Old Testament reading, the peace (introduced into some places with South Indian touching rather than hand shaking[6]), and a eucharistic prayer based on ancient forms. But when CSI was producing its liturgy, these were innovations for many of the constituent denominations. The eucharistic liturgy received high praise from Louis Bouyer: 'this eucharistic liturgy seems much more satisfactory than any other liturgy that emanated from the Reformation. . . . Supposing that validly ordained ministers use it, it seems difficult to say that they would not validly consecrate the eucharist.' His only point of criticism of the liturgy was its lack of reference to the faithful departed and commemoration of the Blessed Virgin and the saints.[7]

Likewise E. C. Ratcliff enthused about the Ordinal: 'the composers have produced rites, the meaning and content of which echo those of the rites of the ancient Church. . . . The new rites resemble the ancient in simplicity of pattern, logic of movement, and economy of prayer and ceremony.'[8] Ratcliff hoped that this Ordinal would be of great influence, and indeed it has been. Through the proposed Ordinal of the English Anglican-Methodist unity scheme (Ronald Jasper being a member of the sub-committee for the draft ordinal), the CSI has influenced the Church of England, the Methodist Church in England, and many other churches of the Anglican Communion.[9]

T. S. Garrett saw that some services reflect family likeness to constituent bodies, the eucharist to the Anglican Church, Confirmation to the Methodist Church, and baptism to the Presbyterian *Book of Common Order*, but the CSI liturgy is 'more than a conflation of traditions'.[10] J. R. MacPhail reports that the

---

[6] See Colin Buchanan, *The Kiss of Peace*, Grove Worship Series No. 80 (Grove Books, Nottingham 1982), pp. 15–18.

[7] 'A Roman Catholic View of the Church of South India', *Theology* 54 (1956), pp. 3–11; quotations from pp. 4 & 6.

[8] 'The Ordinal of the Church of South India', *Theology* 63 (1960), pp. 7–15, reprinted in A. H. Couratin and D. H. Tripp (eds), *Liturgical Studies* (SPCK, London 1960), pp. 173–82; quotation from p. 180.

[9] See Colin Buchanan, *Modern Anglican Ordination Rites*, Alcuin/GROW Liturgical Study 3 (Grove Books, Nottingham 1978), p. 12.

[10] 'Baptism in the Church of South India', *Scottish Journal of Theology* 8 (1955), pp. 385–91; quotation from p. 385.

counsel of Bishop Palmer was in the minds of the compilers, 'do not add heritages together, but restore to India the church of the fathers, and remember that it is provisional till there shall once more be an ecumenical church'.[11]

At the same time the compilers were aware that there was much to do in letting the church be more Indian. 'A truly Indian service book is still to come. At present . . . CSI would not wish to do more than provide interim orders of worship which will prepare the way for its coming.'[12] But the compilers were concerned in a number of ways to address the Indian situation: they rejected the use of the anaphora of the Liturgy of John Chrysostom and adapted the eucharistic preface to respond to Hindu sacrificial beliefs;[13] a prayer based on the Upanishads was added to baptism to show that 'the age-long desire of the heart of India is declared to find fulfilment in baptism';[14] the use of the white garment and the lamp at baptism was seen as a point where 'ancient Christian tradition and Indian religious sentiment meet';[15] and in marriage the *tali* and Seven Steps may be observed. However, CSI has recently begun to produce liturgies with a more Indian outlook,[16] and so perhaps the hopes of the first generation of liturgists are beginning to be born through their successors.

Clearly the Church of South India stands as a model of the relationship between liturgy and ecumenism. In the words of Ronald Jasper, 'it marked a kind of watershed in the history of liturgical revision; it coloured the thinking of would-be revisers; and its influence, whether direct or indirect, was undeniable'.[17]

---

[11] 'Worship in the Church of South India', p. 29.

[12] Garrett, 'Baptism in the Church of South India', p. 391.

[13] Brown, 'The Making of a Liturgy', p. 61.

[14] Garrett, 'Baptism in the Church of South India', p. 389.

[15] ibid., p. 390.

[16] See Sundar Clarke, *Let the Indian Church be Indian* (Christian Literature Society, Madras 1985); K. V. Kennerly, 'The Use of Indigenous Sacred Literature and Theological Concept in Christian Eucharistic Liturgy in India', *Studia Liturgica* 19 (1989), pp. 143–61; George Mathew, 'Whose Culture and Why?', in Kenneth Stevenson and Bryan Spinks (eds), *The Identity of Anglican Worship* (Mowbray, London 1991), pp. 144–55.

[17] *The Development of Anglican Liturgy 1662–1980* (SPCK, London 1989), p. 206.

Another approach to organic unity is that of 'covenanting', of which Wales provides a national model. In 1975 four denominations — the Church in Wales, the Methodist Church, the Presbyterian Church in Wales, and the United Reformed Church — and a group of Baptist churches (now called the Covenanted Baptists of Wales) covenanted together 'to work and pray in common obedience to our Lord Jesus Christ, in order that by the Holy Spirit we may be brought into one visible Church'.

If in South India liturgy came as a result of uniting, in Wales the opposite is happening. The World Council of Churches characterized a distinctive of the Welsh church union negotiations as their liturgical approach. 'Through the creation, authorisation and use of common worship material, the Churches have explored and expressed points of contact.'[18] In 1981 a service of Holy Communion was produced. Baptism followed in 1990, and was accompanied by the report 'Christian Baptism and Church Membership'. As yet the responses to a further report, 'Ministry in a Uniting Church: From Recognition to Reconciliation', have not been digested and the churches are still seeking the way forward to organic unity.

The communion service has been well received, and is used for ecumenical eucharists. Like all Welsh liturgy, it is bilingual, with Welsh and English on facing pages. The confession and absolution are at the beginning of the service, and there is a declaration of forgiveness rather than an Anglican absolution. The eucharistic prayer is unsurprising, except for the anamnesis and epiclesis:

> as we now proclaim his death, resurrection and ascension, we offer to you these your gifts of bread and wine and ask you to accept our sacrifice of praise and thanksgiving. We pray that your Holy Spirit may come upon us and upon these gifts that we, receiving them, may share the body and blood of our Lord.[19]

[18] Thomas F. Best et al., *Survey of Church Union Negotiations 1988–1991*, World Council of Churches Faith & Order Paper No. 154 (Geneva 1991), p. 18.

[19] The Commission of the Covenanted Churches, *The Holy Communion* (1981), p. 25.

Clearly Welsh Anglicans do not have the difficulties in this section of the anaphora that have plagued their English sisters and brothers.

The baptismal rite has a Reformed feel rather than being in the line of the *Book of Common Prayer*. Perhaps the most surprising point is the laying on of hands after the baptism. A group of people lay hands on the candidate as the minister says: 'N. . . . may the power of the Holy Spirit work within you, that being born anew of water and the Spirit, you may be a faithful witness of Jesus Christ.'[20] It is not clear how this relates to Anglican Confirmation (or to Free Church reception into membership). Perhaps the Welsh bishops are indicating that they will accept presbyteral Confirmation, that they are willing to delegate it to their presbyters, and that infants should be allowed to receive Confirmation (and communion).

Inter-Church Bodies

While united churches provide one model for liturgy and ecumenism, a second approach is that of the ecumenical inter-church committee or society. A number of these exist and are influential in bringing liturgical convergence in some areas.

The Joint Liturgical Group (JLG) is one such body, and was founded in large part by Ronald Jasper:

> Dr John Lamb . . . first suggested to me that talking together about liturgy was not enough: creating liturgy together would be more productive: and he firmly believed this offered more opportunity for progress towards Christian unity than any other activity. . . . I took this suggestion up with Donald Coggan privately in December 1960, pleading that it was high time to explore the possibilities of an interdenominational exercise.[21]

The first meeting was in October 1963, and at that meeting Ronald Jasper was elected secretary. The group had this understanding about itself: 'work produced by this Group will have no authority greater than that which its own members give to it by their own weight; but it will be for particular Churches, through their own customary modes of decision, to make use of

[20] The Commission of the Covenanted Churches, *Baptism* (1990), p. 25.
[21] Jasper, *The Development of the Anglican Liturgy*, pp. 227–8.

the results if they are willing to do so'.[22] In some areas the Group has had considerable effect on the churches in Britain. A variety of liturgical material has been produced, including a daily office, calendar, lectionary, and Holy Week services. This has been accompanied by books of essays on such issues as the ministry of the word, children and worship, and hymns. Some of these proposals have been adopted by churches; others have been of less influence.

The Daily Office was a proposal for weekday prayers.[23] Noting that there was some convergence between Anglican and Free Church ministers, the Group suggested a flexible office for daily prayer. To Anglicans the proposals were radical: the psalms were rearranged over a thirteen-week cycle, compared to the monthly one of the *Book of Common Prayer*; different biblical canticles were provided for the morning and evening of each day of the week, with appropriate hymns as alternatives—a Free Church contribution; intercessions were produced for each day of the week, and a new lectionary was provided. This office was well received and went into many editions, suggesting a wide use by people of various denominations. The proposals were incorporated into Anglican liturgy with the result that the *Alternative Service Book 1980* still retains the ethos of the Joint Liturgical Group Office. Although the vision of the introduction was wider, the proposals were directed primarily at clergy, and so while they may have had great influence on the lives of Christians in leadership, they did not bring the sort of changes in the practice of ordinary Christians for which some have hoped. The words of George Guiver set the direction for further co-operation: 'while being thankful, therefore, for present mercies, it seems that we must press on in search for renewal, particularly keeping in view the renewal of the *community's* prayer, and renewal of the divine office as *celebration*'.[24]

Holy Week Services shows a greater influence from Roman Catholics, who moved from becoming observers to full

[22] R. C. D. Jasper (ed.), *The Daily Office by the Joint Liturgical Group* (SPCK/Epworth Press, London 1968), p. 9.

[23] ibid., p. 11.

[24] *Company of Voices* (SPCK, London; Pueblo, New York 1988), p. 146.

participants in the JLG.[25] The aim of this book was to provide services for the week with one eye on the need for ecumenical occasions. Thus, besides the main Holy Week services, a series of thematic services are provided for Monday, Tuesday, and Wednesday. 'Offices like these have a knack of getting people together for a special service at a time when in some traditions daily worship is not normal.'[26] The second edition provided the alternative of trying to follow the biblical events of each day, something that the Church of England later avoided in its own services.[27]

JLG has begun to work on worship in Local Ecumenical Projects (LEPs). These are areas of local ecumenical development, including the sharing of buildings and/or worship and ministry. The canons of the Church of England even allow a priest to lead the rite of a participating denomination and ministers from Free Churches to preside at Anglican eucharists in LEPs.[28] The Church of England's Code of Practice for LEPs says:

> Since 1963 the ecumenical Joint Liturgical Group (JLG) has played a significant part in the consideration of worship in the British Churches and has produced liturgical forms that have been adopted, in whole or in part, in many Churches. . . . Since 1987 the JLG has been in discussion . . . over the production of liturgical forms that might be of service in LEPs or other contexts: consideration is being given to producing a rite of joint Confirmation, a rite for the induction of ministers, eucharistic prayers for use in ecumenical contexts, and the possibility of an ecumenical rite of baptism.[29]

Joint Confirmation is administered by two, three, or more ministers together laying hands upon each candidate and pronouncing the words in unison. Thus the candidate 'becomes a member' of all of the participating denominations at once,

[25] R. C. D. Jasper (ed.) *Holy Week Services by the Joint Liturgical Group* (SPCK, London 1971).

[26] Kenneth Stevenson, *Jerusalem Revisited: The Liturgical Meaning of Holy Week* (Pastoral Press, Washington DC 1988), p. 33.

[27] Donald Gray (ed.), *Holy Week Services: Revised and Expanded Edition* (SPCK, London 1983); *Lent, Holy Week, Easter: Services and Prayers* (Church House Publishing, London 1986).

[28] H. Cross, 'Local Ecumenical Projects in England', *Ecumenical Review* 44 (1992), pp. 48–54.

[29] General Synod of the Church of England, *Ecumenical Relations. Canons B 43 and B 44: Code of Practice* (London 1989), p. 20.

although this does not answer all the questions around Confirmation and membership in the context of a divided church.[30] That JLG has begun to work in this area is a new development in their role. Presently joint Confirmation is administered by local traditions: the new common rite will bring uniformity to a complex area and may enable fuller evaluation.[31]

Liturgical revision inevitably included an examination of the calendar and lectionary. The JLG lectionary[32] developed at a similar time to the Roman Catholic eucharistic lectionary for Sundays, but 'unfortunately there was little contact between the Roman revisers and the JLG until each party had gone too far to withdraw'.[33] The JLG lectionary operates on a two-year cycle, and was developed around three points in the calendar: Christmas, Easter, and Pentecost. For each of the Sundays of the year controlling lessons were selected, the other readings being chosen to fit in with that lesson and so to form a theme. It has been widely used in the British Isles, but not by Roman Catholics.

Its reforms have also come in for severe criticism from some:

> they depart radically from the traditions of the early Church and show little appreciation for the theological meaning of the Christian year as a means of participating in the mystery of Christ. . . . As the Standing Liturgical Commission of the American Episcopal Church has pertinently remarked, 'the inherent fallacy' of such a reconstruction is its 'approach to the Christian Year on a pedagogical rather than a kerygmatic basis'.[34]

[30] See Colin Buchanan, *Anglicans and Worship in Local Ecumenical Projects*, Grove Worship Series No. 101 (Grove Books, Nottingham 1987), p. 10; *Worship the Lord with Joy! Sharing in Worship in Local Ecumenical Projects* (CCLEPE, London 1982), pp. 7–9.

[31] Joint Liturgical Group, *Confirmation and Re-affirmation of Baptismal Faith* (Canterbury Press, Norwich 1992).

[32] R. C. D. Jasper (ed.), *The Calendar and Lectionary: A Reconsideration by the Joint Liturgical Group* (Oxford University Press 1967).

[33] A. R. George, 'The JLG Lectionary', in Donald Gray (ed.), *The Word in Season* (Canterbury Press, Norwich 1988), pp. 97–115; quotation from pp. 98–9.

[34] P. G. Cobb, 'The History of the Christian Year', in C. Jones, G. Wainwright, and E. Yarnold (eds), *The Study of Liturgy* (SPCK, London 1978), pp. 418–19.

The JLG had, however, tried to defend itself from the latter criticism: 'it is tempting to adopt a thematic approach for the post-Pentecost season; but this is to be rejected. . . . Rather must the Bible be allowed to dictate its own conclusions.' While it was admitted that there was a 'subjective procedure in the choice, it was argued that the passages chosen were largely those 'selected and used by the Church through the ages'.[35] Nevertheless, the 'subjective procedure' does leave this and other lectionaries open to feminist criticism, something that future compilers of lectionaries will have to take into account.[36]

The Consultation on Common Texts, another ecumenical liturgical body in North America, has also developed a lectionary, *The Common Lectionary* (*CL*), which is widely used by churches there. *CL* is 'not an original construct but rather an ecumenical response to, and revision of another lectionary system, namely, *Ordo Lectionum Missae* (1969) of the Roman Catholic Church'.[37] Like the Roman lectionary, it divides the year by the distinction between festal Sundays, based around the two feasts of Christmas and Easter, and ordinary Sundays. The Roman 'Ordinary Time' is seen by some as a novel concept and a poor translation of *tempus per annum*.[38] *CL* has turned this into 'Propers'. Neither of them are very evocative names for Sundays, and both will also need some revision if Christmas is seen to extend to Candlemas rather than to Epiphany, as the Church of England's Liturgical Commission is now proposing.[39] *CL* has changed the use of the Old Testament reading in ordinary time to try to put this also on a continuous basis and

[35] Jasper (ed.), *The Calendar and Lectionary*, pp. 18–19.

[36] See Marjorie Procter-Smith, 'Lectionaries—Principles and Problems: Alternative Perspectives', *Studia Liturgica* 22 (1992), pp. 84–99.

[37] Horace Allen, 'Common Lectionary: Origins, Assumptions, and Issues', *Studia Liturgica* 21 (1991), pp. 14–30; quotation from p. 14.

[38] See for example A. R. George, 'The Reconciliation of Calendars', in Gray (ed.), *The Word in Season*, p. 84.

[39] See Michael Perham and Kenneth Stevenson, *Welcoming the Light of Christ* (SPCK, London 1991), p. 94: '*The Promise of His Glory* seeks to rescue it [Candlemas] and give it that pivotal place in the Christian year, looking back to Christmas at the end of an incarnation season and forward to Lent and a season of the passion.'

thus eliminate some of the criticism of the Roman original as being too typological in its use of the Old Testament.[40]

CL has recently been revised,[41] and the JLG has also produced a second lectionary proposal, known as JLG 2, which is based on a four-year cycle and moves away from the use of themes.[42] It is not clear to what extent it will be adopted by the churches in Britain. The Baptists have included it in their worship book,[43] but recent lectionary proposals by the Church of England's Liturgical Commission suggest that they may be moving in a different direction.[44] Does it matter that there are two ecumenical lectionaries in the English-speaking world? Perhaps not: in Kerala, India the three branches obedient to Rome—Latin, Syro-Malabar, and Syro-Malankara—have three different lectionaries and calendars. On the other hand, there might be some value in ecumenical agreement in at least common provision for the key festivals of Easter and Christmas.

Another form of liturgical ecumenical endeavour has been the production of agreed services or prayers between the denominations without their being in any formal ecumenical relationship. One example of this is an ecumenical wedding liturgy in Germany which draws together Lutheran and Catholic traditions and is authorized by both denominations.[45] Unfortunately, such a liturgy has been passed over in England and Wales,[46] but there are examples of similar co-operation in North America. The Consultation on Church Union (COCU), for instance, has produced a series of services, including marriage, Confirmation, and eucharist. One of their eucharistic

[40] See for example G. S. Sloyan, 'Some Suggestions for a Biblical Three-year Lectionary', *Worship* 63 (1989), pp. 521–35.

[41] The Consultation on Common Texts, *The Revised Common Lectionary* (Abingdon Press, Nashville 1992).

[42] Joint Liturgical Group, *A Four Year Lectionary* (Canterbury Press, Norwich 1990).

[43] Baptist Union of Great Britain, *Patterns and Prayers for Christian Worship* (Oxford University Press 1991).

[44] *Patterns for Worship*, GS 898 (Church House Publishing, London 1989), pp. 8–11, 127–30.

[45] *Gemeinsame kirchliche Trauung* (Pustet, Regensburg; Standa, Kasel 1971).

[46] See G. Steel, 'Revising the Marriage Rite', *Liturgy* 15 (1991), p. 104.

prayers,[47] based on the Liturgy of St Basil, has found wide acceptance and is incorporated in the service books of a number of denominations, and Basil is the basis for the fourth eucharistic prayer in the Roman Missal. Actual common use of an agreed eucharistic prayer seems to be a great step forward ecumenically, particularly from the perspective of *lex orandi, lex credendi*. COCU is a North American example of an inter-church body already influencing parent denominations, and perhaps its example will be built on elsewhere. We have already seen that the covenanting churches in Wales have an agreed eucharist and that JLG is considering the possibility of producing common eucharistic prayers for LEPs.

Another dimension of inter-church co-operation has been international, especially in the translation of common traditional texts. Once again Ronald Jasper was involved in the formation of one of these bodies, the International Consultation on English Texts (ICET).[48] This body produced *Prayers We Have in Common*,[49] and its successor, the English Language Liturgical Consultation, produced the later revision, *Praying Together*.[50] Although 'it quickly became clear that with traditional texts like the Lord's Prayer there was no point in acting in a denominationally separatist way', the Church of England proceeded to do just that with the 'unilateral action of amending the ICET text'.[51] This has been a great tragedy, as the modern language Lord's Prayer has been introduced in England in variant versions, leading to its half-hearted adoption, particularly in school prayer.

International agreement can, however, cut across local traditions. For example, the ICET Lord's Prayer has been included in the Mar Thoma *Order of Services* in India.[52] This raises questions about an ancient tradition adapting to modern English.

---

[47] In *Word, Bread, Cup* (Forward Movement Publications, Cincinnati 1978).
[48] See Jasper, *The Development of the Anglican Liturgy*, p. 290.
[49] SPCK, London 1970.
[50] Canterbury Press, Norwich, 1988.
[51] Colin Buchanan, *Recent Liturgical Revision in the Church of England*, Grove Ministry and Worship Series No. 14 (Grove Books, Nottingham 1973, 1984), p. 12.
[52] (The Mar Thoma Sabha Book Department, Tiruvalla 1988), p. viii.

The Syrian Lord's Prayer has used 'give us today the bread we need' and 'deliver us from the evil one', based upon the Syriac translation of the Bible. In using the ICET texts the Mar Thoma Syrian Church has conformed to an internationally agreed English translation, but has moved away from the Syrian tradition, and thus from other Syrian Churches using modern English.[53] This raises the question: how should ancient traditions relate to internationally agreed texts?

International ecumenical endeavour has also occurred at the academic level with the formation of Societas Liturgica, and again Ronald Jasper was involved in its inception.[54] This international body, and various other regional bodies, bring together liturgists from the different churches. Such gatherings help in the convergence of the worship of denominations, not least because the comparative method is embedded in modern liturgical study, forcing liturgists to consider the rites of churches outside their own confession.

Individual Initiatives: Taizé

The Taizé community provides a different model of liturgy and ecumenism. It is neither a united church nor an inter-church committee, but an ecumenical monastic community that grew out of the vision of one man, Brother Roger. Life professions began in 1949, and at first the community was of brothers from Protestant churches—Brother Roger himself grew up in the French Reformed Church. But from its inception Taizé was ecumenical in intention, although it was not until 1969 that a Catholic brother joined. Later, Roman Catholic priests were to make their professions.

The heart of Taizé is prayer: 'our liturgy, that powerful means of moulding us into one communion of faith, and our Rule, are instruments that make it possible for us to live the hope of unity'.[55] Taizé is searching for unity. It is painfully aware that it

[53] See Francis Acharya, *Prayer with the Harp of the Spirit*, Kurisumala Ashram (CMS Press, Kottayam 1980, 1983), p. 21.

[54] See R. S. Loudon 'Recent Developments in Ecumenical Liturgical Studies', *Studia Liturgica* 4 (1965), p. 120.

[55] Brother Roger, *The Dynamic of the Provisional* (Mowbray, Oxford 1981), p. 67.

has not yet arrived, and so the forms of prayer evolve, both in architecture and language. 'Once the brothers were enclosed in solid concrete stalls; now they simply stand or kneel on the carpet. . . . Once French was used, now there are always prayers and readings in a variety of languages.'[56] Style has also changed: 'in our beginnings, we worked out a prayer that was mainly monastic. Then in order to come closer to the people of God, we endeavoured to make it meditative and accessible at the same time, congenial to all generations and as universal as possible.'[57]

For a single monastic community, they have produced a considerable quantity of liturgy. There is a rite of monastic profession, a service of confession, the eucharist, and various editions of the office.[58] Alongside this is the music of the community, composed by Jacques Berthier.[59] It is hard to assess the impact of this community. Taizé rejects being called a movement and does not organize chapters across the world: 'There will never be a "Taizé theology" or a "Taizé spirituality".'[60] Likewise, Brother Roger would reject a 'Taizé liturgy', but clearly both individuals and sometimes groups pray the Taizé office, and some churches have occasional Taizé services. When the brothers organize a pilgrimage, it is possible to fill the cathedrals of Europe with young people to sing and pray, often well on into the night. Also, the music of Jacques Berthier is beginning to enter denominational hymnals.[61]

[56] J. L. G. Baldo, *The Story of Taizé* (Mowbray, London & Oxford 1985), pp. 69–70.

[57] Brother Roger, *And Your Deserts Shall Flower* (Mowbray, Oxford 1984), p. 65.

[58] See Brother Roger, *Parable of Community* (Mowbray, London & Oxford 1980, 1984), pp. 41–5; Max Thurian, *Confession* (Mowbray, London & Oxford 1985), pp. 130–41; *Eucharist at Taizé* (Faith Press, London 1962); M. Thurian and G. Wainwright, *Baptism and Eucharist, Ecumenical Convergence in Celebration* (World Council of Churches, Geneva; Eerdmans, Grand Rapids 1983), pp. 180–2; *The Taizé Office* (Faith Press, London 1966); *Praise in All Our Days: Common Prayer at Taizé* (Mowbray, London & Oxford 1981); *Psalms from Taizé* (Mowbray, London & Oxford 1979); *Praying Together in Word and Song* (Mowbray, London & Oxford 1982, 1985); *Songs and Prayers from Taizé* (Geoffrey Chapman/Mowbray, London 1991).

[59] *Music from Taizé*, 2 vols (Collins, London 1982, 1985).

[60] Brother Roger, *Festival* (Les Presses de Taizé 1973), p. 21.

[61] See for example *Rejoice and Sing* (Oxford University Press 1991). This hymnal for the British United Reformed Church has nine Taizé chants.

It is perhaps the office that has been most influential, as can be seen in the variety of editions published in English, but it is also worthwhile to look at the eucharist. The published text, *Eucharist at Taizé*, is a translation of the 1959 rite, which was itself revised in 1972. Clearly the inclusion of Roman Catholic brothers has sharpened the issue of intercommunion, and seems to have affected the present use of this Taizé eucharist within the community. While some brothers seem to continue to use the Taizé eucharist for mid-week services, the Roman rite now seems to be used for consecrating the reserved sacrament, which is then distributed after morning prayer. Likewise, the Sunday eucharist is now usually a Roman Mass. But in both cases there is a generous interpretation of the Roman Catholic provision for the welcome to those from other communions (on the grounds of their inability to find a minister from their own denomination in this remote part of France).

The Taizé eucharist is remarkable in a number of ways. It was obviously very well researched and is steeped in the principles of the Liturgical Movement. Some of it might now look basic, but it has to be remembered that it was produced in 1959 before the Second Vatican Council and the revisions of many other churches in Europe. There was an attempt to include the whole community in the leadership of the liturgy, and so the rubrics indicate six different ministers. This is something that has been neglected in the revisions of the 1960s and 1970s. Also there was the inclusion of various Orthodox litanies as options within the service; here perhaps it stands closer to the CSI liturgy than many others. But it was in the eucharistic prayer that there was a foretaste of things to come. This prayer contains a series of variable seasonal prefaces which are followed by the Sanctus. There is then a split epiclesis which is justified in the following terms: 'In the Alexandrian tradition (Der-Balyzeh text) the epiclesis . . . immediately precedes Christ's words of institution, uniting in a most happy way the work of the Holy Spirit and the work of Christ in the Eucharist. . . . The form of the liturgy of St Mark is therefore of great ecumenical value.'[62]

[62] *Eucharist at Taizé*, p. 18.

Both the Roman Catholic Church and the Church of England were to follow this form in their revisions, and it may perhaps be not merely coincidental that both Brother Max Thurian of Taizé and Ronald Jasper were observers at the Concilium Liturgicum at the Vatican in 1966. However, it is not clear that this epiclesis is of the ecumenical value that is claimed. Aidan Kavanagh has criticized the division of the hallowing and unifying functions of the Spirit, as well as the fact that the split epiclesis makes a unit that is longer and more consecratory than before. He fears that it may resurrect rather than solve the old divisions between East and West, and commends the united epiclesis in the *Apostolic Tradition* and the Byzantine rite.[63] Richard Albertine points out that Eastern Catholic rites use the epiclesis in the traditional Eastern position and so questions this new innovation in the Roman rite. He suggests that variety is a better solution to the expression of the epiclesis.[64] So at this point it would seem that the Taizé eucharist has led in an unfortunate direction.

The office has gradually become more simple. Although *The Taizé Office* (1966) and *Praise in All Our Days* (1981) follow a similar structure, gone are Terce, Sext, and None, as well as the office of the night and Compline. This leaves only three services in the day: morning, midday, and evening. Brother Roger outlines some of his thoughts on the office in these terms:

> Prayer never changes its essence through the centuries, but it adopts different forms as history unfolds, or at different periods of our lives.[65]
>
> Over the years, the Community has evolved a form of common prayer which is still only a provisional one. . . . The ecumenical nature of the Community and its worship explain a deliberate attempt to draw on many different sources.[66]

The basic structure of the office is: Psalms (Introduction and Psalm); Reading (Old Testament, Gospel, Epistle, and Short Reading); Song (Responses and Hymn); Prayers (Intercession, Collects, Free Prayer, and Blessing). This underlies both the

---

[63] 'Thoughts on the New Eucharistic Prayers', *Worship* 43 (1969), pp. 2–12.

[64] 'Problem of the (Double) Epiclesis in the New Roman Eucharistic Prayers', *Ephemerides Liturgicae* 91 (1977), pp. 193–202.

[65] *A Life We Never Dared Hope For* (Mowbray, London 1980), p. 23.

[66] *Praise in All Our Days*, pp. 7–8.

office books themselves and the shorter books of songs and prayers. There are a number of distinctives features. Firstly, there is the music, 'plaintive, repetitive, almost Oriental chanting'.[67] At Taizé the songs are sung over and over again like waves crashing over the congregation. The prayers include many litanies that can be united with chants and sung, producing a very attractive style of prayer. Secondly, the Church of the Reconciliation has great atmosphere. It is dark. The front is filled with flickering candles. Before evening prayer the room is filled with incense. A few simple icons are located at various points in the church. People sit on the floor, the brothers in the middle of the people. All these points of atmosphere are central to the Taizé office: 'When the mystery of God becomes tangible through the simple beauty of symbols, when it is not smothered by too many words, then a common prayer, far from exuding monotony and boredom, awakens us to heaven's joy on earth.'[68] Thirdly, there is a great place for silence: 'it is best to have just one fairly long period of silence (5 – 10 minutes) during the prayer'.[69] Finally, there is a weekly celebration of the cross and resurrection, with prayers around the cross on Friday. The latter practice has its origins in a visit of Brother Roger to Moscow and was introduced at Taizé on 8 July 1978.

Taizé clearly has had a great impact on many people and has been a place of pilgrimage for thousands of young people since the 1960s. This was not a ministry that was planned, and the community has been forced to adapt its worship for these pilgrims. But what is most significant is that where the office in many churches has been in the doldrums, displaced in part by the eucharist, Taizé is producing a unique ecumenical revival of common prayer.

Conclusion

The experience of worshipping with another Christian tradition often produces the comment, 'It's just like we do it.' This grassroots reaction is one of the more hopeful signs for the Ecumeni-

[67] Baldo, *The Story of Taizé*, p. 105.
[68] *Songs and Prayers from Taizé*, p. 7.
[69] ibid., p. 20.

cal Movement, and is the result of a number of factors. Firstly, the reforms of Vatican II, not least in the emphasis on the vernacular and the ministry of the word (including preaching), have made Roman Catholic worship more accessible to other Christians. Secondly, renewing the liturgy according to the principals of the Liturgical Movement has made liturgies in different traditions agree more closely both in structure and in text. Thirdly, there has been a growing interest in symbol in the Protestant churches and an increasing centrality of eucharistic worship. This may in part be due to the charismatic movement and its 'inchoate sacramentality'.[70] All these factors make the worship of different traditions look much the same, and may lead to the question, 'Why do we remain apart?'

As yet, the Lund principle, to 'act together in all matters except those in which deep differences of conviction compel them to act separately' — often translated into 'not to do separately what can be done together' — has not been uppermost in the actions of denominations in the process of liturgical revision. Lund brings us back to the question of common lectionaries and of co-operation on other rites such as marriage, funerals, and offices. It might even question the need for different sets of denominationally approved hymn-books. Indeed, the rigorous application of this principle might eventually lead to a 'common Western rite'. But while some denominations continue the work of revision without even the interaction of observers, the practice of the churches reveals that liturgy and ecumenism still have far to go.

[70] General Synod of the Church of England, *The Charismatic Movement in the Church of England* (CIO, London 1981), p. 37.

5

Liturgy and Ethics

L. EDWARD PHILLIPS

> To bless God in the churches, brethren, means so to live that each one's life
> may give glory to God. To bless God in word and curse Him in deed is by
> no means to bless Him in the churches. Almost all bless Him with their
> tongues, but not all by their works. But those whose conduct is inconsistent
> with their profession cause God to be blasphemed.[1]

Reflection on the relationship between liturgy and ethics is not a
new phenomenon. Indeed, the Old Testament prophets decry
the 'solemn assemblies' of the people when justice and righteous
were neglected (Amos 5.21–4).[2] In the New Testament, St Paul
criticizes the Corinthians for their scandalous behaviour at their
gatherings for the Lord's Supper: 'When you come together, it is
not really to eat the Lord's supper. For when the time comes to
eat, each of you goes ahead with your own supper, and one goes
hungry and another becomes drunk' (1 Cor. 11.20–1). Paul is
not merely concerned about drunkenness and gluttony, but
about the disregard shown to poor Christians who laboured for a
living by those who had means and could get to their assemblies
early. That is to say, for Paul, this is not a problem of personal
behaviour; it is an issue of justice. The passage from Augustine
cited above was delivered in a sermon to a congregation at worship. For Augustine, blessing God in the church becomes
blasphemy if it is not somehow connected to lives that give glory
to God apart from worship.

If the relationship between liturgy and ethics has never been
entirely neglected, recent years have seen an explosion of inter-

[1] *St Augustine on the Psalms*, trans. S. Hebgin and F. Corrigan, Ancient
Christian Writers 29 (Newman Press, Westminster MD 1960), p. 252.

[2] On the relationship between worship and ethics in the Old Testament, see
Walter Brueggemann, *Israel's Praise: Doxology Against Idolatry and Ideology*
(Fortress Press, Philadelphia 1988).

est in the topic, and not just among liturgical scholars.[3] The 1979 meeting of the Society of Christian Ethics focused on the topic 'Liturgy and Ethics', and included major addresses by such noted ethicists as Paul Ramsey, Margaret Farley, and William Everett.[4] Liberation theologians, such as Tissa Balasuriya[5] and Rafael Avila,[6] have examined the political/ethical dimensions of liturgy as a development of their concern for orthopraxy. The Evangelical theologian Robert Webber, of Wheaton College, and Rodney Clapp, an associate editor of *Christianity Today*, have taken up the issue in a recent book, in which they describe liturgy as the source of the Church's 'depth politics'.[7] Clearly, the interest in liturgy and ethics spans the denominational and theological spectrum.

Given the diverse perspectives of the various authors who treat the topic, it is notable that one central notion runs throughout the literature: there *is* a relationship between liturgy and ethics. Virtually no one takes the position that liturgy and ethics have nothing to do with each other. But *how* are liturgy and ethics related? Not surprisingly, the nature of the relationship and its relevance is approached differently by different writers. At the risk of over-simplification, since this essay cannot possibly evaluate the entire corpus of literature on the topic, the possibilities seem to fall into three categories: liturgy is a source for ethics; liturgy is an object of ethics; liturgy itself is an ethic.

Liturgy as a Source for Ethics

Liturgy can function as a motivation for ethical behaviour or as a source for ethical reflection. That is to say, liturgy may function as a norm for the way Christians live the good life and how they think about questions of right and wrong, good and bad, justice, virtue, and so forth.

[3] See the lengthy annotated bibliography published by Mark Searle, *Studia Liturgica* 21 (1991), pp. 220–35, to which this present essay is greatly indebted.

[4] Papers published in *Journal of Religious Ethics* 7 (1979), pp. 139–248.

[5] *The Eucharist and Human Liberation* (Orbis, Maryknoll NY 1979).

[6] *Worship and Politics* (Orbis, Maryknoll NY 1981).

[7] *People of the Truth: The Power of the Worshipping Community in the Modern World* (Harper & Row, San Francisco 1988), pp. 68ff.

How liturgy functions in this capacity is not a simple issue and raises several questions.[8] First, what aspect of liturgy is taken to be normative and why? For example, are the texts normative as written or as performed? Does ritual have priority over text, or historical meaning over present meaning? These related questions help to clarify the source to which appeal is made, since any appeal to liturgy assumes, explicitly or implicitly, certain boundaries about what actually functions as the norm for ethical thought and behaviour. Second, how is the liturgy to which appeal is made brought to bear on ethical concepts? For example, is it used as a proof-text to buttress arguments already in place? Does it function as a motivation for particular kinds of ethical action? Does it shape Christian character which then grounds moral discernment?[9] This second set of questions clarifies the way in which the norms function, once they are identified. Third, what is the larger context of the liturgy under consideration? What sociological, historical, and cultural factors come to bear? These questions recognize that 'liturgy' in a general sense is an artificial construct; actual liturgy takes place in concrete communities. The historical background and present circumstances of particular communities influence their understanding and practice of worship.[10]

Geoffrey Wainwright provides us with an example of liturgical text as a source for ethical discussion. In his article 'Eucharist and/as Ethics', he cites a passage from the Byzantine liturgy, which comes before the Creed, in which the congregation is addressed directly: 'Let us love one another, that with one mind we may confess the Father, the Son, and the Holy Spirit.'[11]

[8] In this regard, the problem is parallel to the use of scripture in theology and ethics. David Kelsey has demonstrated that there is not one, but an irreducible number of ways in which scripture is employed by theologians. Kelsey develops several questions to map out the use of scripture which have been adapted here for our purposes. See *The Uses of Scripture in Recent Theology* (Fortress Press, Philadelphia 1975).

[9] See John Howard Yoder, 'Sacrament as Social Process: Christ the Transformer of Culture', *Theology Today* 48 (1991), p. 33.

[10] James White, for example, has demonstrated how very differently worship and sacrament function in the contexts of various Christian traditions. See *Protestant Worship: Traditions in Transition* (Westminster/John Knox Press, Louisville 1989).

[11] *Worship* 62 (1988), pp. 123–37; quotation from p. 130.

Wainwright notes that this applies, first of all, to the 'personal relations in the local congregation'. Going beyond this, he finds in the admonition a warrant for all Christians to work for the reuniting of the Church of Christ in order to overcome 'our sadly divided Christendom'. What aspect of this liturgical text is normative for Wainwright? It certainly is not just its use by a particular deacon addressing a particular congregation —the liturgy as actually performed. Rather, he sees the text of the Byzantine liturgy as transcending the particular Orthodox congregations which use it. But, since Wainwright is a Methodist rather than an Orthodox Christian, he must make a further universalizing move to claim that the text has relevance for the Ecumenical Movement. It seems fair to say that someone who did not already have an understanding of the value of ecumenism would be hard pressed to find in this Byzantine diaconal admonition a warrant for the unity of all Christian bodies. Thus, Wainwright is using this passage from the Byzantine liturgy as a proof-text for his already established commitment to ecumenism.[12]

The use of liturgy as proof-text may be the most characteristic use of liturgical texts in ethics. This no doubt results from the simple fact that liturgy, like the New Testament, does not present an organized ethical system.[13] While a few liturgical texts contain something like a system of morality, such as Anglican liturgies which quote the Decalogue, these still must be interpreted within a larger ethical framework. For example, 'honouring the Sabbath' is never taken in its original Old Testament sense, but requires a particularly Christian interpretation for it to have meaning for Christians.[14] The use of the Sabbath commandment in a Christian liturgy does not inform Christian

[12] I do not use 'proof-text' in a pejorative sense, but to indicate the citing of texts as support for positions already established. I must acknowledge here that Wainwright's development of the relationship between liturgy and ethics is much more thorough and complex than this brief extract might indicate.

[13] Ernst Käsemann has observed to 'what small degree the New Testament possesses an "ethic" . . . i.e., a system of morality developing logically out of a single nucleus'. See 'Worship and Everyday Life: A Note on Romans 12', in *New Testament Questions of Today* (Fortress Press, Philadelphia 1969), p. 180.

[14] Though we should acknowledge that Seventh-day Adventists do accept the original sense of this commandment.

ethics; rather, a Christian ethical interpretation is required for that commandment to make sense in Christian worship. Thus, the use of liturgical texts seems to function in ethics on the level of supporting evidence, rather than primary source.

Liturgy, of course, is not merely text, but also ritual action. As with texts, liturgical actions may be used as a sort of 'proof-case' for established ethical systems. For instance, Wainwright cites the ancient practice of the kiss of peace, which has found its way into recent liturgical practice as a 'sign of peace', as an example of how Christians understand their fellowship at the table to be a demonstration of their harmonious fellowship.[15] Likewise, William Willimon cites the action of the eucharist as a demonstration of the early Church's 'protest against the way the world dealt with hunger, food, and community'.[16]

Theodore Jennings, on the other hand, has argued from the standpoint of ritual studies that liturgy functions as more than a secondary-level example of theological or ethical meanings which are already in place. Rather, 'liturgical actions . . . generate meanings which form or pattern action and meaning outside liturgical space and time'.[17] Jennings demonstrates how this works in his investigation of the Christian ritual of communal confession and absolution. He calls this ritual sequence 'the liturgy of liberation', because it demonstrates 'that Christian existence continually struggles against the forms of bondage and brokenness from which Christ came to liberate humanity'.[18] He observes:

> We engage together in this sequence of actions when we come together to perform the liturgy of the *ekklesia*. In the repetition of this action, we become practiced in these actions — in the recognition of our situation, in the renunciation of bondage, in the turning toward freedom, in the pronouncement and performance of liberation.[19]

[15] *Doxology* (Epworth Press, London; Oxford University Press, New York 1980), p. 402.

[16] *The Service of God: How Worship and Ethics are Related* (Abingdon Press, Nashville 1983), p. 130.

[17] 'Ritual Studies and Liturgical Theology: An Invitation to Dialogue', *Journal of Ritual Studies* 1 (1987), pp. 37–8.

[18] *The Liturgy of Liberation: The Confession and Forgiveness of Sins* (Abingdon Press, Nashville 1988), p. 52.

[19] ibid., p. 60.

According to Jennings, this liturgical pattern of confession/absolution becomes the pattern for the Christian life in the world; it shapes Christians' ethical behaviour.[20]

In employing ritual as norm, just as in employing text as norm, the particular aspect of ritual action which is brought to bear must be delineated. Is the ritual action normative as it is actually performed, or as it was originally intended (if we could ever know that), or as it ought to be intended (employing a theological critique)? Jennings is very aware of these difficulties. For this reason, he maintains that ritological investigation of practice requires the critical evaluation of liturgical theology when it comes to examining the questions of normative Christian practice.[21] Ritual practice by itself can never set the standard, because performing a ritual does not guarantee that a worshipper will understand or adopt the ethics which are enacted.

Liturgy as an Object of Ethics

The main problem with employing liturgy as a source for theology and ethics is that liturgy is by nature ambiguous. It must be scrutinized by extra-liturgical standards.[22] This leads to a second way in which the relationship between liturgy and ethics is approached: liturgy as an object of ethics. As such, liturgy may be approached in two ways: (a) as the object of ethical critique, or (b) as a tool for expressing ethical ideals.

Liturgical theologians and Christian ethicists recognize that there ought to be a positive correspondence between, in Wainwright's words, 'the vision and values celebrated in worship and the practical attitudes and behaviour of the worshippers before and after the liturgy'.[23] But can the liturgy itself perpetuate ethical attitudes and behaviours which are at odds with the gospel? A positive correspondence could result in unchristian ethical

---

[20] See the use of Jennings' work by Theresa F. Koernke, 'An Ethics of Liturgical Behavior', *Worship* 66 (1992), pp. 25–38.

[21] 'Ritual Studies and Liturgical Theology', p. 42.

[22] This is probably why liturgical theologians typically express the dictum of Prosper of Aquitaine, *legem credendi lex statuat supplicandi*, with the more dialectical formula, *lex orandi, lex credendi*.

[23] *Doxology*, p. 399.

standards if the liturgy, in fact, does not truly embody Christian
ethical standards. This is the sort of critique which, historically,
Protestant theology has brought to liturgy when it evaluates *lex
orandi* from the standpoint of *lex credendi*, and which Catholic
liberation theologians have now taken up in their concern for
orthopraxy.

For liberation theologians, justice among Christians must be
established as a prior condition in order for worship to be
authentic, or else worship will merely perpetuate the situation of
injustice, since both the oppressed and the oppressors are often
ostensibly members of the Church. Gustavo Gutiérrez comments on liturgy in situations of injustice:

> Under such circumstances, life in the contemporary Christian community
> becomes particularly difficult and conflictual. Participation in the eucharist,
> for example, as it is celebrated today, appears to many to be an action
> which, without authentic Christian community underlying it, becomes an
> exercise in make-believe.[24]

Such an evaluation has led some liberation theologians to question whether the eucharist can actually be celebrated when the
circumstances indicate that the Church 'humiliates those who
have nothing' (1 Cor. 11.22).

Feminist theologians raise similar questions about the per-
petuation of patriarchy and misogyny in the liturgy. On one
level, this critique addresses the sort of liturgical language used
to refer both to the worshipping community and to God. Such a
critique is increasingly reflected in the official liturgical books
published by Christian denominations.[25] Many feminist
theologians, however, are questioning whether tinkering with
liturgical language sufficiently addresses the deeper problems of
sexism. For example, does a lectionary which includes stories
about violence towards women perpetuate that violence? Does a
liturgy which stresses obedience to God continue to relegate

---

[24] *A Theology of Liberation* (Orbis, Maryknoll NY 1973), p. 137.

[25] For instance, in *The United Methodist Hymnal* (1989), the hymn 'Good
Christian Men Rejoice' appears as 'Good Christian Folk Rejoice', and several
other hymns and prayers avoid the use of 'Father' for God, though 'Father' language has by no means been eliminated completely. United Methodists continue to debate the use of traditional trinitarian language in their rites.

women to positions of subordination? Does a prayer which acknowledges Jesus, a male, as '*The* Lord' authorize male supremacy?

Marjorie Procter-Smith demonstrates the complexity of the feminist critique in her evaluation of the 'birth' imagery connected to baptism:

> Granted that these images are female, to what extent are they feminist? . . . Indeed, one might well argue that in appropriating childbirth imagery for baptism, the patriarchal church implicitly devalues actual women's lived experience of pregnancy and childbirth, suggesting that the nature [sic] event must be supplemented, if not supplanted, by birth into mother church. Moreover, since motherhood is the only explicitly female image found in the church's liturgical tradition, it runs the risk of becoming an umbrella image for women's lives, in spite of the fact that not all women are or choose to be mothers.[26]

According to Procter-Smith, pointing out or adding feminine imagery to a liturgy which is otherwise patriarchal will only perpetuate the problem of sexism. In order for liturgy to be 'emancipatory' , women's experience must be valued on its own terms, and women must be 'remembered and respected, not as marginal to the tradition, but as a necessary part of it'.[27] This requires women to develop their own liturgies in communities of women who are willing to struggle to remember (she employs the term anamnesis) what the Christian tradition has largely ignored, hidden, or maladapted.

While the critique of liberation and feminist theologians demonstrates the need for ethical evaluation of Christian liturgy, it also recognizes that liturgy can be a tool in the development of ethical concepts and behaviour. On a simplistic level, this use of liturgy takes such forms as Roman Catholic Masses for world peace or Protestant 'litanies' for social justice.[28] On the other hand, the use of liturgy as a tool for ethical motivation may be very powerful. James Cone notes that participants in marches

---

[26] *In Her Own Rite: Constructing Feminist Liturgical Tradition* (Abingdon Press, Nashville 1990), pp. 158-9.

[27] ibid., p. 35.

[28] See 'The World Methodist Social Affirmation' in *The United Methodist Hymnal*, which is full of 'consciousness-raising' language about social justice issues.

during the American civil rights movement sang 'Negro spirituals' because of the 'empowerment and courage they bestowed upon the marchers'.[29] Here the liturgical act of singing was employed as a motivational tool in an extra-liturgical setting, not unlike, perhaps, the motivational use of singing in the Arian controversies in fourth-century Constantinople. More recently, Nicholas Wolterstorff has described a South African liturgy 'in which, at the time of the offertory, not only were bread and wine brought forward, but along with them a set of chains, a rubber bullet, and a passbook'.[30] In this example, the offering of the signs of the oppression of apartheid employed the liturgy to do something other than the liturgy usually intends. As Wolterstorff observes, this demonstration turned the eucharist from a thanksgiving into a lament. While it would be hardhearted to object to this use of liturgy, we must recognize that such demonstrations are effective precisely because they are *not* what we expect; they could never really become standard ritual practice.

Liturgy as Central to the Christian Ethos: Liturgy as Ethics
When liturgy is approached as a source for ethics or as an object of ethics, the underlying assumption is that liturgy and ethics occupy two distinct realms, and that a relationship must be established. The ethicist John Howard Yoder begins with a different assumption. He argues that what we call liturgy and ethics are virtually identical ways in which the Christian community lives out the gospel. For example, according to Yoder, the eucharist as an act of table-fellowship is essentially Christian economic ethics. He comments on the institution of the Lord's Supper in the New Testament:

> What the New Testament is talking about in 'breaking bread' is believers actually sharing with one another their ordinary day-to-day material substance. It is not the case, as far as understanding the New Testament accounts is concerned, that, in an act of 'institution' or symbol-making, God or the church would have said 'let bread stand for daily sustenance.' It is not

[29] *For My People: Black Theology and the Black Church* (Orbis, Maryknoll NY 1984), p. 69.
[30] 'Liturgy, Justice, and Tears', *Worship* 62 (1988), p. 396.

even merely that, in many settings, as any cultural historian would have told us, eating together already stands for values of hospitality and community-formation, these values being distinguishable from the signs that refer to them. It is that bread *is* daily sustenance. Bread eaten together *is* economic sharing. Not merely symbolically, but in actual fact, it extends to a wider circle the economic solidarity that normally obtained in the family.[31]

Thus, according to Yoder, in the New Testament Church the eucharist did not inform or motivate Christian ethics; rather, it *was* Christian ethics. In its eucharistic liturgy the New Testament Church was merely doing what the Church always does — sharing food as a family of brothers and sisters in Christ.

Yoder's example provides support for the ethicist Stanley Hauerwas' assertion that 'the church does not have a social ethic; the church is a social ethic'.[32] Yet, while Yoder stresses sacraments as observably verifiable ethical actions, Hauerwas stresses the narrative aspect of liturgy as the foundation of Christian community: liturgy, and especially the sacraments, 'enact the story of Jesus and, thus, form a community in his image'.[33] Christians become a part of that story by their participation in liturgy and sacraments, and so carry out the on-going work of Christ:

> These rites, baptism and eucharist, are not just 'religious things' that Christian people do. . . . Instead of being motives or causes for effective social work on the part of Christian people, these liturgies *are* our effective social work. For if the church *is* rather than has a social ethic, these actions are our most important social witness.[34]

For Hauerwas, the performance of liturgy is the Church's ethical work in the world because it defines the church community as distinct from the world around it. Nevertheless, Hauerwas recognizes that this identification of liturgy with the social work of the Church is not automatic. In order for this witness to be credible, the Church and its worship require a people who are able to demonstrate the virtues of 'charity, hospitality,

[31] 'Sacrament as Social Process', pp. 36–7.
[32] *The Peaceable Kingdom: A Primer in Christian Ethics* (University of Notre Dame Press 1983), p. 99.
[33] ibid., p. 107.
[34] ibid., p. 108.

and justice'.[35] There must be a consistency between the Church's worship and the ethical demands of the gospel. Thus Hauerwas admits that it is certainly possible for the Church's worship to be inauthentic.

This last observation raises a problem with the 'liturgy-as-ethics' approach. How do we identify what is normative for Christian ethics in worship, if the actual worship of the Church is not always consistent with Christian ethics? Yoder reaches back to the New Testament community to find his examples of how sacraments and social ethics are unified activities, and he makes some useful points about how the New Testament Church can provide paradigms for contemporary churches. Yet, even in the New Testament, the ethical meaning of the eucharist was capable of being misunderstood by the Church itself, as Paul demonstrated in 1 Corinthians 11. While Hauerwas refers to contemporary liturgical practice, his approach is circular: the liturgy is the on-going story which forms God's holy people, but the people must demonstrate some degree of holiness (evidenced by charity, hospitality, and justice) in order for liturgy to be credible. While both Hauerwas and Yoder demonstrate an integral correspondence between liturgy and ethics, they nevertheless find it necessary to critique liturgy from the standpoint of ethics. That is to say, they also indicate that it is necessary to make ethical assumptions about what a liturgical community must demonstrate in order to be authentic.

Some Concluding Observations

This brief overview of the three approaches to liturgy and ethics has indicated that each has a place in the discussion as well as certain limitations. Several observations may now be offered in an attempt to further the discussion.

1. The relationship between liturgy and ethics is not always obvious. All three of the approaches given above indicate that the connection must be demonstrated. Historically, this is what the Church refers to as catechesis. Theologians in the fourth century recognized this when they lectured newly initiated Christians on the meaning of the rites they had just experienced.

[35] ibid., p. 109.

Participation in the rites themselves did not sufficiently communicate their full meaning; this meaning had to be explained through mystagogy.[36] Despite the insistence of some liturgical theologians and ritologists that liturgy 'forms' ethical behaviour, without proper catechesis liturgy will not be sufficient as an agent of ethical formation, as the overwhelming testimony of church history bears witness. Wealthy Christians all too easily can participate in the eucharist with poor Christians and not understand the justice issues inherent in this act. Christians can pray, 'give us this day our daily bread', and not understand the limits this places on the consumption of food resources. As noted above, ritual is inherently ambiguous, and perhaps it is most ambiguous to those who participate in it regularly. Therefore, today, as in the fourth century, the ethical relevance of liturgy must be periodically explained in order for worshipping Christians to make the connection.

2. This leads to a second observation: in any discussion of liturgy and ethics, a distinction must be made between their primary functions and the reflection upon these functions. As regards liturgy, this is the distinction between worship as *theologia prima* (first-order theology) and *theologia secunda* (second-order reflection). As regards ethics, this is the distinction between right action and the systematic evaluation of what constitutes right action (using deontological or consequentialist reasoning, for example). That is to say, a distinction must be made between liturgy *per se* and liturgical theology, as well as between right action and ethical theology or philosophy. Therefore, the discussion of the relationship of liturgy and ethics must include a discussion of their relationship to theology: *lex orandi, lex credendi, lex bene operandi*.[37] These three go together in the life of the Church and each maintains its own particular function. It is pointless to try to rank their importance as if one could

---

[36] See Edward Yarnold, *The Awe-Inspiring Rites of Initiation* (St Paul Publications, Slough 1971).

[37] See Teresa Berger, 'Lex orandi — lex credendi — lex agendi: Auf dem Weg zu einer ökumenisch konsensfähigen Verhältnisbestimmung von Liturgie, Theologie, Ethik', *Archiv für Liturgiewissenschaft* 27 (1985), pp. 425–32.

some how supersede the others.[38] To use an analogy, there is no reason to argue which is more important to a human body, the heart, the liver, or the lungs. Without all three in reasonably good working order, the whole human body will suffer. Likewise, liturgy, theology, and ethics have a vital relationship, and no one can be neglected without affecting the others.

3. A problem with many approaches to liturgy and ethics is the tendency towards reductionism on the liturgy side: only those aspects which are ethically relevant appear to count. This ignores the gratuitous element of worship. Yet, as Willimon has stated, 'We do not worship God in order to become better people. Christians worship God simply because we are God's beloved ones. Christian worship is an intrinsic activity.'[39] This suggests that any discussion of the relationship between liturgy and ethics must acknowledge the ways in which they are *not* related. The quotation from Augustine with which we began is relevant here. Augustine recognized that it is entirely possible for a worshipper formally to bless God with words in church while living a life that does not bear witness to the gospel. For Augustine, this turned the blessing uttered in church into blasphemy. Augustine does not suggest that the blessing in church forms the ethical life; rather, the ethical life authenticates the blessing in church. Yet, this does not lead to the opposite conclusion that an ethical life without liturgy is sufficient. Augustine does not call for the ethical life to the neglect of worship, for the blessing in church indeed has its essential place.

This observation certainly does not deny that there are ethical dimensions to liturgy, since liturgy involves human beings who are called to ethical living. Likewise, there are liturgical dimensions to ethics, since ethics is not merely our duty, but our delight—our thankful response to God.[40] Nevertheless, I suggest that the most important relationship between liturgy and ethics is not direct or causal, but is to be found on a higher level in their common goal, the faithful service of God. Because they

---

[38] See the critique by Vigen Guroian, 'Seeing Worship as Ethics', in *Incarnate Love: Essays in Orthodox Ethics* (University of Notre Dame Press 1987), pp. 51–2.

[39] *The Service of God*, p. 37.

[40] See Wainwright, 'Eucharist and/as Ethics' (above, n. 11), p. 128.

have a common goal, a critical principle may be formulated: sound liturgical practice will never subvert Christian ethics, nor will proper Christian ethics denigrate liturgy, because each is necessary for God to be well served. This is why it is important to recognize the degree to which liturgy and ethics are *not* related; by keeping them distinct we may give each the proper attention it deserves.

At the heart of the consideration of liturgy and ethics from Augustine to the present is the longing for deeper human faithfulness to God. We may examine the ways we pray or believe or act to find clues for some formula that will produce faithfulness, holiness, and sanctification. But, finally, we must acknowledge that there is no formula. The work of sanctification belongs to God, and how God accomplishes this work will always be a mystery, out of our control, and beyond our complete understanding.

6

Liturgy and the History of Christianity

GRANT SPERRY-WHITE

The study of both the history of Christianity and the history of Christian liturgy have progressed considerably since the famous dictum of Dean Inge. Historians today cannot ignore the witness of the many early texts of liturgical provenance when reconstructing the history of the ancient Christian movement. For their part, historians of Christian liturgy have begun to approach the raw materials of their discipline with more critical acumen than in the past. Thanks to the work of Geoffrey Cuming, Ronald Jasper, Georg Kretschmar, Juan Mateos, Marcel Metzger, Robert Taft, Gabriele Winkler, and Paul Bradshaw (a former student of Ronald Jasper), to name a few, the study of the history of Christian worship has attained a level of scientific rigour largely lacking in the past.

Unfortunately, few histories of ancient Christianity written in the past twenty years have integrated liturgical evidence into their reconstructions of early Christian communities. For example, the recent *Festschrift* for W. H. C. Frend[1] discusses early Christian worship only as a portion of a larger chapter on 'Ministry, Worship, and Christian Life'. Even then, the bibliography cited at the chapter's conclusion evinces absolutely no cognizance of liturgical scholarship since World War II. On the other hand, there are some exceptions: Jaroslav Pelikan and Elizabeth Clark attempt to take liturgical sources into account in their respective histories of early Christian doctrinal development and the Origenist controversy.[2] Doubtless, this relative

---

[1] *Early Christianity: Origins and Evolution to AD 600*, ed. Ian Hazlett (SPCK, London 1991; Abingdon Press, Nashville 1992).

[2] Jaroslav Pelikan, *The Christian Tradition*, vols 1 & 2 (University of Chicago Press 1971, 1974); Elizabeth A. Clark, *The Origenist Controversy: The Cultural Construction of an Early Christian Debate* (Princeton University Press 1992).

absence of liturgical sources in recent treatments of the history of early Christianity is due in part to the notorious slipperiness of many ancient Christian liturgical texts. Their use in the reconstruction of the fabric of early Christianity is fraught with difficulties stemming from the fact that often the most basic questions of their date, authorship, and provenance remain open. This situation is particularly true for the liturgical texts most often cited by historians of early Christianity, those contained in the church order literature.[3]

Fortunately, liturgiological scholarship of the past two decades has begun to shed some light on the methodological issues pertaining to the interpretation of ancient Christian liturgical texts. Robert Taft's massive study of the pre-anaphoral rites of the Byzantine eucharistic liturgies has set the standard for rigorous study of liturgical evidence.[4] The work of Frans Van de Paverd, Juan Mateos, and Gabriele Winkler provide other examples of the comparative approach to the study of liturgy, a methodology founded by the Austrian liturgiologist Anton Baumstark (1877–1948).[5] Most recently, Paul Bradshaw has proposed a set of methodological guidelines for the interpretation of early Christian liturgical materials.[6] According to Bradshaw, early Christian liturgical texts, like any other early Christian literary product, must not be read naively, as if they dispassionately reported the liturgical activities they describe. Rather, liturgical texts are to be subjected to the same historical-critical investigation which applies to any other early Christian text. They must be viewed in light of the push and pull of the theological, sociological, and political forces which occasioned or at least influenced their production. It is precisely these

[3] On church orders, see Paul F. Bradshaw, *The Search for the Origins of Christian Worship* (SPCK, London; Oxford University Press, New York 1992), pp. 80–110; and Bruno Steimer, *Vertex Traditionis: Die Gattung der altchristlichen Kirchenordnungen* (Walter de Gruyter, Berlin/New York 1992).

[4] *The Great Entrance* (Pontificium Institutum Orientalium, Rome 1978).

[5] Frans van de Paverd, *Zur Geschichte der Messliturgie gegen Ende des vierten Jahrhunderts* (Pontificium Institutum Orientalium, Rome 1970); Juan Mateos, *Le Typikon de la Grande Eglise* (Pontificium Institutum Orientalium, Rome 1962, 1963); Gabriele Winkler, *Das armenische Initiationsrituale* (Pontificium Institutum Orientalium, Rome 1982).

[6] *The Search for the Origins of Christian Worship*, pp. 56–79.

aspects of ancient Christian liturgical remains which render them useful to the historian of early Christianity.

Therefore, liturgical texts should not be viewed as unmediated witnesses to the worship practice of ancient Christian communities. Instead, they must be approached with the same caution with which one approaches any other ancient Christian literary product. This methodological principle will have major consequences for the use of early Christian liturgical materials: no longer can they be mustered as proof-texts for a single interpretation of the character and development of ancient Christian worship.

Liturgical Sources for the History of Early Christianity

What can liturgical texts offer to the historian of Christianity? There is not, of course, one answer to that question. Liturgical texts comprise a wide spectrum of literary genres: isolated prayer texts, collections of prayers, homilies, mystagogical and catechetical texts, legislative-canonical materials, lectionaries, and rules. These texts originate in a variety of settings: the so-called 'great church', heterodox and Gnostic communities, ascetic and monastic groups, and individuals associated with those communities. Let us take a closer look at some of these sources.

Isolated Prayer Texts

These are both the simplest and the most problematic of early Christian liturgical sources. Sometimes liturgical evidence of this type is the easiest for the historian to draw on. When such prayers appear to have been committed to writing specifically for the purpose of use in worship, so there is a direct correlation between the text and its function, and when such texts can be dated and assigned to a particular locale, they make for excellent liturgical and theological evidence. At other times, however, their origin is difficult to determine. For example, it is often impossible to ascertain if the leaf of papyrus or other material on which a prayer is preserved once belonged to a liturgical codex or to a text not meant for liturgical use at all. Such is the case with some of the fragments of the anaphora of

St Mark or its predecessors, such as the famous Strasbourg papyrus *gr.* 254.[7]

It should be noted that the preservation of prayer texts in isolated form apparently was not limited to the great church; the Coptic Gnostic codices from Nag Hammadi contain, among other things, 'The Prayer of the Apostle Paul' (Nag Hammadi Codex I, 1),[8] 'The Prayer of Thanksgiving' (Nag Hammadi Codex VI, 7),[9] and two fragmentary prayers which may be meant for a Gnostic eucharist (Nag Hammadi Codex XI 43, 20–38; XI 44, 1–37).[10] Their preservation in codices alongside non-liturgical texts also makes it difficult, if not impossible, to determine their origin. In this situation, their value as evidence for the development of Gnostic liturgical practice is reduced.

Collections of Prayers

Perhaps the most famous collection of prayers in ancient Christianity is that which exists under the name of Sarapion, a fourth-century bishop of the Egyptian town of Thmuis.[11] Although it is unique in that it contains only liturgical texts, it is not the only early Christian source containing a large proportion of prayers and/or liturgical directions. At least some of the documents traditionally placed under the umbrella category of church orders also contain liturgical materials: *Didache*, *Apostolic Tradition*, *Canons of Hippolytus*, *Apostolic Constitutions*, and *Testamentum Domini*. The euchologion of Sarapion and the above church orders appear to represent in different

[7] For further details, see G. J. Cuming, *The Liturgy of St Mark* (Pontificium Institutum Orientalium, Rome 1990).

[8] For an English translation of all the Nag Hammadi texts, see James Robinson (ed.), *The Nag Hammadi Library in English*, 2nd edn (Harper & Row, San Francisco 1988). The Coptic texts of the Nag Hammadi documents have been published in *The Facsimile Edition of the Nag Hammadi Codices*, 13 vols (Brill, Leiden 1972–1990).

[9] Coptic text in Douglas M. Parrott (ed.), *Nag Hammadi Codices V, 2-5 and VI: with Papyrus Berolinensis 8502, 1 and 4* (Brill, Leiden 1979).

[10] Facsimile of the Coptic text in Charles W. Hedrick (ed.), *Nag Hammadi Codices XI, XII, XIII* (Brill, Leiden 1990); see also Jacques E. Menard, *L'exposé Valentinien les fragments sur le baptême et sur l'eucharistie (NH XI, 2)* (Presses de l'Université Laval, Québec 1985).

[11] See Maxwell E. Johnson, 'A Fresh Look at the Prayers of Sarapion of Thmuis', *Studia Liturgica* 22 (1992), pp. 163–83.

ways the tendency in early Christian communities to commit prayers to writing, even if the reasons for that activity are not always clear.[12]

Homilies, and Mystagogical and Catechetical Texts

Homilies have long been recognized as sources for evidence concerning early Christian liturgical practice. They provide a context for references to liturgical practices, and the historian can be reasonably sure that they are reliable.[13] By the mid-fourth century, some Christian communities had developed extensive systems of pre-baptismal teaching and post-baptismal explanation of the initiatory rites.[14] But why and how do those practices come into existence at that particular point in time, and not before? The traditional explanation notes the influence of the pagan mystery cults, and the presumed desire of Christian leaders to provide a viable alternative to their chief religious competition.[15] Enrico Mazza, the most recent scholar to study the subject of Christian mystagogy, suggests that Canon 46 of the Council of Laodicea (in the second half of the fourth century) may be responsible for the development of mystagogy in its own right, although admitting that his theory is 'fragile'.[16]

A number of points could be made against it, perhaps the strongest being the fact that the Council of Laodicea seems to have been called to deal with liturgical and canonical problems only within a portion of Asia Minor.[17] The extent to which the canons of the council were meant to apply to analogous liturgi-

[12] For a study of this phenomenon, see Allan Bouley, *From Freedom to Formula* (Catholic University of America Press, Washington DC 1981).

[13] See for example Van der Paverd, *Messliturgie*, where the shape and content of the eucharistic rite of Antioch is deduced from the writings of John Chrysostom, many of which are sermons.

[14] For an introduction to these catechetical elements, see Edward Yarnold, *The Awe-Inspiring Rites of Initiation* (St Paul Publications, Slough 1971).

[15] See for example the brief discussion in Yarnold, *Awe-Inspiring Rites*, pp. 55–62. He concludes that while the Christian rites themselves were probably not affected by the mystery cults, their explanation (in mystagogy) was.

[16] *Mystagogy* (Pueblo, New York 1989), p. x.

[17] On the Council of Laodicea, the date of which is still disputed, see the entry (with bibliography) in Angelo Di Berardino (ed.), *Encyclopedia of the Early Church* (James Clarke, Cambridge; Oxford University Press, New York 1992), pp. 472–3.

cal situations outside Asia Minor is open to debate. Part of the answer to the question may indeed lie in the competition between pagan mysteries and a Christianity still struggling to some extent for adherents. Other possible sources for Christian mystagogy may be earlier Christian instructional and homiletic traditions utilizing typological and allegorical methods of interpretation. Such traditions appear to have existed both in non-Gnostic and in Gnostic Christian communities.[18]

Legislative-Canonical Texts

A number of ancient Christian texts attempt to prescribe liturgical practice under the colour of a variety of types of authority. The church orders do so, usually by invoking the authority of the apostles, or even that of the Lord himself.[19] Into this category also fall the *acta* of the various local, regional, and ecumenical councils of the fourth and fifth centuries; in the case of those texts (some of which pre-date the later church orders), the authority invoked is that of the collective episcopacy.[20] The

[18] As evidenced by the sermon *On the Pascha* of Melito of Sardis (second century), and by the (probably Valentinian) *Gospel of Philip* (Nag Hammadi Codex II,3), which contains among other things teaching on the meaning of the eucharist and of initiatory rites. See Othmar Perler, *Méliton de Sardes: Sur la Pâque et fragments*, Sources chrétiennes 123 (Editions du Cerf, Paris 1966). For older studies of the *Gospel of Philip*, see J. E. Menard, *L'évangile selon Philippe* (Université de Montréal, Faculté de Théologie 1964), and R. M. Wilson, *The Gospel of Philip* (Mowbray, London 1962). A more complete bibliography of works relating to the *Gospel of Philip* can be found in David M. Scholer, *Nag Hammadi Bibliography 1948–1969* (Brill, Leiden 1971), and in annual supplements to *Novum Testamentum*, beginning with volume 13.

[19] See A. F. Walls, 'A Note on the Apostolic Claim in the Church Order Literature', *Studia Patristica* 2 (1957), pp. 83–92. His theory of the development of the apostolic claim must be modified in the case of the *Testamentum Domini*, which he alleges represents the zenith of the appeal to authority in the church orders. For example, the second-century *Epistula Apostolorum*, like the *Testamentum Domini*, derives its claim to dominical authority from its use of a post-resurrection dialogue between Jesus and his disciples, a literary device found almost exclusively in Gnostic literature. It may be more accurate to view the claim of dominical authority as a literary phenomenon entirely separate from the trajectory of the appeal to apostolic authority, which appears as early as the New Testament (e.g., 1 & 2 Timothy, 2 Peter).

[20] For a critical edition of the council texts, see Périclès-Pierre Joannou, *Discipline generale antique*, 4 vols (Tipografia Italo-Orientale 'S. Nilo', Rome 1962–4).

canons of church councils are valuable, of course, for the comparative ease with which they can be dated and located; thus the liturgical practices they legislate can be fixed chronologically and geographically. It must be kept in mind, however, that most if not all legislative-canonical texts by their very nature are not descriptive, but prescriptive. That is, they do not attempt to describe liturgical practice, but rather seek to impose 'correct' practices upon a situation not currently meeting the standards of the group responsible for the legislation. Thus these texts may have a dual value for the historian, for they indirectly describe liturgical practices which have evoked a response from ecclesiastical authority.

Lectionaries

Lectionaries comprise perhaps one of the most under-used liturgical sources of early Christianity. Scholars of the New Testament utilize lectionaries in their study of the text of the New Testament,[21] but they remain largely untapped by liturgical historians. Perhaps the most complete work to date which makes use of lectionary evidence is that by Thomas Talley on the liturgical year.[22] The value of early Christian lectionaries lies in their witness to the association of the scripture text to specific liturgical feasts, and in their witness to the development and utilization of exegetical traditions in specific cities or regions (e.g., Jerusalem, North Africa, or East Syria).

Ascetic and Monastic Rules

The monastic rules of the fourth and fifth centuries provide valuable evidence for the development of liturgical practice in ascetic communities. They also bear witness to the use of anterior liturgical traditions and to their relationship to the

[21] See for example Bruce M. Metzger, *The Text of the New Testament: Its Transmission, Corruption, and Restoration*, 3rd edn (Oxford University Press, Oxford/New York 1992), pp. 30–1.

[22] *The Origins of the Liturgical Year* (Pueblo, New York 1986). At the end of his study (pp. 237–8), Talley suggests further topics for study involving early Christian lectionaries.

sociological structure of the monastic or ascetic community.[23] Ascetic and monastic rules may be related to church orders; it would be worthwhile to analyse the genesis of such rules within the context of the emergence of the church orders of the late fourth century.

Liturgy and the Dynamics of Early Christianity

The history-of-religions approach to the history of early Christianity has become a widely accepted methodology, although it is not without its critics.[24] By viewing the Christian movement as one among many religious movements to emerge in late antiquity, historians are able to interpret it in a much wider context than that provided by the disciplines of church history or systematic theology. It seems that, by and large, liturgiologists have been reluctant to adopt a similar approach to the history of early Christian worship, leaving it to scholars of the New Testament and other early Christian literature to suggest theories based upon an examination of early Christian liturgical texts from a more general history-of-religions perspective.[25] One can only speculate upon the reasons for this. Perhaps it has something to do with the historically close relationship between the study of the history of liturgy and the nineteenth- and twentieth-century movements (especially among Western churches) for liturgical reform and renewal.[26]

[23] For a discussion of the value of the Rule of Pachomius as a historical source, see Philip Rousseau, *Pachomius: The Making of a Community in Fourth-Century Egypt* (University of California Press, Berkeley/Los Angeles 1985), pp. 48–53.

[24] See Kurt Rudolph, 'Early Christianity as a Religious-Historical Phenomenon', in Birger A. Pearson (ed.), *The Future of Early Christianity: Essays in Honor of Helmut Koester* (Fortress Press, Philadelphia 1991), pp. 9–19. On the history-of-religions school, see Rudolph's entry in Mircea Eliade (ed.), *Encyclopedia of Religion* (Macmillan, New York 1986), vol. 10, pp. 230–9.

[25] See for example Adela Yarbro Collins, 'The Origin of Christian Baptism', *Studia Liturgica* 19 (1989), pp. 28–46; Reinhart Staats, 'Die Sonntagnachtgottesdienste der christlichen Frühzeit', *Zeitschrift für die neutestamentliche Wissenschaft* 66 (1975), pp. 242–63.

[26] See Teresa Berger, 'Liturgical Movement', and Balthasar Fischer, 'Liturgical Reforms' (and the bibliography attached to each), in Nicholas Lossky et al. (eds), *Dictionary of the Ecumenical Movement* (WCC Publications, Geneva; Eerdmans, Grand Rapids 1991), pp. 616–22.

It may be worthwhile, however, for liturgiologists to take a fresh look at the history-of-religions school and what it can offer to the effort to reconstruct the development of early Christian worship. In one sense, that methodology is already being utilized by scholars who study the relationships between the varieties of Christian worship attested in late antiquity and the diverse Jewish liturgical forms from the same period.[27] However, the areas in which liturgiologists fear to tread are the realms of liturgical practice of pagan and Gnostic communities which certainly coexisted with Christian communities during the period under consideration here.

In a very real sense, the liturgical landscape implied by the above paragraph is misleading, for it does not seem to be the case that for the early Christian movement such neat divisions between 'Christian', 'pagan', and 'Gnostic' existed. As Walter Bauer[28] and scholars who belong to his school have demonstrated, many groups in the first, second, and third centuries considered themselves Christian: Valentinians and other Christian (as opposed to Jewish and pagan) Gnostics, Jewish-Christian communities, ascetic groups, and others. Christianity is a highly syncretistic religion, absorbing elements from the religious and philosophical systems around it. Therefore, to understand the development of Christian worship it is necessary to supplement the liturgical witnesses of the great church with sources belonging to other communities also claiming to be Christian.

The above methodological presupposition leads to the conclusion that the trajectory is the most appropriate model for describing the development of Christian worship in the ancient period. The task of the historian of early Christian worship will be to describe the formation and development of Christian liturgical traditions within the diverse communities of the Christian movement in late antiquity. The use of trajectories in the analysis of early Christian liturgical history is rare: it has

[27] See Bradshaw, *The Search for the Origins of Christian Worship*, pp. 1–29.
[28] *Orthodoxy and Heresy in Earliest Christianity* (Fortress Press, Philadelphia 1971).

been attempted recently for early Christian meal traditions by Berndt Kollmann.[29]

Related to the heuristic model of the trajectory is Bauer's regional approach to the history of ancient Christianity, which has been adopted in the past sixty years by historians of early Christianity.[30] The recognition that early Christian traditions can to a certain extent be associated with specific regions of the Roman Empire or even the Persian Empire has found its way into other fields, including liturgiology. This idea has been particularly fruitful for the study of the most ancient texts pertaining to baptism and the eucharist.[31]

What now follows are two examples of how a liturgical document can be utilized in the study of early Christian history. Both concern the *Testamentum Domini*, a collection of liturgical, canonical, and apocalyptic materials which probably dates from the last quarter of the fourth century, and which survives today in Syriac, Ethiopic, and Arabic versions.[32]

The Testamentum Domini: Text and Ecclesiastical Motive

Of particular interest to the historian of Christianity are the liturgical and canonical repositories known as church orders. On the surface, these texts appear to provide a window into the legal and liturgical construction of early Christian communities. Yet, as Paul Bradshaw has demonstrated, the church orders are

[29] *Ursprung und Gestalten der frühchristlichen Mahlfeier* (Vandenhoeck & Ruprecht, Göttingen 1990). See also the review of Kollmann by Hal Taussig, *Journal of Biblical Studies* 111 (1992), pp. 733–5.

[30] See Bauer, *Orthodoxy and Heresy in Earliest Christianity*, Appendix 2, which summarizes and discusses the reception of Bauer's thesis and its subsequent influence upon New Testament scholarship.

[31] See especially Winkler, *Initiationsrituale*, and Paul F. Bradshaw (ed.), *Essays in Early Eastern Initiation*, Alcuin/GROW Liturgical Study 8 (Grove Books, Nottingham 1988).

[32] What follows is an expansion of some material from my 'Daily Prayer and its Ascetic Context in the Syriac and Ethiopic *Testamentum Domini*' (unpublished Ph.D. dissertation, University of Notre Dame 1993). In the following notes, R refers to the page and line number of the Syriac version edited by Ignatius Ephrem Rahmani, *Testamentum Domini Jesu Christi* (Kirchheim, Mainz 1899 = Olms, Hildesheim 1968), and B refers to the page and line number of the Ethiopic text edited by Robert Beylot, *Testamentum Domini éthiopien* (Peeters, Louvain 1984).

not bare descriptions of ecclesiastical practice, but complex documents reflecting the predilections of 'armchair liturgists' as much as they describe ecclesiastical life at the time of their composition.[33] That some of the church orders may have emanated from a single person or from a small group by no means vitiates their value as historical sources. In fact, the very particularity of each church order may make the genre as a whole particularly useful for the historian.

A good case in point is the *Testamentum Domini*, which since its rediscovery by Western scholars in the nineteenth century has generally been thought of as a clumsy reworking of an earlier church order, the *Apostolic Tradition*. In reality, the *Testamentum Domini* is a complex collection of apocalyptic, ascetic, and church order material from a variety of periods. Perhaps the major question surrounding it concerns the reason for its composition. Of particular interest in this regard is the juxtaposition in the documents of materials from two very different Christian communities: ascetic, represented by the prayer texts and instruction on times of prayer prescribed for widows, presbyters, and the bishop (Syriac I.22, 32, 43); and ecclesial, represented by the material from the *Apostolic Tradition* (which provides the skeleton of the text). When the ascetic texts are read within the context of the document as a whole, it appears that the redactor has attempted to bring ascetic traditions within the ambit of ecclesiastical authority. The *Testamentum Domini* recasts male and female ascetic authorities (presbyters and presbyteresses) in the mould of the ecclesiastical presbyter and widow by juxtaposing materials concerning the authority and responsibilities of the senior man and senior woman (from another source) with the *Apostolic Tradition* chapters on the presbyter and widow.

Thus the chapters on the widow, presbyters, and bishop reveal the sometimes clumsy attempt by a person or community to harmonize two different traditions of Christian community

[33] *The Search for the Origins of Christian Worship*, pp. 71–3. The question of the genre's definition is still open; for another recent contribution to the debate, see Julian Hills, 'A Genre for I John', in Pearson (ed.), *The Future of Early Christianity*, 367–77.

and authority. Whether or not such a congregation as described by the *Testamentum Domini* actually existed is unknown; in a sense, that question is unimportant. The significance of the document lies in its preservation of a strand of thought concerning the relationship between ascetic and congregational traditions in fourth-century Christianity that does not appear in the ascetic or canonical literature of the period.

Liturgy and the Anthropomorphite Controversy

Ascetic practice and theology played an increasing role in Christian debates from the late fourth century. Recent scholarship has focused particularly upon the sources of fourth-century monasticism, pre-Constantinian Christian asceticism, the role of ascetic women, and the diversity of ancient Christian ascetic thought and practice.[34] Liturgical texts add to the knowledge of how certain monastic and ascetic communities organized their daily lives around cycles of communal and private prayer, usually centring upon psalmody, and sometimes evincing a close relationship to older patterns of Christian private prayer, as well as to the daily prayer of congregations, the so-called 'cathedral office'. The daily office thus provides a way into exploring the larger self-understanding of each community, and the use made by each group of anterior or contemporary theological, historical, and euchological traditions.[35]

Elizabeth Clark has recently taken a fresh look at the evidence for the so-called Anthropomorphite controversy which

[34] For an overview of the varieties of early Christian asceticism which takes into account the scholarship of the past forty years, see the article by Jean Gribomont in *Theologische Realenzyklopädie* 4 (Walter de Gruyter, Berlin 1979), pp. 204–25. See also Ruth Albrecht, *Das Leben der heiligen Makrina auf dem Hintergrund der Thekla-Traditionen* (Vandenhoeck & Ruprecht, Göttingen 1986); Peter Brown, *The Body and Society: Men, Women and Sexual Renunciation in Early Christianity* (Columbia University Press, New York 1988); and Philip Rousseau, *Ascetics, Authority, and the Church in the Age of Jerome and Cassian* (Oxford University Press 1978).

[35] See Paul F. Bradshaw, *Daily Prayer in the Early Church* (SPCK, London 1981; Oxford University Press, New York 1982), pp. 93–110; idem, 'Cathedral vs. Monastery: The Only Alternatives for the Liturgy of the Hours?', in J. Neil Alexander (ed.), *Time and Community* (Pastoral Press, Washington DC 1990), pp. 123–36; and Robert Taft, *The Liturgy of the Hours in East and West* (Liturgical Press, Collegeville 1986), pp. 57–140.

took place in the last decade of the fourth century.[36] As described by the fifth-century church historian Socrates, the debate centred around the opposition of Theophilus, patriarch of Alexandria, to the supposed belief of certain monks in the Nitrian wilderness, that since human beings were made 'in the image' of God, God must possess human form. Contemporary scholars have questioned the traditional interpretation of the Egyptian monks' views about the image of God, and some have suggested that Socrates misrepresents the views they actually held.[37]

The controversy over the use of images which erupted in the late fourth century encompassed debate over Origenist theology, asceticism, and ecclesiastical politics in Egypt. In particular, as Elizabeth Clark has demonstrated, the Origenist theological heritage as developed by Evagrius Ponticus played a major role in arguments against making an image of God in the mind during prayer. Proponents of this position held that the use of any mental image of God was blasphemous, as the image naturally attempted to circumscribe the One who transcended all images. Evagrius Ponticus and John of Lycopolis are the major witnesses to the practice of imageless prayer.[38] What has been lacking, however, is any liturgical evidence for the practice.

A prayer in the *Testamentum Domini* may hint at the controversy over the image of God in prayer. Among its texts is a tripartite prayer to be said daily by the presbyters of the church. The third strophe of the prayer ends on a note of praise which appears to articulate the self-understanding of those who are praying: 'We unceasingly praise you in our hearts always, as we depict in ourselves the image of your kingdom.'[39] Behind this thought seems to stand a Platonic understanding of the world, in which the ascetics, through their practice (which includes

[36] *The Origenist Controversy*, pp. 43–84.

[37] See Graham Gould, 'The Image of God and the Anthropomorphite Controversy in Fourth Century Monasticism', in Robert J. Daly (ed.), *Origeniana Quinta* (Louvain University Press 1992), pp. 549–57.

[38] Clark, *The Origenist Controversy*, pp. 68–70.

[39] Syriac I. 32: R 78.6. The Ethiopic (B 73.16) reads 'images'.

prayer) reflect or 'depict' (as in a painting)[40] their heavenly prototypes, perhaps the angels. The 'image of the kingdom' also appears elsewhere in the *Testamentum Domini*. Jesus' response to the question of Martha, Mary, and Salome about what they are to do in order to live is: 'in all things be images of the kingdom of heaven';[41] and the third strophe of the first early dawn hymn describes the tripling of praise to God as 'for the image of your kingdom'.[42]

The correct interpretation of the phrase 'image of the kingdom' is not immediately clear from the contexts in which it appears. It may somehow be related to traditions concerning the androgyny of the pre-Fall Adam, the restoration of which appears to be at the heart of some ancient Christian ascetic traditions articulated as early as Galatians 3.28 and the *Gospel of Thomas*.[43] Such an understanding of what the kingdom of heaven entailed would be quite appropriate for the *Testamentum Domini*, in which both women and men ascetics are given prominent place in the church. Another interpretation of the phrase is also possible. A notable feature of several the *Testamentum* texts pertaining to daily prayer is their use of ascetic terminology which can best be described as belonging to the Origenist theological heritage, especially as interpreted by Basil, Gregory of Nyssa, and Evagrius Ponticus. It may be that the reference to the depiction of the kingdom of God, rather than of God *per se*, is to also be interpreted in an Evagrian, anti-Anthropomorphite sense. Thus the *Testamentum Domini* may

[40] The Syriac verb employed here is used in Exod. 32.4 to refer to the casting of the image of the golden calf, and in 1 Kings 7.15 for the casting of the pillars of bronze in the Temple. See Robert Payne Smith et al., *Thesaurus Syriacus* (Oxford University Press 1879, 1901), col. 3384.

[41] Syriac I.16: R 18.22–3.

[42] R 52.12.

[43] On the widespread use of the imagery of androgyny in early Christianity, see especially Wayne A. Meeks, 'The Image of the Androgyne: Some Uses of a Symbol in Earliest Christianity', *History of Religions* 13 (1974), pp. 165–208; Dennis R. MacDonald, *There Is No Male or Female* (Fortress Press, Philadelphia 1987); and K. L. King (ed.), *Images of the Feminine in Gnosticism* (Fortress Press, Philadelphia 1988). For a brief overview of ancient Christian understandings of salvation which involved a flight from femininity, see Harold W. Attridge, ' "Masculine Fellowship" in the Acts of Thomas', in Pearson (ed.), *The Future of Early Christianity*, pp. 409–11.

preserve an echo of the polemics involved in the Anthropomorphite debate, and demonstrate one way in which an anti-
Anthropomorphite position could be articulated liturgically.

Conclusion

As the foregoing pages make clear, the relationship between the
study of liturgy and the study of early Christianity is not simple.
There is a relatively large amount of liturgical material waiting
to be tapped more extensively by historians of early Christianity,
and there are several methodological approaches utilized by
them which historians of liturgy could adopt with profit. Both
disciplines can learn from each other, perhaps with the result
that they will come to share more academic ground than in the
past.

7

Liturgy and Language: The Sacred Polis

CATHERINE PICKSTOCK

The cosmos is poised on the edge of the abyss.[1] In order that there be an enclave at a remove from the vast and undefined space of the chaotic quotidian where events are caught up in the cataract of paratactic time, an enclave where words are continuous with their referents and where the violence of time is suspended, the sacred polis must perpetually reaffirm creation. There are various linguistic and semiotic devices which liturgical language employs to keep chaos at bay. Of these, I shall consider stylization, performativity, and repetition. These three have implications for the eventfulness of language, the initiation of a sacral temporal order, and the creation of a cohesive community where there is a synaxis or 'coming together' of the disparate into a single unit.

All rituals are a declaration against indeterminacy.[2] The chaos which the formalized and recursive nature of liturgy eschews is by implication its central concern.[3] Every invocation betrays an absence, but it also embodies the reparation, since to call is to anticipate an answer, and to name is to bring into being. Ritual is paradoxical in that it constitutes one of the most contrived forms of social contact, drawing attention to its own artifice, yet at the same time deflecting challenge. Its message is established as unverifiable, since it is synaesthetically performed, and, once engaged, it offers its own immutable cosmos. The sacred polis remains unperturbed by the atonal clamour of

[1] K. Burke, *The Philosophy of Literary Forms: Studies in Symbolic Action* (Vintage Books, New York 1957), pp. 87–113, 317–18.

[2] See S. F. Moore, 'Uncertainty in Situations, Indeterminacies in Culture', in S. F. Moore and B. Myeroff (eds), *Symbol and Politics in Communal Ideology: Cases and Questions* (Cornell University Press, Ithaca 1975), pp. 210–39.

[3] See S. Freud, 'Obsessive Acts and Religious Practices', in his *Collected Papers*, vol. 2 (Hogarth Press, London 1924), pp. 25–50.

the chaotic quotidian which seeks always to render the performative infelicitous and the repetition lexically diminished. The sacred polis sets as its task to hold in rapture not only the cosmos, but also chaos itself.

The Chaotic Quotidian

The chaotic quotidian, whether seen as a historical process or as a universal, qualitative distinction, attempts in various ways to simulate cosmos. These include the reliance upon the *verifiable given* as its substance, *textualization*, and *repetition*. These attempts prove abortive, since they are based on a harnessing of the present moment at the expense of the past. Any momentary order this may produce soon disintegrates into chaos.

(i) Quotidian reliance upon constative truth

The language of the secular quotidian is contingent upon an external reality, and its function is to maintain a mimetic, analytic vigil on that reality. Liturgical language, by virtue of its performativity,[4] provides the substance of representation, constituting an unending reality by being uttered, while quotidian language merely fastens itself to an eroding reality. The constative[5] language of the quotidian describes and names things independent of their descriptions and names, effecting nothing more substantive than a slight perturbation of air. Performatives do not describe situations but create them. The referent does not exist without the words. Performatives in the quotidian arena, however, do not guarantee their referents. In the utterance of a promise, intentions are often only implicit; the lack of clear delineation of status between the participants earns each the right to question the verity of each other's utterances. All participants require a shared understanding of the rules governing promises[6] and of the meanings of the words used in

---

[4] See J. L. Austin, 'Performative Utterances', in his *Philosophical Papers*, ed. J. O. Urmson and G. J. Warnock (Oxford University Press 1970), pp. 233–52.

[5] See J. L. Austin, *How to do Things with Words* (Clarendon Press, Oxford 1962), p. 3.

[6] See L. Wittgenstein, *Philosophical Investigations* (Blackwell, Oxford 1991), para. 431, 505.

articulating the promise. Intentions rarely coincide with actions.[7] Speakers and hearers of promises are subject to too many conditions to make fulfilment of a quotidian promise a likelihood.

Quotidian language views liturgical language with suspicion, reducing it either to the elaborative and expressive, or the representative, forgetting that metaphor precedes the literal. The quotidian attempt to isolate abstract truth is bound to founder because the performative-constative dichotomy is not watertight;[8] J. L. Austin challenged the Saussurian sign-referent discontinuity by asserting the performative aspect of *all* utterances. The identity between speaking and doing is as true of 'I state that' or 'I say that' as of 'I bet that'.[9] The former two assertions establish just as much a congruence between word and referent as the latter explicit illocution. Austin's speech-act theory departs from the fabrication of abstractions towards a parallactic contextualization of truth of which the language is both the mode of communication and the actualization.

For example, that Spain is an 'arid square'[10] is arrant nonsense for a geometrician, but true for an activist in the Spanish Civil War. Abstract truth and falsehood upon which quotidian language relies do not stand for anything simple at all, but only for a vague dimension of being a right or proper thing to say given particular circumstances. In the story of the emperor's new clothes, so long as the subjects refuse to acknowledge the nudity of the emperor for fear of appearing to lack the virtue to perceive his clothes, the referential fact of his nudity is collectively non-existent. His attire is *performed* by a community which is willing to speak and act as if he were clothed. Similarly, the child's proclamation of the emperor's nudity, by virtue of its performativity, denudes him. Meanwhile, the emperor's referential

---

[7] cf. M. Berman, *All That is Solid Melts into Air: The Experience of Modernity* (Verso Editions, London 1983), pp. 208–9, 278, on Dostoevsky and Mandelstam.

[8] See Austin, *How to do Things with Words*, p. 20. Cf. J. Ladrière, 'Language of Worship: The Performativity of Liturgical Language', *Concilium* 2.9 (1973), pp. 50–62.

[9] See Austin, *How to do Things with Words*, p. 55.

[10] See W. H. Auden, 'Spain' (1937), in V. Cunningham (ed.), *Spanish Civil War Verse* (Penguin Books 1980), pp. 97–100.

condition remains constant before and after the proclamation, but his constative identity alters. Considered as acts, utterances change in conjunction with the conventions which they invoke and by which they are assessed. They are part of interactive, collective existence in history, standing opposed to any immutable, synchronic abstraction of truth. So, any quest to establish referential accuracy will be discountenanced since the prerogative to determine the felicity of truth resides in the collective.

(ii) Textualization

In an attempt to harness the transcience of reality, and to fix the spoken word, the quotidian engages in textualization. This freezing of language precludes the possibility of eventfulness. The moment that language is separated from its author, it is laid out like a cadaver, dismembered (interpreted), and then cast aside. The quotidian, in spite of its emphasis upon the given, finds itself stuttering. The printed word is left open to the ravages of market forces and eisegetical delirium.[11] It is erroneous to suppose that interpretation will yield clarity, since interpretation refers only to the imposition of the oscillating, solipsistic self, as if this constituted an unmediated transmission of the author's intentions to the hearer. This does not mean conversely that the original intention is in command of language, or that the author owns the text, but rather that the separation of an author from his words precipitates a closure of his speech. In the Eden myth, we see that to question God's words and to reinterpret the meaning of divine speech amounts to hubris and the loss of eventful language. The serpent begins with an exaggeration implicit in his question, 'Did God *really* say "You shall not eat from *every* tree in the garden?" ' (Gen. 3.1). This exaggeration provokes exegesis, for Eve is prompted to interpret God's instructions (3.3).[12] During the fleeting hiatus between the utterance and its reception, the serpent imposes a series of teasing exegetical sciolisms ('You will not *surely* die?' [3.4]). His

[11] See Plato, *Phaedrus and Letters VII and VIII* (Penguin Books 1973), 275b.
[12] See G. von Rad, *Genesis: A Commentary* (Westminster Press, Philadelphia 1961), p. 86.

interrogatives release the instability of definition, God's command stutters, and is rendered impotent. The moment exegesis enters the language, lexical authority is questioned, and human beings are estranged from the certainty of their own words.

Interpretation has to do with the imposition of definitions and meanings, which can only result in the reduction or closure of the open-ended event. Textualization does not render the event permanent, but rather widens the chasm between word and referent. The text cannot coincide with the event; at best, it consigns traces of it. The posteriority of the text does not permit recourse to the event, since it issues from it, assuring us no more than a negative of it. This discontinuity either dispenses with the referent (as in literature, we say that the characters exist only in the text), or else announces its abolition (as in the writing of historical texts). Theology claims that its referent is neither merely linguistic nor abolished. The liturgical text exists to open up access to the referent, even though this referent consists in the historical death and resurrection of Jesus Christ. In order that the liturgy be precluded from foreclosing the historical event, that is, rendering it mute, the text must be balanced with orality, the given with the hypothetical.

Jacques Attali equates exact reproduction made possible by modern methods of recording (which is an audible equivalent of textualization) with the totalitarian monologue of power. Texts are to do with stockpiling, and facilitate the 'triumph of the copy'.[13] Attali regards this sinister form of textualization as a means of hypnosis, of syncretic levelling, silencing, and of the distribution of normalized speech. It is in the interests of power to maintain predictability and a tonal lullaby of similarity, in order to eradicate any maenadic locus of subversion. Extempore risk of error and the unforeseen disappear into repetition, abstract perfection, and artificial, unidimensional differentiation. Textualization is a means of mutation and isolation. The text exists because of the absence of speakers, and the reader cannot participate in its monologue. In a sense, the reader is outside language. Since verbal and social reality are closely

[13] See J. Attali, *Noise: The Political Economy of Music* (University of Minnesota Press, Minneapolis 1985), p. 89.

related, textualization might be said to have colluded in the fragmentation of society.

Attali's suspicion of textualization is not a modern phenomenon. In Plato's *Phaedrus*, Socrates and his interlocutor discuss the inferiority of the written to the spoken word. In contrast to the process of dialectic whereby truth is elicited by means of conversation, textual communication is no more than an aid to recollection of a truth already discovered. In the dialogue, Socrates argues that 'those who acquire [the accomplishment of writing] will cease to exercise their memory and become forgetful', that the text is a receipt for recollection, not for memory. Truth can never be guaranteed, since texts consist of empty words, unaccompanied by their author, and if one were to ask a text what it means by something, it would simply return the same answer over and over again.[14]

The vastness and fluid nature of the semantic resource, the flexibility of registers, the modern facility of mass communication, the proliferation of texts, and the extra resource permitted in chaotic quotidian language of qualifications, irony, equivocation, conditions, and deception, all these options conspire to impede rather than facilitate communication,[15] to render limited and restrained what is most vast and free. Textualization transposes language from the realm of communication into the abstract, generalized agora of exchange and commodity, representing a reality by a form, semantics by a syntax.[16] This presupposes the existence of an objective scale of value, and dupes its consumers into believing in a cosmos of stable links of equivalence. One might suppose that quotidian language would be simple and lucid, being as it is fastened to the verifiable given,[17] and that any change which occurs consists only of a rearrangement of that given. That it proposes to construct the constructed and understand the understood might lead us to imagine there to be linguistic and conceptual security in this realm. But in spite of this short-circuited dynamic, there can be

[14] See Plato, *Phaedrus and Letters VII and VIII*, 275a.
[15] cf. Berman, *All That is Solid Melts into Air*, pp. 209ff.
[16] See Attali, *Noise*, p. 57.
[17] See Austin, *Philosophical Papers*, p. 233.

no last word; the analysis and the exegesis can never be satisfied. Xyrphe Delawey describes this bleak open-endedness of modernity: 'I could replace any one of these words with another, and still it would be the same. Such is the endless entrapment of the Modern. There is no point at which you might say to me, "Yes, and now you have finished. Your work is complete".'[18]

(iii) Quotidian repetition, the parody of divine excess

The quotidian is characterized by a levelling out of difference by means of a suppression of the hypothetical, and a codification and proliferation of the given. Repetition based solely in the given perpetuates 'the same sameness',[19] difference being artificially simulated in the excessive multiplication of semi-identical objects. There are various manifestations of quotidian repetition, such as scientific repetition of experiments, technical proliferation of commodities, habitual repetition, recursive motifs or genres, and repetition compulsions. In spite of the varied nature of these occurences, the aim of quotidian repetition is to achieve identity between things. Recent liturgical revision has been influenced by this quotidian conformity, where minor modification of a precedent parades as innovation and eventfulness. Similarly, a fear of contrastive, synaesthetic language can be perceived in the much-criticized 'flat' register of the *Alternative Service Book 1980* of the Church of England. Trapped in identity, language ceases to be substantial, and is reduced to the mimetic. The consequences of this proliferation of the given and shattering of differences is mutation and uneventfulness. Constantin Constantius describes the stasis of this negative repetition as beginning 'with a loss; the reason it is safe and secure is that it has nothing to lose'.[20] It resides at the end instead of the beginning. People often talk about the speed with which society changes, but that is because the past is incarcerated aoristically in anteriority, and is slipping away forgotten. The mass production and stockpiling of the present

[18] *The May Anthology* (Dillons, London 1992), p. 117.
[19] S. Kierkegaard, *Repetition*, ed. & trans. H. V. and E. H. Hong (Princeton University Press 1983), p. 170.
[20] ibid., p. 136.

leads to an obliteration of the past. If society seems unpredictable and fast-moving, and if the future seems uncertain, perhaps it is because nothing happens, nothing, that is, except simulacra.[21]

The quotidian avoids acknowledgement of the past by means of paratactic repetition. That is, it favours juxtapositive, linear recurrence in which causal, temporal, and modal hierarchies are obscured. Hypotactic rationalizations and figural anaphorae are avoided. Every resumption of the repetition is complete and uncontingent, resulting in an unteleological sense of history. This paratactic construction is related to Henri Bergson's notion of the habitual. Bergson describes how the mind often fails to make the total response to a situation which is the guarantee of its freedom. Economy of effort leads the individual to become an 'automatic conscient' who responds mechanically to impressions and sensations and who abdicates his or her liberty of action as part of a programme of temporal budgeting.[22] In Bergson's thought, the role of habit is unambiguously opposed to free creativity, and represents a threat to autonomy. The automatic is always ready to usurp the living and the free. Marcel Proust also regards habit as being among the various mental tendencies which anaesthetize and distract us from the elucidation of our experience of life. The people and places he has known are obscured because they have become habitual.[23] However, Proust is more ambivalent than Bergson, seeing habit as a curious amalgam of deprivation and protection. While a breaking of habit can overcome the 'vitesse acquise', he is predisposed to protect himself from all that is unfamiliar. The intensity of sensitivity, not 'blasé par l'habitude', which makes artistic creation possible, also makes him vulnerable to suffering.[24]

Attali, Bergson, and Proust isolate a disruptive, regressive, amnesiac type of repetition which engenders aphasia. The hec-

[21] See Attali, *Noise*, p. 89.

[22] 'Essai sur les données immédiates de la conscience', in *Oeuvres* (Presses Universitaires de France, Paris 1970) vol. 30, p. 126. Cf. Kierkegaard, *Repetition*, p. 179.

[23] *Le Temps Retrouvé* (Gallimard, Paris 1954), III.897. See also I.650ff.; II.85, 754.

[24] ibid., I.916. Cf. also I.678, 679, 681; II.754.

tic, linear temporal order of the everyday runs parallel with the mass-production of semi-identical commodities. As the innovative and the obsolete continually outrun each other, so the violence of time obliterates the past and eschews figural recurrence and commemoration.[25]

It is an irony that there is such uniformity beneath the apparent diversity of modernity; stasis in the midst of indeterminate flux; uncertainty in the midst of the given; forced-forgetting and alienation in the midst of freedom; and silence in spite of advanced communication devices. Attali attributes society's acceptance of identity in mass-production to fear of alienation: 'unanimity becomes the criterion of beauty'.[26] Quotidian language, then, is rooted in the mythic given; it is discontinuous with its referent and with its author. It is a commodity, whose purpose is not to communicate but to be bought and sold. It is codified, and can respond neither to its reader nor to change. The three features of quotidian language which I have discussed have to do with its attempt to harness cosmos and to save itself from the ravages of time, but such an attempt will be thwarted unless it is tackled by means of eternity. The abstract, powerless language of the quotidian leaves reality untouched. Where language is mute, only deeds can talk, and only violence can cast reality.

The Language of the Sacred Polis

Once things have happened, there remain only words. Liturgical language sets as its task the perpetual renewal of creation. In order that this be possible, it must set itself apart from the finitude, composite, and stasis of the quotidian. Nearly all the world religions have been marked by a deliberate separation from the 'drift'[27] of secular language by means of the use of archaic and ritual registers or even foreign languages, such as Latin in the Roman Catholic Church[28] and Hebrew in the

[25] See P. Connerton, *How Societies Remember* (Cambridge University Press 1989), p. 64.

[26] *Noise*, p. 121.

[27] See E. Sapir, *Language* (Harcourt, Brace, & World, New York 1921), pp. 147ff.

[28] See A. Bugnini, *The Reform of the Liturgy 1948–1975* (Liturgical Press, Collegeville 1990), ch. 20.

synagogue.[29] Liturgical rites are at a further remove from quotidian proceedings by virtue of their occurrence at special times, their limited duration, their performance in a marked-off arena, and their following of a predetermined, formalized order.[30] Stylization, performativity, and repetition are three ways in which the language of the sacred polis achieves its renewal of creation, offering temporary perfection in the midst of chaos.

(i) Stylization

Liturgical language is characterized by the use of a restricted semantic and syntactic field.[31] Orchestrated sequencing and set responses initiate a succession of linguistic and semiotic cues which facilitate continuation of the rite and cognitive orientation of its participants. There is no provision for the indeterminacies of irony, retraction, or deception. The language is given further support by means of consolidatory paralinguistic gestures such as genuflection, crossing, shaking hands, and kneeling. These indices do not perform a commentary on the ritual but reveal and embody the message itself, as well as the disposition of the participants, in the tangible, unequivocal presence of the body.[32]

Liturgical language does not constitute communication in the secular sense of the transference of new information from one human being to another.[33] Instead, liturgical language is stylized and consists of predictable formulae. Its conventionalized action and the reduction of the random by restraint have the effect of distancing the participants from the ritual enactment. The subjective intentions of the individual are subordinated to the common telos of the polis. This deprioritization of the psyche enables the polis to be stable, for the psyche is contingent, diffuse, irresolute, and demurring. This psychic distancing is a

[29] See Connerton, *How Societies Remember*, pp. 66–7.

[30] See S. J. Tambiah, 'A Performative Approach to Ritual', *Proceedings of the British Academy* 65 (1979), pp. 113–69; see esp. p. 117.

[31] See G. Hughes, *Words in Time* (Blackwell, Oxford 1988), ch. 1.

[32] See Connerton, *How Societies Remember*, pp. 66–7.

[33] See H. P. Grice, 'Meaning', *Philosophical Review* 66 (1957), pp. 377–88, on Information Theory; cf. also D. W. J. Corcoran, *Pattern Recognition* (Penguin Books 1971), p. 33.

means of producing the 'articulation of feelings',[34] that is, a permanent attitude, rather than a hysterical, fleeting Aristotelian catharsis.

The message of the liturgy is regarded as immutable, so it is a necessary corollary that its rites be couched in a non-mystifying fixed form, and be transmitted relatively unchanged through time. The condensed semantic, syntactic, and gestural resource is by no means a communicative hindrance. The diversity of the quotidian tongue yields nothing but opacity, instability, and conflict, and as such could precipitate a communicative collapse.[35] The iterability of liturgical language is a necessary criterion for the second category of liturgical language, performative speech acts,[36] the felicity of which relies upon the exactitude of the utterance, the following of conventional rules, and the consent of the collective as to the form and import of the utterance.

(ii) Performativity

The special use of pronouns which accompanies speech acts has an important synactic function. The community is *performed* by means of pronominal expressions of mutual acknowledgement, in the words 'we' and 'us'. To enact a rite at all is to give consent to its message, and collective pronouns awaken in the participants an affective disposition which discloses a specific field of reference, fortifying the participant's general preparedness in concrete form, enacting 'a form of constitutive receptivity . . . [which] prepares the soul to hear what they propose and effect'.[37] Personal pronouns deictically commit speakers to spatio-temporal and doctrinal locations. In pronouncing 'I' or 'we' the speaker fastens his or her volition to the ensuing

[34] See S. Langer, *Philosophy in a New Key* (New American Library, New York 1951), p. 125.

[35] See Tambiah, 'A Performative Approach to Ritual', p. 151.

[36] See Austin, *How to do Things with Words*, pp. 13–14; cf. idem, *Philosophical Papers*, p. 238, and Wittgenstein, *Philosophical Investigations*, para. 206.

[37] Ladrière, 'The Performativity of Liturgical Language', p. 57.

proposition. The participants express their ratification of the rite by their very presence within the physical boundaries allotted the ceremony.[38] But there is also an abstract enclave, the boundaries of which are drawn by their speech acts.[39] Liturgical language does not form an expression of a prior community, nor is it descriptive of that community. Rather, the language and the community institute a mutually constitutive reciprocity. By participating in the liturgical meal, communicants are incorporated into Christ's body. This movement from multiplicity to unity, the synaxis, is counterbalanced by a movement in the opposite direction, linked with the incarnation. Pseudo-Dionysius describes the symbolic actions of the celebrant: 'The bread which had been covered and undivided is now uncovered and divided into many parts. Similarly, he shares the cup with all, symbolically multiplying and distributing the One.'[40] It is by means of the incarnation, without undergoing any change in himself, that Jesus Christ beneficently becomes a composite and visible reality and accomplishes for us a unifying communion with himself. This ultimate community is no longer merely linguistic, but is signified proleptically in the language.

Speech-act theory demonstrates the reconciliation of apparently incompatible entities, such as words and deeds, individual and collective, but this only occurs when the individual participates perceptibly in communality. The word 'liturgy' derives from its use in the ancient Greek polis where *leit-ourgos* referred to the public act of citizenship. When a society does things with words, the deeds and words affirm the society just as its conventions unite the deeds and words. To be sure, when words do things, they actualize their users as well as their referents. The illocutionary lexicon effects the same democratic collectivity it requires, because speech acts, speakers, and hearers interact all at once. The dialectic between illocutionary

---

[38] cf. Richard Fenn's correlation of the closed linguistic resource and the physical structure of the church, in *Liturgies and Trials: The Secularisation of Religious Language* (Blackwell, Oxford 1982), p. xv.

[39] See Connerton, *How Societies Remember*, p. 58.

[40] *Eccl. Hier.* 3.3.12; English translation in *The Complete Works*, trans. C. Luibheid and P. Rorem (SPCK, London; Paulist Press, New York 1987), p. 222.

felicity and collective consent conveys the solidity of connections among speakers, but it also conveys the precariousness of such connections, as can be seen in the case of greetings. Most illocutions perform the speaker's participation in collective existence, but greetings have performance of sociability as their sole reason for being, that is, a greeting has no referential value beyond itself. Promises, wagers, and protestations are transitive ('We protest that . . .', 'I promise that . . .'), whereas greetings are intransitive; they just greet. The propositional content, or implicit constative reference, of transitive speech acts enables them to conceal any lack of communal ties. However, the absence of constative reference in a greeting makes this act of concealment impossible. A refusal to greet constitutes a withdrawal from the community[41] and a breakdown of communication.

The common teleological beliefs and the closed arena ratified by the attendance of the participants and defined by their speech acts enable the sacred polis to achieve a cohesive certainty unknown in the vast and undefined space of the quotidian. The reality-constitutive element of performative language means that participants can suspend their hermeneutic doubts. Sacraments and performatives are unambiguous, serious, and binding. The performative does not have its referent 'outside of itself or, in the event, before and in front of itself'.[42] Rather, in the sacred polis substantive action and verbal articulation are simultaneous. It is this continuity between word and deed which makes liturgical language eventful. With reference to transubstantiation, G. B. Sanguire remarked that 'all these miracles and prodigies that nature can only contemplate with dread are worked by means of three or four little words emitted from the

---

[41] cf. Stanley Fish, 'How to do Things with Austin and Searle: Speech-Act Theory and Literary Criticism', in idem, *Is There a Text in this Class?* (Harvard University Press, Cambridge 1980), p. 213.

[42] J. Derrida, 'Signature Event Context', in idem, *Limited Inc.* (Northwestern University Press, Evanston 1988), p. 13.

mouth of a man'.[43] Doing things with words, like doing things by other means, can construct or deconstruct reality.

Performativity is part of the oral component of the sacred polis. Utterers accompany their words, and the dialogic, participatory dynamic precludes the possibility of monologic, textual alienation.[44] However, the liturgy reconciles text and orality, since the written, static, monologic text of scripture is just as integral to the proceedings as the open-ended, unmediated use of speech acts. So, the given and the hypothetical, the established and the possible (in the liturgy, even the impossible is possible) are juxtaposed. The quotidian restricts itself to the *legible* —the abstraction and silence of statistics and polls. The *audibility* of liturgical language defeats secularity because sound can neither be owned nor made a commodity. Audible language, like music, is part of inhabited time; it cannot be stockpiled. Like the image in a mirror, it is an immaterial production, always anterior to concrete production. It is 'the mark of something missing, a shred of utopia, a collective memory . . . affirmed in time with a beat'.[45] Further, the absence of codified meaning is the presence of all meanings, a construction beyond the confines of the given.

The quotidian is wary of anything uncodified, but orality is not chaotic. It is shielded from delirium in two ways. First, it is shielded by the fact that utterances are accompanied by the utterer. Both speaker and recipient are present together in a specific context, and the sender's intentions are encoded in linguistic representation and in the consciousness of the listener to whom this representation communicates. In fact, the principle criterion of an oral situation is presence: speaker and listener, meaning and intention, words as phonetic and mental reality.[46]

Secondly, eucharistic language is spared delirium by virtue of the presence of the Word to support its narrative: 'While they

[43] *Erario della vita Cristiana e religiosa* (N. Pezzana, Venice 1711), part 3, p. 292, cited in P. Camporesi, 'The Consecrated Host: A Wondrous Excess', in M. Feher, R. Naddaff, and N. Tazi (eds), *Fragments for a History of the Human Body* I (Urzone, New York 1989), p. 232.

[44] 'Death alone is silent. Nothing essential happens in the absence of noise' (Attali, *Noise*, p. 3).

[45] ibid., p. 9.

[46] See Plato, *Phaedrus*, p. 276a.

said these things, he himself stood among them' (Luke 24.36). The eucharist is the superlative sacred polis in that every word is accompanied by its author, and every utterance occupies the site of the Word. The Christian assembly which celebrates the eucharist unceasingly adheres to the undifferentiated referent, the original event. The participants listen to the given word, first the Old Testament lesson, a figural prolepsis of the Word (Luke 24.27), then the New Testament, as a fulfilment and annulment of its precursor, then the hermeneutic of the Word which the homily verbally executes. Finally, the community, having heard the text, passes through it as the carnal, esculent Word comes to the community, and the community into him. While quotidian pabulum transforms itself into our own substance and becomes one with us, the divine victual 'transforms us into itself'.[47] No referent is ever more directly apprehended, since 'by eating his divine flesh with his bones, we become, through this conjunction, even more specifically the limbs of his divine body'. Unlike other sacraments, 'the eucharist, having assumed the shape of food and drink, is received internally, and, as such, brings Jesus himself inside our chest'.[48] Catholic theologians of the seicento Italian Baroque believed so fervently in this direct incorporation that the stomach became a hidden altar where the communicant is transformed into the Host, a zone of liturgical mediation between the divine and the bestial.[49]

The language of the sacred polis is directly apprehensible because of its stylistic predictability, its performativity, its orality, and the presence of the Word. The linear structure of a rite means that its language must be immediate, since there is no opportunity during the service to peruse the liturgy. The proceedings of the polis are made still more direct by means of another form of performativity, that is, a dramatic, dialogic dynamic. The language of liturgy, like that of theatre, *produces* rather than *depicts*. Like drama, the liturgy palpably involves col-

[47] Alessandro Diotallevi, *La beneficenza di Dio verso gl'uomini e l'ingratitudine degli uomini versa Dio considerazioni* (A. Poletti, Venice 1716), pp. 253, 258, in Camporesi, 'The Consecrated Host', p. 227.

[48] Fulgenzio Cuniliati, *Il catechista in pulpito* (T. Bettinelli, Venice 1768), p. 232, in Camporesi, 'The Consecrated Host', p. 229.

[49] See Camporesi, 'The Consecrated Host', p. 232.

lective experience. However, the theatre demands neither the assent nor the active participation of its collective. Further, liturgical language makes present, not as a spectacle or a picturing-forth, but as a reality the efficacy of which is once-and-for-all, and which is taken into the daily lives of the participants. The confession of faith takes the form of a proclamation whose illocutionary power expresses ratification and dedication. The enunciation of the creed presents and actively manifests the mystery in the space of its own words. While drama is a representation of actuality, the liturgy constitutes actualization in itself.[50] In the Institution Narrative, the celebrant repeats the words of Jesus Christ at the Last Supper, and, by their very articulation, Christ's words are vivified to their original efficacy.[51]

While an audience remains passively engulfed in darkness, the liturgical congregation is acknowledged and actively participates in the rite by means of dialogic responses to greetings, invitations, blessings, exchanges of the peace, and utterance of the affirmative 'Amen', as well as participating in singing and prayers. Further, a reciprocal dialogue is established between the worshipper and God. First-person pronouns indicate the concrete act of illocution and locate the speaker, while second-person pronouns establish the addressee, opening up a channel of reciprocity, effecting a location of interlocution. God is addressed as 'you' or 'thou' in spite of not being perceptibly present. Liturgical language is designed around this special fact: the invisibility of the divine interlocutor. Throughout the text, second-person pronouns are anaphorically supported and substantiated by terms of invocation such as 'Lord' and 'Father'. When this dialogic structure is interrupted by monologue, this communicative 'collapse' can be seen as a mark of social transformation. The Institution Narrative, a monologic delineation culminating in Christ's words given in direct speech, is not illocutionary so much as dislocationary.

God's deeds are identical with God's speaking: 'And God said, "Let there be light", and there was light' (Gen. 1.3); 'Out of

---

[50] cf. L. Lévy-Bruhl, *Primitives and the Supernatural* (Dutton, New York 1935), pp. 123–4, on representation.

[51] See Ladrière, 'The Performativity of Liturgical Language', p. 61.

his mouth comes a sharp sword' (Rev. 19.15). Gregory of Nyssa argues that creation is 'the true mute language of God, although unlike human language it is completely indivisible from his will'.[52] God's words and their fulfilment are simultaneous: 'The order is itself an operation.'[53] However, the eventful language of God must not be muddled with human speech acts. While both do what they say, they derive their authority to act from wholly incommensurable sources. Where God is, the illocution falls mute. God's voice moves eventfully through the world independent of our ratification. He is atemporal, acontextual,[54] not social but 'natural'.[55] The doctrine of transubstantiation enables us to see Christ's words at the Last Supper as simultaneously analytic and synthetic. The statement, 'This is my body . . .', is on the one hand definitive, and on the other, transformatory. The words dislocate the natural laws connecting substances and their accidents. With these few words, the substance perishes while its accidents (colour, shape, and flavour) survive the annihilation of their former identities. These words transform the inanimate into the animate, the dead into the beatifying. But even saying that these words are simultaneously analytic and synthetic betrays the stuttering of human speech, for in God's terms they are not synthetic at all. For God, these four words merely disclose what the bread always was, atemporally and acontextually. God can construct a state merely by declaring it to exist. God's language, then, is the optimum fiat.

(iii) Repetition

Quotidian repetition is a means by which differences are obscured. It consists of a paratactic proliferation of the given, and is static and uneventful. However, the repetition of occasion, content, and form which occurs in the sacred polis is

[52] Cited in A. J. Milbank, 'Theology without Substance: Christianity, Signs, Origins', *Journal of Literature and Theology* 2 (1988), p. 131.

[53] Basil, *Hexaemeron* I.7.

[54] See J. R. Searle, *Speech Acts: An Essay in the Philosophy of Language* (Cambridge University Press 1969), p. 18, on the divine exception.

[55] cf. Fish, 'How to do Things with Austin and Searle', p. 217, on Coriolanus.

axiomatic to the cohesion of its community,[56] to its assertion of cosmos over chaos, and to its establishment of a sacral temporal order.

Repetition can be located at semantic, syntactic, and phonetic levels of expression; it can take the form of repeated sequences, either within the same rite, or between a series of rites, and recurrent words such as 'Amen'. Roman Jakobson has noted, with reference to Finnish and Russian oral poetry, the pervasive device of parallelism in all idioms of formal speaking, chanting, greeting, farewells, petitions, and blessings.[57] Parallelism in these dialogic, reciprocal tableaux is iconic with the equal exchange between speakers which is required in a greeting or a farewell. As well as the obvious mnemonic advantages of a recursive structure in an oral context,[58] repetition has implications beyond mnemonics.

The recursive structures to be found in liturgical language can be divided into two groups, paratactic and hypotactic. These terms refer to successively juxtaposed independent elements on a linear plane, and elements embedded in a hierarchy of prototypic, figural relations on a vertical plane, respectively.

Paratactic repetition occurs within the text of the sacred polis in its local repetitions of greetings, blessings, and doxologies; and on the larger scale of the diurnal, hebdomadal, and annual cycles. These predictable rhythms have implications for the community in that they convey permanence and unanimity by means of harmonious movement through patterns. The recursive structure is an iconic analogue of the perpetual processes of the cosmos, both in its spatio-temporal regularity and in its cumulative effect. The repetition of a familiar form also deflects questioning, and participants lose sight of the fact that rites are evanescent cultural constructs.

[56] See A. R. Radcliffe-Brown, *The Andaman Islanders* (Free Press Paperback Edition, New York 1964), p. 246.

[57] 'Grammatical Parallelism and its Russian Facet', *Language* 42 (1966), pp. 398–429. Cf. J. J. Fox, 'On Binary Categories and Primary Symbols', in Roy Willis (ed.), *The Interpretation of Symbolism* (John Wiley & Sons, New York 1975), pp. 127–8.

[58] cf. Tambiah, 'A Performative Approach to Ritual', p. 134.

Paratactic repetition counteracts temporal erosion by means of the multiplication of simultaneous present moments. For Constantin Constantius, the category of repetition is necessary in preventing life from dissolving 'into an empty meaningless noise'.[59] He believes that the cosmos continues because it is a repetition, and imagines the chaos of a world in which nothing is ever the same: 'Who could want to be a tablet on which time writes something new every instant or to be a memorial volume of the past? Who could want to be susceptible to every fleeting thing, the novel, which always enervatingly diverts the soul anew? If God himself had not willed repetition, the world would not have come into existence.'[60] It is a quotidian error to suppose that repetition requires identity between things, for 'if everything in the world were absolutely identical there would be no repetition'.[61] Positive repetition, then, emerges from difference, and it constitutes development; each new assertion of an element, over and against the disparate world, has absolute significance in relation to what has gone before.[62]

Repetition of a rite does not mean that its efficacy is of finite duration. With reference to prayer, Constantius notes that 'it was quite right once to sink into God and then remain there, but since man is a finite being, to pray means continual striving'.[63] With the perpetual threat of quotidian chaos clamouring at the gateway of the sacred polis, the cosmos must be continually reasserted. The cosmic creation itself was not a single, aoristic event opposed to repetition. Rather, it was 'an activity which ultimately implies return and repetition rather than simply linear accomplishment'.[64] Commemorative repetition cannot be dissociated from the event to which it refers. There was repetition in the original event of the Last Supper, not simply in the parallelism of Jesus' words, but also in his repetitive call to repeat and to remember. Without that provision for repetition,

[59] Kierkegaard, *Repetition*, p. 149.

[60] ibid., pp. 132–3.

[61] ibid., p. 274.

[62] ibid., p. 307.

[63] ibid., p. 327.

[64] E. W. Said, *Beginnings: Intention and Method* (Basic Books, New York 1975), p. xiii.

the event itself would be incomplete. Further, when Christ's words are repeated by the celebrant, it is not mere citation but rather the resumption into acts of the here-and-now of words uttered in the past.

While in the quotidian arena paratactic repetition signals a decline in meaning, proliferation forming a broad-scale grammaticalization, sacral repetition produces an intensification of meaning, a perpetual lexical reassertion, the cumulative effect of which is the suspension of mundane time. Events are transposed from linear time into a perspective of eternity. Constantius notes that in a recursive structure, 'present and future contend with each other to find an eternal expression'.[65] This kind of repetition is eternity's flowing back to the present. Heedless of the passing events subject to the violence of time, incessant ritual (itself, and within itself) effects the initiation of a supratemporal order. Although each resumption of a repetition works through linear time, the identity of each moment to its predecessor and successor appears to effect the quiescence of time.[66]

Beside the creation of simultaneous present moments, there are two other ways in which repetition can relinquish linear duration, first, by re-presenting the past through remembrance, and secondly, by making the past perfective, that is, meaningful to the present through figural interpretation. These two methods pertain to hypotaxis since they belong to a vertical, atemporal vision of events. In quotidian chaos, each successive moment supersedes its precursor by violent means, and repetition in this realm is amnesiac since it annihilates the past. Remembrance, however, is creative. Ritual repetition, though it acknowledges the passing of time by moving through it, and the anteriority of the event by commemorating it, brings with it reparation, since event and commemoration are one. The event is not reproduced as a memory but as itself, an event. To think of remembrance as the commemoration of a dead person in order to spare him the further humiliating death of oblivion is to misinterpret the anamnesis.

---

[65] Kierkegaard, *Repetition*, p. 137.

[66] See M. Eliade, *The Myth of the Eternal Return* (Pantheon, New York 1954), p. 76.

The event of the Last Supper is less a past fact than a pledge given in the past so as to appeal to a future advent which governs even today. Instead of a regressive dynamic, ritual remembrance constitutes a positive negotiation with the future. Far from being an accomplished actuality, the past, seen figurally, orders through its anteriority a today which, without it, would be meaningless. The memorial makes of the past a decisive reality for the present (1 Cor. 15.17–18), that is, it renders this day tenable. Further, ritual memorial presses always forward towards the Parousia; we do these things in remembrance of Christ, 'until he comes' (11.26). The pledge which the past memorial sets into action now anticipates the future, so that the present occurs as this anticipation concretely lived. The eucharist, then, is both analepsis and prolepsis, the first fragment of the new creation, the *figura nostra*, the figure of what will be, though we cannot yet figure it. The memorial and the epektasis traverse the present from end to end, ceaselessly abandoned and taken up again with each paratactic repetition, perpetually consigning and rescinding it in a hypotactic network of vertical continuity. Hypotactic repetition presupposes a dispossession of the quotidian here-and-now, and a reappraisal of the present on the basis of prefiguration, as a fulfilment of the past and as an eschatological invocation which provokes its accomplishment. Not a single moment stands in isolation; nor can it derive its meaning from itself alone, but is always incomplete and always searching. The past remains, but radically and perfectively thought of in terms of the present. The eucharistic present does not persistently enter the repeated interstices of our diurnal order to reside passively in them, but rather to transpose the horizontal into the vertical, the quantitative into the qualitative, *chronos* into *kairos*. Every event is already fulfilled in God and has existed from all eternity. Figures or events, repeatedly taken up, are tentative forms of something timeless, pointing not only to an eschatological future, but to something which is at all times present.[67]

[67] See E. Auerbach, 'Figura', in idem, *Scenes from the Drama of European Literature* (Manchester University Press 1984), pp. 11–78.

Repetition in the sacred polis seeks to harness the present not by annihilating the past, but rather by vivifying it, and by setting the present in the context of eternity. The cumulative effect of such recursive present moments is to suspend the ravages of mundane time and to establish a vertical plane where each event points simultaneously behind and in front of itself, filling each moment of history with meaning and purpose.

Divine Excess and the Logos
Liturgical language, unlike the quotidian with its verification obsession, gives credence both to the given and the hypothetical. The reading of sacred texts, the recitation of catechisms and creeds, and the superlatively verifiable re-presentation of events are set in the context of unverifiable mystery, since the addressee is neither visible nor palpable, and not fully known. As Pseudo-Dionysius writes, theological tradition 'has a dual aspect, the ineffable and mysterious on the one hand, the manifest and more evident on the other . . . the inexpressible is bound up with what can be articulated'.[68]

Quotidian reliance upon the given would never suffice in the sacred polis, where definition must be abandoned. Any attempt to restrain the hypothetical, either by means of textualization or of definition, silences the Word, since 'love of the letter is but the mask of . . . impiety'.[69] One must instead forget 'what is behind and strain towards what is ahead' (Phil. 3.13b). A gift, and the gift of the Logos above all, does not require that we define it, but rather that we receive it. The haste to explain discloses a nervous refusal of love, a refusal which will in any case be thwarted since he even 'comes lovingly to those who have turned away from him'.[70] The acceptance of hypothesis and metaphor will not precipitate indeterminate chaotic groping, but rather the disclosure of possibilities already realized in the Logos but not yet in our words.

The liturgical text is unlike any other text in that it can pass unimpeded to its referent. Once an event has occurred, there

[68] *Ep.* 9.1.
[69] Gregory of Nazianzus, *Orationes* 31.3.
[70] Pseudo-Dionysius, *Ep.* 8.1.

remain only words. Like the disciples hearing rumours of events, we cannot peel back the biblical text as far as that at which it aims because no hermeneutic could yield anything but an interpretation. As such, our desire for an unmediated apprehension of the epiphanic referent remains unrequited. However, the divine Logos, the unspeakable Word, is the one referent which can transgress the text, and possesses the optimum authority to interpret it for us. To be sure, it is not so much that he explains the text, but explains himself by means of it, or through it. Inexplicably, he is simultaneously referent, locutor, spoken and speaking. This unimpeded passage occurs at the moment when the unspeakable speech of the Logos is uttered, 'This is my body . . .' The Word intervenes in person to accomplish the perfect hermeneutic, to support and sustain his words, and to protect them from the delirium of discontinuity. Christ abolishes in himself the chasm between sign and referent, utterance and text.[71] Each sign is filled to overflowing with its optimum referent, and exceeds incommensurably the limits of its mundane, quotidian usage. Christ does not say the word, but he says himself, the Word. He says himself, and that is all, for nothing else remains to be said outside the Word, since the Word accomplishes all. Further, he has nothing to say in order to say everything, since he incarnates the dictum in saying it.

[71] See J.-L. Marion, *God Without Being* (Chicago University Press 1991), ch. 6.

8

Liturgy and 'Living Literature'

PAUL BRADSHAW

It has often been suggested that liturgical texts are in a class by themselves and cannot easily be compared with other literary forms. Unlike, for example, the classics of English literature, these texts are not simply to be read by individuals but used within the ritual life of a community, and what is more, they are subject to periodic change and revision in a way that is totally foreign to other literary compositions. It is the contention of this essay, however, that claims of this kind about the unique character of liturgical texts may be over-stated, and that on the contrary there are at least some literary works that display a measure of similarity to such texts. To these we may perhaps give the collective name 'living literature'.

This term seems to have been first coined by Stanislas Giet,[1] who used it to describe the ancient church order known as the *Didache*, because it apparently was not the work of a single author but had been subjected to successive stages of alteration and amplification as it passed through different hands.[2] This phenomenon, however, is not unique to the *Didache*, but as I have already suggested elsewhere,[3] the designation may fittingly be extended to include a wide range of ancient (and even some not so ancient) literary material, which though diverse in many other respects, has in common the fact that it circulated within a community, forming a part of its heritage and tradition, but underwent periodic revision and rewriting in response to changing historical and cultural circumstances.

[1] *L'Énigme de la Didachè* (Ophrys, Paris 1970), p. 257.

[2] For a discussion of some theories of its evolution, see F. E. Vokes, 'The Didache still Debated', *Church Quarterly* 3 (1970), pp. 57–62.

[3] *The Search for the Origins of Christian Worship* (SPCK, London; Oxford University Press, New York 1992), p. 74.

Ancient Church Orders

Among the ancient church orders, the *Didache* is not alone in appearing to have been revised and expanded by different hands. On the contrary, this is something which is characteristic of the whole genre. Both the individual documents and the various composite collections of the material were subject to a process of emendation and 'correction' by successive editors, copyists, and translators. Indeed, most of the church orders are not independent compositions at all, but themselves constitute a further stage of the rewriting of an earlier text in the series.[4]

The marks of living literature can especially be seen in the case of the document usually identified as the *Apostolic Tradition* of Hippolytus. While several of the other church orders (the *Apostolic Constitutions*, the *Didascalia*, and the *Testamentum Domini*) bear the clear stamp of the work of a single major redactor, even if they have also been affected by minor 'improvements' by other hands, this text more closely resembles the *Didache* in several respects. It is characterized by the same terse style, abrupt changes of subject-matter, grammatical switches of person (e.g., from the third person to the second person singular), and absence of signs of the controlling influence of a single editorial hand that also mark the *Didache*. According to Marcel Metzger, these traits constitute further reasons for doubting its traditional attribution to Hippolytus.[5] What is more important for our present purposes, however, is that in this and in other ways it shows evidence of having been built up over a considerable period of time into the later forms found in extant manuscripts.

Scriptural and Apocryphal Texts

A similar process of composition can also be seen within much of the canonical and early extra-canonical literature of the

4 For further details, see ibid., pp. 80–110.
5 'Enquêtes autour de la prétendue *Tradition apostolique*', *Ecclesia Orans* 9 (1992), pp. 7–36. See also his article 'A propos des règlements écclesiastiques et de la prétendue *Tradition apostolique*', *Revue des sciences religieuses* 66 (1992), pp. 249–61; and his earlier work, 'Nouvelles perspectives pour la prétendue *Tradition apostolique*', *Ecclesia Orans* 5 (1988), pp. 241–59, and esp. p. 257, where he describes this church order as 'littérature vivante'.

Jewish and Christian traditions. A very obvious example is in the book of Isaiah, where scholars are generally agreed that the original nucleus consisted only of chapters 1–39, with the remainder (chs 40–66) being added by a later hand, or according to many scholars by two later hands. Even within the first part of the work, chapters 36–9 form a prose appendix to the prophetic material, and contain a historical narrative which displays close verbal parallels with 2 Kings 18.13–20.19, though there are some significant differences between the two versions: for instance, 2 Kings 18.14–16 are missing from the Isaiah text, while Hezekiah's psalm occurs only in Isaiah (38.9–20) and not in Kings. Here, then, we have a further example of living literature, with two different recensions of the same material. The books of Chronicles, of course, provide yet a further version of much of the material in the books of Samuel and Kings, once again with some parts of the one not appearing in the other and vice versa.

Living literature, therefore, may be characterized either by quantitative differences (i.e., longer and shorter versions of the same material) or by qualitative differences (i.e., various ways of saying the same thing), or often by a combination of the two. Frequently it will be obvious which of the various recensions is the original text and which are the later revisions, but sometimes there will be no clear indication that a single *Urtext* ever existed behind the various extant versions. Some scholars would take this point of view, for example, with regard to the parallel material found in Matthew and Luke which is not derived from Mark. While these resemblances are commonly attributed to a hypothetical source-document designated as 'Q', it is not at all clear which of the two evangelists has preserved the original reading of this source and which has modified it, or whether both may not have refashioned it, thus making the original inaccessible to us, or indeed whether there really ever was a single written text at all to account for these similar passages in the two gospels.[6]

[6] For some other examples of living literature, see Robert A. Kraft, 'Reassessing the "Recensional Problem" in Testament of Abraham', in George W. E. Nickelsburg (ed.), *Studies on the Testament of Abraham* (Scholars Press, Missoula MT 1976), pp. 121–37.

Comparison of the variant texts of instances of this kind of literature suggests that the motives of the redactors were often to present an alternative interpretation of the earlier material or to bring it up to date in some way. Thus, for example, the various additions made to the Greek version of the book of Esther are designed to give a more religious cast to a story which in the Hebrew version never actually mentions God. The Greek additions rectify this and attribute the deliverance of the people not to Esther's courage and beauty but to God's response to the prayers of Mordecai and Esther. God is shown to be in control of events by the device of Mordecai's dream at the beginning, which predicts what will happen, and its interpretation at the end. Contemporary concerns of Jewish piety are also revealed in the text of Esther's prayer, which asserts that she has never eaten at the table of the pagan king (which would have violated Jewish dietary laws—but cf. Esth. 2.18; 5.5; 7.7).

The inclusion of much of this material in the Jewish and Christian canons of scripture naturally put an end to the process of its revision and amplification.[7] Yet in another sense it can be argued that it did not really cease to be living literature. While the documents themselves may have become frozen, their interpretation did not, and so changes to the texts were now replaced by constantly changing understandings of their meaning, in both Jewish and Christian traditions. This is particularly evident in the case of the Jewish tradition, where early rabbinic midrash on the scriptural texts was gathered into formal collections, which themselves were subject to periodic revisions and updating; the Mishnah, for example, is thought to have gone through perhaps three different stages of evolution, and the Talmud another two. But the same process is no less true of the Christian tradition, where biblical exegesis, commentary, and homily offering ever-changing perspectives on the sacred text have continued to flourish through the centuries.

[7] The approach to biblical study known as canonical criticism, pioneered by Brevard Childs and refined by James Sanders, is of assistance in understanding this further evolution of the literature. See for example James A. Sanders, *From Sacred Story to Sacred Text: Canon as Paradigm* (Fortress Press, Philadelphia 1986).

All this presents some interesting parallels to liturgical texts, which have also been subject to change and revision in the course of time in order to reinterpret earlier traditions or to bring them up to date in some way. In the case of liturgical texts too, it is often possible to trace ancestry by observing quantitative differences — how earlier texts were expanded by later additions — or to discern some relationship between two or more texts displaying qualitative differences from one another, sometimes leading to the hypothesis of a common source and sometimes not. In some instances, as for example the *Book of Common Prayer* of the Church of England after 1662 or the post-Tridentine Roman Catholic rites, liturgical texts also became frozen in time and, as it were, canonized by their religious community, with the result that here too, like the Bible, an unchanging text was subject to changing interpretations.

Liturgical texts not only resemble scriptural texts in the manner of their composition, but also to a considerable extent in the functions which they exercise within a religious tradition. Both alike tell the stories that are constitutive of that tradition; both are the bearers of its values and norms; both are the principal means by which those values and norms are communicated and reinforced within it; and as changes occur within the tradition and its values, so too must the liturgical and scriptural texts undergo modifications in their forms, or at least in their interpretation so as to keep in step with the tradition that they are meant to reflect. All these parallels, therefore, suggest possibilities for a whole range of comparative studies not so far undertaken between scripture and liturgy within Judaism and Christianity.

Folk-tales

We must not assume, however, that the phenomenon of living literature is restricted only to a religious context. On the contrary, the same process can be seen in some types of secular literature, and especially in folk-tales. Widely divergent forms of what is still recognizably the same story can be seen both at different historical periods and also at the same historical period in different geographical regions and cultural settings. As a simple example, we may refer to the well-known legend of Lady

Godiva's ride through the city of Coventry. While this tale may indeed have some historical basis to it, the form of the early versions of the story, dating from the twelfth and thirteenth centuries, already shows the influence of various familiar folk motifs. For example, tales of a dutiful wife who performs some humiliating task at the bidding of her husband in order to benefit the common people turn up in connection with other places in England, including Dunster and Tichborne. Similarly, folk-tales of a clever wife or maid who fulfils apparently impossible conditions, or of a noble heroine miraculously saved from shame, containing some other parallels to the Godiva story, are found in many parts of the world. Later versions of the Godiva legend, from the seventeenth century onwards, add to it the mention of a man who dared to peep at the naked Godiva as she rode through the city. Variously described at first as a groom or a tailor, this character was eventually given the name of Peeping Tom, and once again there are parallels to this motif in other folk-tales from other parts of the world.[8]

The dominant method in the study of folk literature has been what has been called the Finnish historical-geographical school, which attempts by comparative analysis to trace variant forms back to a hypothetical single original tale. The standard means of classification of the material has been the Aarne-Thompson tale-type index, which grouped stories first according to the basic type to which they were perceived to belong (e.g., magic, romantic, religious) and then by the constituent motifs or events which various stories were thought to possess in common with one another (e.g., The Foolish Bridegroom; The Unjust Partner).[9]

However, the approach adopted by scholars of this school has been criticized as inadequate by others on at least two grounds. First, their notion that a single original *Urtext* must lie behind all similar stories has been seriously questioned:

[8] See further Hilda Ellis Davidson, *Patterns of Folklore* (D. S. Brewer, Ipswich; Rowman & Littlefield, Totowa NJ 1978), pp. 80–94.

[9] Antti Arne and Stith Thompson, *The Types of the Folktale: A Classification and Bibliography*, Folklore Fellows Communications no. 184 (Helsinki 1961).

We must remember that a folktale is the sum of its versions; the versions are not partial reflections or evolved examples of an original, ideal text. Also, in their zealous attempt to trace minute connections between geographically or historically related tales, they overanalyze individual versions at the expense of the larger pattern that manifests itself in the tale; their studies are not examinations of how individual folktales are constructed but instead are detailed lists of the traits found in various versions.[10]

Secondly, it has been argued that the constituent units into which they chose to divide stories for the purpose of comparison had a fundamentally subjective character and were not always found in every version of a story. Consequently, the work of Vladimir Propp, *Morphology of the Folktale*, first published in Russian in 1928 and translated into English in 1958, pioneered a new school of structuralist analysis, based not on the variable elements of motifs or *dramatis personae* but on the invariable elements of action or function within the narrative.[11] More recently, Steven Swann Jones has attempted to combine elements from both schools into a synthesized approach which also makes use of the ritual patterns identified by Arnold van Gennep,[12] while others have criticized all formalist studies of folklore for an excessive concentration upon the similarities in archetypal features, repetitive patterns, and generalized meanings shared by tales from various cultures and different historical periods to the neglect of the creativity and uniqueness of individual stories, and have proposed a semiotic approach as a means

[10] Steven Swann Jones, 'The Structure of "Snow White" ', *Fabula* 24 (1983), p. 57, n. 4; reprinted in Ruth B. Bottigheimer (ed.), *Fairy Tales and Society: Illusion, Allusion, and Paradigm* (University of Pennsylvania Press, Philadelphia 1986), p. 182, n. 3.

[11] See for example Alan Dundes, 'From Etic to Emic Units in the Structural Study of Folktales', *Journal of American Folklore* 75 (1962), pp. 95–105; Bertel Nathhorst, *Formal or Structural Studies of Traditional Tales: The Usefulness of Some Methodological Proposals Advanced by Vladimir Propp, Alan Dundes, Claude Lévi-Strauss and Edmund Leach* (Stockholm 1969).

[12] See the article cited in n. 10 above, and Joseph Campbell, *The Hero with a Thousand Faces* (Princeton University Press 1968), where van Gennep's ritual pattern is also applied to folk-tales.

of overcoming this failing.[13] Analyses from other perspectives have also been attempted.[14]

Just as in the case of biblical literature, all this again offers further interesting possibilities for the comparative study of liturgical texts and living literature. In particular, the methodological debate described above should serve as a warning against the dominance of an analytic approach to texts which is based exclusively upon the existence of a putative common source. Although a literary connection often exists between different liturgies, as it does between many folk-tales, that is not always the case, and liturgical scholars are just as capable as folklorists of falsely imagining such a link merely on the basis of tenuous similarities. In any case, whether or not a literary relationship can be traced, other ways of analysing the material have much to contribute to our understanding of it, and the comparable experiences of those engaged in folklore research may thus serve to give encouragement to the as yet fledgling attempts to analyse liturgical texts by other methods.[15] Furthermore, because folk literature, like some biblical material, has its ultimate roots in oral and not written communication, the discernment of which elements tend to be constant and which instead incline to variation in that tradition[16] may be of assistance in understanding in what ways liturgical forms also preserved or modified their primitive character during their period of oral transmission.

Yet liturgical texts and folk literature have more in common than merely parallel methods for their study. Both alike are the carriers of the norms and values of a culture or society. It is true that the norms and values reflected in many folk-tales are often somewhat different from those in religious literature. Indeed, in their early, unexpurgated forms even what we call fairy-tales

[13] See for example Anna Tavis, 'Fairy Tales from a Semiotic Perspective', in Bottigheimer (ed.), *Fairy Tales and Society*, pp. 195–202.

[14] See further the other essays in Bottigheimer (ed.), *Fairy Tales and Society*.

[15] See for example Lawrence Hoffman, *Beyond the Text: A Holistic Approach to Liturgy* (Indiana University Press, Indianapolis 1987).

[16] See for example Propp's *Morphology of the Folktale*, and Albert B. Lord, *The Singer of Tales* (Harvard University Press, Cambridge 1960).

(which were manifestly not originally intended for children) often contain strongly erotic—not to say pornographic—elements and deal with such subjects as cannibalism, incest, rape, and sodomy. For instance, in an early French version of 'Sleeping Beauty' the prince, who is already married, ravishes the princess, who bears him several children without waking up, and the prince's mother-in-law later attempts to eat the illicit offspring.[17] But this earthiness of the genre should not blind us to certain similarities to liturgical texts.

For example, fairy-tales often function as a paradigm whereby the listeners or readers can be helped both to understand their society and to determine and develop appropriate behavioural patterns and personality within it. They thereby exercise a conditioning or formational function not unlike that of a liturgical text. Not surprisingly, a number of scholars have also suggested that the telling of these tales fulfils an important psychological function, helping individuals to come to terms with powerful inner emotional forces and conflicts (although unfortunately their analyses have all too often lacked a critical historical perspective).[18] Here, too, we may discern a parallel with the role of liturgical texts that might warrant further investigation. Moreover, many such tales suggest that events may develop in a way that diverges sharply from the common daily experience of the listener or reader, and so present an alternative, more optimistic vision of life in which, for instance, good always triumphs over evil and the poor are raised up to sit among princes. In this way they may be compared with the eschatological dimension inherent in both scriptural and liturgical texts.

Like liturgies, folk-tales may also be put to the service of less laudable ends. When fairy-tales were expurgated, romanticized, and for the first time directed primary at an audience of children

[17] For this and other examples, see Robert Darnton, 'Peasants Tell Tales: The Meaning of Mother Goose', in *The Great Cat Massacre and Other Episodes in French Cultural History* (Basic Books, New York 1984), pp. 14–15.

[18] Among the more influential scholars in this field have been Erich Fromm, *The Forgotten Language: An Introduction to the Understanding of Dreams, Fairy-Tales, and Myths* (Rinehart, New York 1951), and Bruno Bettelheim, *The Uses of Enchantment* (Knopf, New York 1976). But cf. the critical comments of Darnton, *The Great Cat Massacre*, pp. 10–13.

in nineteenth-century Germany, it was not for the sake of mere amusement but in the service of pedagogical utility and a political ideology, as part of the 'recovery' of a German culture which would foster the myth of German primordiality and assist in forging the national unity of the German people. But in fact what was passed on was not identical to the value system that had been expressed in the traditional forms of the tales.

These earlier stories, as we have indicated above, frequently articulated a vision of a changed society in which oppressed people overcame the power of rich and exploitative rulers, and hence they could embody an element of political protest. But the later versions instead teach preponderantly nineteenth-century bourgeois social virtues—diligence, moderation, cleanliness, obedience, contentment with one's lot, and gratitude. In this process of transformation the Brothers Grimm played a not inconsiderable part. Most people assume that their *Kinder- und Hausmärchen* were faithful reproductions of traditional German stories, and indeed in the preface to the first edition of the first volume the brothers insisted that this was the case: 'No particular has been either added through our own poetic recreation, or improved or altered.' But scholarly research has demonstrated otherwise.[19] Similarly, the living, and hence changeable, character of liturgical texts may also be used to forge a sense of national identity and/or to embody values advantageous to the shapers of a particular culture rather than those of the Christian gospel. The choice of lectionary texts, for example, provides a case in point.[20]

On the other hand, the process can also work in the opposite direction. Folk-tales may be revised so as to incorporate elements and motifs that challenge the *status quo* and encourage a more revolutionary spirit. For example, traditional fairy-tales inevitably tend to carry social norms and values belonging principally to a patriarchal society and a feudal age. When, therefore, the point was reached that the paradigms which they

[19] See the detailed study by John M. Ellis, *One Fairy Story Too Many* (University of Chicago Press 1983).

[20] See Bryan D. Spinks, 'Christian Worship or Cultural Incantations?', *Studia Liturgica* 12 (1977), pp. 1–19.

offered no longer corresponded sufficiently with the expectations of certain groups, radical reinterpretations or rewritings inevitably began to appear. Clear signs of this can be seen in Germany in the 1970s, as well as in feminist circles throughout the Western world. As well as challenging the gender-stereotyping found in many current forms of fairy-tales, feminists have responded by composing original stories with more aggressive heroines, by reworking old tales in new ways, and also by publishing lesser-known traditional stories which do redress the balance by giving women a more active role.[21] This presents an interesting point of comparison with the process of the revision of liturgical texts which began to be undertaken in Christian and Jewish circles at about the same period. That process, too, involved the composition of new liturgical formulae, the reworking of older ones, and the recovery of ancient texts that had fallen out of use.

The Performing Arts
The tendencies which we have observed so far become even more marked in the case of written texts that were intended not simply to be read by individuals but to be publicly performed in some way. Here, even the known existence of an original author does not guarantee that there is only one authentic, normative version of a composition. It is interesting, for example, that William Shakespeare's plays do not exist in one single definitive form. In particular, the earliest printed versions of several of them, including *Hamlet* and *Romeo and Juliet*, differ markedly from the later printed texts of those same plays in such things as overall length, the arrangement of scenes, the names and speech mannerisms of characters, literary style and diction, stage properties, and movements. The editors of the 1623 folio edition of the plays maintained that all previously printed texts were 'stolne, and surreptitious copies, maimed, and deformed by the frauds and stealthes of injurious imposters, that expos'd them', and this claim has been widely accepted by modern textual critics. As Steven Urkowitz has said,

[21] See Kay F. Stone, 'Feminist Approaches to the Interpretation of Fairy Tales', in Bottigheimer (ed.), *Fairy Tales and Society*, pp. 229–36.

their usually unstated hypothesis is that Shakespeare composed only a single full-length version of each play, that he took no important part in theatrical revision or adaptation of his own scripts, and that the providers of the 'stolne, and surreptitious copies' were ignorant, incompetent, and insensitive to the drama and poetry of Shakespeare's 'perfect' originals.[22]

Here we have an interesting parallel to the *Urtext* theory of the composition of folk-tales or early liturgical texts.

Urkowitz and others, however, have challenged this consensus, and sought to revive an older view that the different versions of the text of the plays reflect successive revisions by the author together with his acting company.[23] In other words, playwriting in the Elizabethan age was not so much the once-for-all creation of a masterpiece by the author which was then presented in its pristine perfection on the stage, but something much more akin to the process which Shakespeare himself comically portrays in 'Pyramus and Thisbe', the play-within-a-play of *A Midsummer Night's Dream*. Here, as the cast engage in rehearsal for its production (Act 3, Scene 1), substantial changes and rewritings are necessary in order to deal both with problems raised both by the staging of the play (moonshine and a wall) and by the supposed sensibilities of the female members of the audience towards the portrayal of acts of violence on stage.

In any case, whatever the truth in this particular debate, what is indisputable is that in the seventeenth and eighteenth centuries the texts of Shakespeare's plays were frequently modified and adapted with great freedom by other people. Thus, to cite just two examples from many, Nahum Tate, the famous translator of the Psalter, wrote an 'improved' *History of King Lear* in 1680 which was so successful that it kept Shakespeare's original version off the stage for more than 150 years;[24] and

[22] 'Good News about "Bad" Quartos', in Maurice Charney (ed.), *'Bad' Shakespeare: Revaluations of the Shakespeare Canon* (Associated University Presses, London/Toronto 1988), p. 190.

[23] See for example the essays by Ernest A. J. Honigmann and Michael J. Warren in Jerome J. McGann (ed.), *Textual Criticism and Literary Interpretation* (University of Chicago Press 1985), pp. 1–54.

[24] See Nancy Klein Maguire, 'Nahum Tate's *King Lear*: "the king's blest restoration" ', in Jean I. Marsden (ed.), *The Appropriation of Shakespeare: Post-Renaissance Reconstructions of the Works and the Myth* (St Martin's Press, New York 1991), pp. 29–42.

John Sheffield, Earl of Mulgrave and Duke of Buckingham, completely rewrote *Julius Caesar* in the early 1700s as two plays, *The Tragedy of Julius Caesar, altered,* which revises Shakespeare's first three acts, and *The Tragedy of Marcus Brutus,* which was based on acts 4 and 5.[25]

The motives behind many such adaptations of the Bard's tragedies and histories were strongly political. Versions in the early Restoration period, for instance, celebrated the newly restored monarchy by displaying a vigorous Royalist tone; and versions after 1678 were responses to the crisis caused by attempts to exclude the Roman Catholic James II from succeeding to the English throne. But other factors were at work, too. For example, with the reopening of the London theatres in 1660 women rather than boys began to play the female parts in plays, and Shakespeare's plots were reworked to take advantage of the new dramatic possibilities that this offered. These adaptations included both an increase in the number of roles in which female characters dressed as men, so that the clearer view of the women's legs might provide titillation for the audience, and also the addition of

> scenes featuring helpless female virtue, ennobled by love and fraught by fear. With the possible exception of Desdemona and Ophelia, both of whom appeared virtually unaltered on the Restoration stage, Shakespeare's women are rarely meek and seldom passive. . . . the same is not true of female characters in the adaptations. Instead, the plays recreate a patriarchal system in which women have no power beyond the masochistic ability to arouse sympathy by their suffering, an ability mirrored in the audience response to pathos. This suffering is rarely caused by the heroine's own wrong-doing; it results instead from her selfless love or from her passive attempts to defend her virtue against malefactors.[26]

In the nineteenth century, however, there emerged the phenomenon of bardolatry which prevented too much liberty being taken with the text of the plays thereafter—another example of the effect of canonization upon living literature. Nevertheless, theatrical productions still regularly modified the

[25] Michael Dobson, 'Accents Yet Unknown: Canonisation and the Claiming of *Julius Caesar*', in ibid., pp. 11–28.

[26] Jean I. Marsden, 'Rewritten Women: Shakespearean Heroines in the Restoration', in ibid., pp. 43–56; quotation from pp. 45–6.

playwright's original version in numerous ways, often introducing substantial cuts, sometimes amounting to hundreds of lines, and this practice continues down to the present day.[27] Thus the text as performed can differ markedly from the text as written —a further parallel with liturgy, where the same is frequently true.

To this we may add the effect of the transfer of the performance from stage to film or television. Not only are new dramatic and interpretative possibilities opened up by this change of medium, but new expectations and requirements are also imposed upon a play by the conventions proper to that medium, so that the televising of a play exactly as performed in live theatre is rarely found to be as satisfactory as an adaptation specially made for the small screen (e.g., while theatre audiences are content for characters in a stage-play to describe action supposedly going on off-stage, film and television viewers need to see it happening). This transfer, then, brings about alterations in both the stage directions and speeches of the written text, and has its parallel in the celebration of liturgies in settings and buildings for which they were not originally intended, where changes of a similar kind can also be observed.

When a novel or short story is dramatized for the theatre, cinema, or television, what happens is not just a change of form but also of meaning, and this adds yet a further twist to some living literature. Walt Disney's portrayals of fairy-tales in animated films, for example, differ as much from the versions by the Brothers Grimm as those published texts did from the earlier forms of the tales. So too, efforts by Cecil B. de Mille and others to capture biblical epics in cinematic form add yet another layer of text and interpretation to this living literature. Nor should we forget that the scores of musical compositions, operas, and ballets also belong to the category of living literature, as they also are interpreted by succeeding generations of arrangers, conductors, choreographers, and performers.

All such changes constitute a part of the same continuing process of reinterpretation to which the works of Shakespeare

[27] See, for just one example, Ann Thompson, 'Cymbeline's Other Endings', in ibid., pp. 203–20.

and other classic playwrights are subjected, sometimes out of a concern to make the text more intelligible, relevant, and meaningful to a contemporary audience, sometimes out of a yearning to uncover meanings and nuances supposedly buried deep within it, and sometimes out of a desire to go back and recover what is thought to be the original meaning lost through successive layers of interpretation. Here, too, we may see comparable motives at work in much liturgical revision and renewal.

Conclusion

Although liturgical texts may have some unique features, they are not entirely *sui generis*. The category of living literature joins them to a variety of other texts with which they share a number of features, and consequently opens up many possibilities for comparative and interdisciplinary studies. Thus, methods already adopted in the analysis of other literary forms belonging to this genre may also be employed to enrich our understanding of liturgical texts; the discernment of the motives responsible for the evolving character of other examples of the literature should encourage a search for similar influences at work behind liturgical changes; the functions which other forms of living literature are seen as exercising within a culture offer a basis for examining the role of liturgical rites within the life of a community; and so on.

As well as pointing to new avenues of research in liturgical studies, the concept of living literature also suggests that the idea either of an unchanging liturgy, as advocated by conservative groups in many Christian denominations, or of a normative liturgy, as presupposed by many involved in the ordering of liturgical life in different ecclesiastical traditions, is not in accord with what has actually been the case in other value-bearing literary forms. While supposedly embodying the constitutive heritage and principles of a culture or tradition, these texts have nevertheless been subjected to periodic reformation in accordance with the changing times, and have appeared in quite different guises in different contexts.

As we have seen, even where attempts have been made to canonize such literature in one way or another and so make its text normative and unchangeable for all time, that did not put an end to the process. Its reinterpretation has continued unchecked, and the more so where the text in question formed the basis of some kind of public performance, whether that might be as the scriptural foundation of the preacher's exposition or as the script of a dramatic production. It is therefore ironic that those seeking to preserve the heritage of the 1662 *Book of Common Prayer* in England have often likened it to the Bible and to Shakespeare. For they turn out to be right—but in ways that they never imagined.

9

Liturgy and Society: Cultural Influences on Contemporary Liturgical Revision

RUTH MEYERS

The latter half of the twentieth century has been a time of widespread liturgical revision. New liturgical books have appeared in many different worshipping traditions, and in several of these traditions there were successive revisions issued over the course of two or three decades. For example, several American Lutheran bodies collaborated in issuing the *Service Book and Hymnal* in 1958, and then the Inter-Lutheran Commission on Worship, formed in 1966, produced the *Lutheran Book of Worship* (1978). The first *Book of Worship* in the American Methodist Church, published in 1945, was replaced by the 1965 *Book of Worship* and 1966 *Hymnal*. Further work resulted in *We Gather Together* (1980), *The Book of Services* (1985), and finally *The United Methodist Hymnal* (1989). A similar process of revision in England led to *The Methodist Service Book* (1975) and *Hymns and Psalms* (1983). A number of books have been published by churches with roots in the Reformed tradition: in the Presbyterian churches in the United States, *Service for the Lord's Day* (1964), *The Book of Common Worship: Provisional Services* (1966), *The Worshipbook: Services* (1970), and *The Worshipbook: Services and Hymns* (1972); *The Book of Common Order* (1979) of the Church of Scotland; *A Book of Services*, issued in 1980 by the United Reformed Church in England. New books in the Anglican Communion include *The Book of Common Prayer* (1979) and *The Hymnal 1982* of the Episcopal Church in the United States, *The Alternative Service Book 1980* of the Church of England, and *The Book of Alternative Services* (1985) of the Anglican Church of Canada. In the Roman Catholic Church, the reforms of the Second Vatican Council, especially *Sacrosanctum Concilium*, the Constitution on the Sacred Liturgy (1963), prepared the way for significant revisions of liturgical texts.

It is not only liturgical texts that have undergone substantial revision. Virtually every aspect of the liturgy, including ritual action, congregational participation, hymnody, architecture, and the use of visual arts, was subject to extensive experimentation. Although some of the more extreme forms of liturgical expression were abandoned, many of the changes endured and have been generally accepted as elements of contemporary worship.[1]

A number of factors can be said to have contributed to this widespread liturgical experimentation and revision. The twentieth-century Liturgical Movement, with its emphasis on liturgy as the work of the whole body of Christ, provided an impetus for liturgical change in many churches. Liturgical scholarship of the nineteenth and twentieth centuries yielded insights from newly discovered ancient texts and provided new theological understandings. Gregory Dix's *The Shape of the Liturgy* established the pattern for many eucharistic rites developed since its publication in 1945.[2] The Ecumenical Movement fostered exchange of the riches of diverse traditions and prompted efforts to achieve common understandings and to develop common texts. In this ecumenical climate, many Roman Catholic reforms initiated by Vatican II have been adopted in Protestant traditions.[3]

But the causes for this liturgical reform cannot be located solely within the churches. Churches exist in the wider framework of culture and society, and their worship is always situated in a particular historical context. Hence when revision occurs in a number of different worshipping traditions during the same period of time, it is likely that socio-cultural factors have been a crucial stimulus for change. German Martinez points out that the interplay between 'religious-theological ideas and socio-cultural phenomena' has been the basis for the evolution of worship throughout Christian history: 'The style of worship and its understanding by people has been in fact structured at every stage by that complex system of interdependent theological and

[1] See James F. White, *Protestant Worship: Traditions in Transition* (Westminster/John Knox Press, Louisville 1989), pp. 55–57, 77–8, 114–16, 167–70.

[2] See Kenneth W. Stevenson, *Gregory Dix — Twenty-Five Years On*, Grove Liturgical Study 10 (Grove Books, Nottingham 1977), p. 24.

[3] See White, *Protestant Worship*, pp. 34–5.

cultural ideas that permeate and are permeated by the predominant Christian vision of the day.' Martinez suggests that there have been several shifts in ritual paradigms as Christians have reinterpreted their faith and their symbol systems in the context of the evolving cultural framework. However, he attributes the most recent paradigm shift primarily to the Second Vatican Council and mentions only in passing the impact of modern culture upon the Council and the ensuing reforms.[4] This seems inadequate to explain the liturgical change which occurred simultaneously in so many different Christian traditions.

To consider the causes of this pervasive liturgical experimentation and revision, this essay explores societal and cultural shifts during the twentieth century. That liturgical change occurred in churches in many countries suggests that global factors affected this ritual paradigm shift. Nevertheless, since worship is always located in and affected by particular historical and cultural contexts, it is likely that the impact of these global influences varied somewhat in different parts of the world. Hence this study focuses on socio-cultural factors affecting liturgical revision in the United States.

Societal and Cultural Change during the Twentieth Century

It is apparent to even a casual observer that the twentieth century has been a time of monumental change and global crises. Two world wars and an intervening economic depression were followed by the dawn of the nuclear age and the threat of global annihilation. Scientific and technological change has proceeded at an ever-increasing pace, as Arthur M. Schlesinger, Jr, points out:

> A boy who saw the Wright brothers fly for a few seconds at Kitty Hawk in 1903 could have watched Apollo 11 land on the moon in 1969. The first rockets were launched in the 1920s; today astronauts roam outer space. The first electronic computer was built in 1946; today the world rushes from the

---

[4] 'Cult and Culture: The Structure of the Evolution of Worship', *Worship* 64 (1990), pp. 406–33; quotation on p. 408.

mechanical into the electronic age. The double helix was first unveiled in 1953; today, biotechnology threatens to remake [humankind].[5]

The twentieth century has seen the rise of mass communications, the development of ever more rapid transportation, and the growth of an entertainment industry as movies, radio, and television have come to the fore. All of these changes have affected the way we live and the way we perceive ourselves and our world. Our horizons have been expanded, and at the same time the world has 'shrunk' as the nightly news brings worldwide events into our living rooms and modern transportation permits global travel with an ease never before known.

The United States has been affected by these global changes and has experienced its own crises which have dramatically altered the shape of society. The demand for labour in the defence industry during World War II increased the participation of women in the work-force and encouraged the migration of blacks from the rural South to urban industrial centres in the North, Midwest, and West. The decade following World War II was a time of relative prosperity and expansion of cities and suburbs, although even this post-war period of recovery was disturbed by the emerging Cold War and the Korean War, by the anti-Communism led by Joseph McCarthy, and by racial tensions, evident in the 1954 Supreme Court decision striking down separate but equal schools, the forced integration of schools in Little Rock, Arkansas, and the Montgomery, Alabama, bus boycott. Yet this upheaval was mild in comparison to the 1960s. One study catalogued the changes of this decade:

> the election of the first Roman Catholic as President of the United States and his tragic death in 1963; the continuation and escalation of the cold war, including both the Berlin Wall and the Bay of Pigs; rapid technological advances . . . ; the full flowering of the civil rights movement—sit-ins, freedom rides, white citizens' councils, bombings, racial murders, the March on Washington, and the passage of the 1964 Civil Rights Act; the urban riots of the late 1960s and the assassinations of Martin Luther King, Jr., Malcolm X, and Robert Kennedy; antiwar protests over Viet Nam; the rise of student protests against both the military-industrial complex and the

[5] *The New York Times Magazine*, 25 July 1986, p. 20, cited by John Booty, *The Episcopal Church in Crisis* (Cowley Publications, Cambridge MA 1988), pp. 12–13.

universities; the beginnings of the women's liberation movement; and, finally, the rise of the counterculture, including the search for alternative life styles, drug use, communes, and a variety of new religious movements.[6]

In short, the 1960s were a time of massive social and cultural disturbance.

Church life in the United States followed a pattern similar to the broader socio-cultural changes. The 1950s were a time of renewed vigour for churches, with rapid growth in church membership and a rise in the construction of new church buildings. The cataclysmic events of the 1960s were accompanied by widespread questioning of institutional church structures, of essential theological principles, and of traditional understandings of morality. Church membership and attendance and the importance people attached to traditional religion declined markedly, but there was also increasing church involvement in social justice issues, including civil rights and anti-war protests. The massive upheaval of the 1960s yielded to disillusionment and despair in the early 1970s. Energetic social activism was replaced by concern for personal fulfilment. Participation in mainstream Protestant and Roman Catholic churches continued to decline, although George Gallup found that levels of religious belief continued to be extremely high. By the end of the 1970s the decline appeared to have halted, and the 1980s were a time of relative stability.[7] But the relationship of church and culture had undergone a fundamental change, often described as a shift to a post-Christian era.

A 1968 sociological study of American religious commitment led its authors to draw this conclusion:

> the religious beliefs which have been the bedrocks of Christian faith for nearly two millennia are on their way out; this may very well be the dawn of a post-Christian era. . . . The new reformation in religious thought reflects

[6] Jackson W. Carroll, 'Continuity and Change: The Shape of Religious Life in the United States, 1950 to the Present', in Jackson W. Carroll, Douglas W. Johnson, and Martin E. Marty, *Religion in America: 1950 to the Present* (Harper & Row, San Francisco 1979), p. 6.

[7] ibid., pp. 6–37; Sydney E. Ahlstrom, *A Religious History of the American People* (Yale University Press, New Haven 1972), pp. 1079–96; George Gallup and Jim Castelli, *The People's Religion: American Faith in the 90's* (Macmillan, New York 1989), pp. 8–17.

the fact that a demythologized modernism is overwhelming the traditional, Christ-centered, mystical faith.

The authors of this study pointed out that challenges to traditional Christian tenets had been discussed by theologians at least since the time of Kierkegaard, but in the 1960s this criticism of traditional Christian beliefs was being popularized by theologians, for example, Bishop J. A. T. Robinson in *Honest to God* and Harvey Cox in *The Secular City*.[8]

To understand the changes in religion in the United States since World War II, Robert Wuthnow has turned to theories of religious evolution, which emphasize a qualitative shift in the character of religion rather than a simple linear decline in religious institutions.[9] As society becomes increasingly complex and differentiated, so too religions become more and more complex and differentiated, and thus adapt to the changing social and cultural milieu. Modern religion is characterized by heightened self-awareness with respect to symbolism. For example, many contemporary theologians emphasize the symbolically constructed character of reality, and at the popular level growing numbers of believers stress personal interpretation rather than strict adherence to official creeds and theological tenets.

While theories of religious evolution are borne out by sociological studies, Wuthnow cautions that the theories are highly abstract and tend to imply that religious evolution results from its own internal dynamics. Hence they do not offer insight as to how specific social conditions relate to particular forms of religious differentiation. Wuthnow suggests that a number of factors play a role in facilitating the emergence of new ideas. Environmental factors include the size, access to material resources, and social location of a potential audience for change; the availability of a medium by which new ideas can be communicated to this audience; and the symbolic or mental capa-

[8] Rodney Stark and Charles Y. Glock, *American Piety: The Nature of Religious Commitment* (University of California Press, Berkeley/Los Angeles 1968), pp. 204–10; quotation from p. 205.

[9] *The Restructuring of American Religion: Society and Faith Since World War II* (Princeton University Press 1988), pp. 297–307; *Rediscovering the Sacred: Perspectives on Religion in Contemporary Society* (Eerdmans, Grand Rapids 1992), pp. 83–105.

cities with which the audience can process the new ideas. The institutional context for change refers to the availability of material and cultural resources and the particular organizational constraints as well as relationships between institutions. Action sequences suggest that ideas are produced in response to specific crises or triggering events and that particular persons or groups work to bring about specific changes.[10]

Wuthnow does not address in depth the question of liturgical change, but his identification of sets of variables offers some guidance in exploring factors influencing contemporary liturgical experimentation and revision. His analysis suggests that religious change results from complex and interrelated factors, and thus multiple factors affected the pervasive liturgical change of recent decades.

Worship in a Secular Age

The changing relationship between church and culture during the 1960s was described not only as a shift to a post-Christian era but also as 'secularization', a term that was widely used but often not explicitly defined. In a secular world, the supernatural or transcendent was viewed with scepticism, and hence traditional beliefs and practices seemed irrelevant to the contemporary world where science and technology were accorded more and more importance. A secular world-view had been emerging since the Enlightenment or even since the Renaissance, but it came to full flower in the years after World War II owing to socio-cultural changes during the post-war years. International competition and accelerating achievements in science and technology led to greater emphasis on education in these areas, and the federal government played an important role in providing financial resources for higher education. Mass communication permitted widespread dissemination of theological challenges to traditional Christian beliefs, including talk of the 'death of God'.[11]

---

[10] Wuthnow, *Rediscovering the Sacred*, pp. 105–8, 122–6.

[11] See Joseph L. Allen, 'Continuity and Change: The Church and the Contemporary Social Revolution', *Interpretation* 22 (1968), pp. 464–9; Booty, *The Episcopal Church in Crisis*, pp. 18–19; Leigh Jordahl, 'Secularity: The Crisis of Belief and the Reality of Christian Worship', *Dialog* 9 (1970), pp. 16–18; Wuthnow, *The Restructuring of American Religion*, pp. 314–17.

The impact of secularization on worship was interpreted in different ways. At the 1968 Assembly of the World Council of Churches, the Section on Worship considered a document entitled 'The Worship of God in a Secular Age'. Objections to the emphasis on secularization came from the Orthodox Theological Society of America, who disputed the assumption that '*only* a world-centred and world-orientated Christianity is possible and permissible for Christians today'. The Orthodox theologians asserted their tradition that worship is a retreat from the world, the Church being in but not of the world. Members of other traditions also objected to secularizing theology. Some Anglicans called for more emphasis on the transcendental dimensions of worship, and some Lutherans requested greater stress on preaching as a proclamation of God's forgiveness of sin which corrupts life in secular societies. The debate between these conservatives and secularizing radicals eventually led to agreement upon a report simply entitled 'Worship'.[12]

In a chapter headed 'The Challenge of Secularization', the report on worship acknowledged both negative and positive possibilities inherent in secularization. In a negative sense, secularization implied a closed world-view, limiting reality to that which can be seen, touched, and controlled. In a positive sense, secularization affirmed the reality of the world and the possibilities and limitations of the world given by God in creation and disclosed by Jesus Christ. Secular theology welcomed relativity in thought patterns and thus maintained an open view of the future. This positive view of secular theology, also expressed by other theologians during the 1960s, saw secularization as an appropriate challenge to a view of religion as separate from the world and as an opportunity to reclaim an incarnational theology. Accordingly, worship must acquire new meaning in relation to the contemporary world.[13]

[12] David Edwards, 'Personal Comment on the Work of the Section on Worship', in Norman Goodall (ed.), *The Uppsala Report 1968: Official Report of the Fourth Assembly of the World Council of Churches, Uppsala, July 4–20, 1968* (World Council of Churches, Geneva 1968), pp. 83–5 (emphasis in original).

[13] 'Worship: The Report as Adopted by the Assembly', in *The Uppsala Report 1968*, pp. 79–80; Fred M. Hudson, 'Worship in a Secular Age', *Foundations* 7 (1964), pp. 316–34; Jordahl, 'Secularity', pp. 22–5; Herman Schmidt, 'Liturgy and Modern Society—Analysis of the Current Situation', in Herman Schmidt (ed.), *Liturgy in Transition = Concilium* 62 (1971), pp. 14–29; Massey

Although secularization was a primary concern of theological discourse during the 1960s, Martin Marty observed that the very opposite of the secular was also present in the contemporary culture: a new religiosity, evident in the growing popularity of such phenomena as astrology, mysticism, the occult, yoga, and zen. Marty commented, 'Their coexistence [i.e., secular and religious perspectives] points to the protean and evanescent aspects of a culture which is uncertain about authority and direction.' In this culture, both the significance of tradition and the reality of the supernatural receded into the background, while immanence and the immediacy of the spiritual experience were stressed. What had become important was the 'here and now'.[14]

As Marty's remarks suggest, much liturgical experimentation in the 1960s reflected the demand for 'relevance'. Social and cultural upheaval was accompanied by a rejection of much of the tradition, or at least radical questioning of its significance for contemporary people. Liturgical experimentation was rampant in some places, and almost nothing was too extreme to be attempted. Urban Holmes recalled that a eucharist giving thanks for the life and witness of James DeKoven included a procession to DeKoven's grave with each worshipper carrying a helium-filled balloon.[15] Robert Bellah described a eucharist at a university chapel:

> in a number of respects—the use of music with sexual and aggressive over-tones, the coffeehouse atmosphere, the movies, the political activism of the San Francisco Mime Troupe—what was being included was not merely the religiously neutral but the consciously profane. . . .
>
> The basic structure and much of the language of the service was provided by the Episcopal Liturgy of the Lord's Supper with its thoroughly traditional symbolism. However, the continuous switching between the

---

H. Shepherd, 'The Dimension of Liturgical Change', *Anglican Theological Review* 51 (1969), pp. 241–56.

[14] 'The Context of Liturgy: Here and Now, There and Then', *Worship* 43 (1969), pp. 465–71; quotation from p. 468.

[15] 'Education for Liturgy: An Unfinished Symphony in Four Movements', in Malcolm C. Burson (ed.), *Worship Points the Way: A Celebration of the Life and Work of Massey Hamilton Shepherd, Jr* (Seabury Press, New York 1981), p. 132.

words of the prayer book and such things as 'The Fool on the Hill' or 'Hey Jude' was itself a central device of the service. . . . The sermon was conspicuously absent and the Mime Troupe performance in no way took its place. . . . The atmosphere of spontaneous disorganization was so complete as to be almost contrived.[16]

Leigh Jordahl criticized the trend in contemporary worship whereby 'the liturgical assembly becomes a kind of group dynamics or sensitivity training session, but in a religious context'. According to Jordahl, advocates of such worship called for small and intimate worshipping communities gathered in a relaxed atmosphere for liturgy which emphasized interpersonal dynamics: the confession of sin might acknowledge failure to be open with one another; the sermon was eschewed in favour of sharing of thoughts; prayer was another opportunity to name personal needs, frustrations, and hopes; and the group experience culminated in the sharing of the communion meal.[17]

There is no doubt that some of the liturgical experimentation of the 1960s was extreme and appropriately did not endure. Urban Holmes reported a comment made to him by the Bishop of Milwaukee as they walked in procession at the liturgy commemorating James DeKoven: 'Terry, don't you *ever* tell anyone what we're doing.'[18] James White notes that many of the liturgies written during the late 1960s and early 1970s were verbose and are 'now almost immediately recognizable as dated'.[19]

While more sentimental and introspective forms of worship are no longer as prevalent, other innovations have been more widely accepted. The visual dimensions of worship were enhanced: liturgical colours were more widely used, and banners adorned church buildings. Banners are no longer as prominent, but a new emphasis on visual aspects of worship is evident, for example, in a comparison of colours and objects in Methodist church-supply catalogues of the 1980s with those of the 1950s. Contemporary folk and pop music was sung, accompanied by guitars rather than the organ. This music has not replaced tradi-

[16] *Beyond Belief: Essays on Religion in a Post-Traditional World* (Harper & Row, New York 1970), pp. 212–13.

[17] 'Secularity', pp. 21–2.

[18] 'Education for Liturgy', p. 132.

[19] *Protestant Worship*, p. 78.

tional hymnody and organ music, but many hymnals produced after the 1960s include a much greater diversity of music. Greater attention was given to movement and action. The passing of the peace has been accepted in many congregations. In some parishes charismatic renewal has introduced other forms of active participation, such as singing with raised hands. Liturgical dance was introduced as another form of experimental worship, and although it has not become commonplace, dance is still included in worship at least occasionally in some places.[20]

Jonathan Lindsey attributed these innovations of the 1960s to a developing awareness of a 'festival spirit' in worship, the goal of which was to provide worshippers with a new cognizance of their participation and involvement in worship.[21] Massey Shepherd also pointed out that experimental worship emphasized corporate participation and 'joy and fellowship in hope and witness'.[22]

One explanation for this new emphasis on active participation and greater sensory involvement can be found in the work of Marshall McLuhan, who postulated a major cultural shift as the result of the twentieth-century development of mass media. According to McLuhan, the culture arising from the Gutenberg era of movable type was a 'hot' culture, one based upon the written and spoken word and hence linear and logical. A hot medium is filled with information and thus requires low participation by the audience. The advent of electronic media was transforming the culture into a 'cool' one, in which media provided a low level of information and necessitated much greater participation by the audience. Viewing liturgy as a medium of communication, Thomas O'Meara characterized post-Reformation liturgy as 'hot' liturgy:

> It contains a great deal of content, of information; it is low on personal involvement; it repeats itself over and over; it keeps the same structure, filling it out with different blocks of detailed information about God and saints; it dictates our responses. . . . The liturgy is a disciplined and orderly

[20] See White, *Protestant Worship*, pp. 56–7, 78, 114–15, 168–70.
[21] *Change and Challenge* (McGrath Publishing Company, Wilmington NC 1977), pp. 48–51.
[22] 'The Dimension of Liturgical Change', p. 254.

structure, and the individual can become involved with this liturg
first entering the structure. The liturgy remains hot in a cool geneɪᴀ.
—high in detailed content, low in creative involvement.

This hot liturgy was ineffectual for the new cool generation:

> Our generation ... looks for high involvement, and this involvement comes
> not through much information but through a lasting, significant, experi-
> enced message, which in turn stimulates authentic involvement and honest
> human commitment. This experienced message ... is mediated not through
> distinctions and analysis but through realization—through life, colors, pic-
> tures, and their person-stimulating interrelationships.

For this cool generation, O'Meara recommended liturgy with
a high degree of involvement and much less content. Some of his
proposals were similar to those of proponents of secular theology. Liturgy should make use of contemporary art and the
secular world, rather than evoking a supernatural world separate
from daily life. Liturgy should have more spontaneity, inviting
worshippers to express their individual faith, needs, and hopes.
Through the use of a variety of media, liturgy should bring worshippers into dialogue with God rather than presenting fixed
truths about God to a largely passive audience.[23]
Others drew upon McLuhan's theories to propose liturgical
change. Commenting upon the 'Liturgy of the Lord's Supper'
which was approved in 1967 for trial use in the Episcopal
Church, E. Raymond McClain called for liturgical expression
which involved all the human faculties. He recommended that
liturgy not rely solely on words, but make full use of the arts,
including architecture, painting, sculpture, dance, and music.[24]
Massey Shepherd suggested that in the emerging cool culture
sacraments became of primary importance because they
'provide an outlet for all aspects of sensory excitement—visible
and tangible no less than auditory'.[25]
McLuhan's theories do not fully explain the development during the 1960s of liturgies described by James White as verbose.

[23] 'Liturgy Hot and Cool', *Worship* 42 (1968), pp. 215–22; quotations from
p. 217.
[24] 'Liturgy in an Electric Age', *St Luke's Journal of Theology* 12 (1969),
pp. 47–50.
[25] 'The Dimension of Liturgical Change', p. 255.

Perhaps these can be understood as the use of a hot medium to meet the demands for relevance and personal involvement. As Jordahl noted, some liturgical experimentation emphasized introspection and interpersonal dynamics, and liturgical texts were developed in response to that demand.

Those who discussed McLuhan's theories observed that it was the 'younger generation', that is, those born after World War II, to whom the theories were most applicable. Not only was this generation influenced by electronic media, its members also received more education than preceding generations. Wuthnow found that the 1960s were a time of enormous expansion in higher education, owing to vast growth in science and technology. Both the overall number of students on college campuses and the proportion of young adults attending college increased significantly. Furthermore, higher educational levels correlated to liberalization of attitudes on matters ranging from divorce and premarital sex to politics and economics. Persons with higher levels of education tended to have more egalitarian views with regard to gender, race, sexuality, and religious preference.[26]

It was the younger and more educated generation in particular who enthusiastically welcomed innovation in worship. Much of the liturgical experimentation of the 1960s occurred on college and university campuses. This may reflect not only the liberalization associated with education, but also the availability of an audience open to new forms of worship. Campuses provided a location where significant numbers of students were gathered, and thus offered a critical mass of people able to consider new liturgical ideas.

The larger number of students on college campuses during the 1960s is not by itself adequate to explain the widespread liturgical experimentation. Using Wuthnow's analysis of factors contributing to the emergence of new ideas, the audience must also be receptive to the new ideas and have the mental or symbolic capacities to process the ideas. To explain the attitudinal shifts of the 1960s, Jackson Carroll postulated a 'cohort difference', that is, the entrance into the young adult population of a new cohort (i.e., a new generation) very different from the

[26] *The Restructuring of American Religion*, pp. 153–64.

preceding young adult population. Carroll cited a study which found that college students of the 1950s had a cluster of values and commitments focused on personal and private concerns, including a tendency to conform to the norms and expectations of others, high commitment to family life, and low interest in political activity. The values of students of the 1960s were diametrically opposite: emphasis upon individual freedom and autonomy rather than conformity to social norms, experimentation with new forms of marriage and family life-styles, and political activism to bring about social change. Furthermore, the majority of adults over the age of thirty maintained more traditional values during the 1960s. Carroll suggested that the formative life experiences of the younger generation were significantly different from those of their elders, causing them to respond differently to the historical crises of the 1960s. Mass communication and the large numbers of students on college campuses were additional factors facilitating the dissemination of new ideas.[27]

Carroll's analysis does not fully explain why the younger generation responded so differently to historical events. But it does indicate that an audience receptive to new ideas was present on college and university campuses during the 1960s, while many older adults were less receptive to new ideas. This suggests that non-university parishes may have been less amenable to liturgical innovation. Other scholars have commented that liturgical experimentation was accepted to varying degrees in different settings. It may have been more common in atypical settings, but some mainstream parishes also permitted experimentation. Leigh Jordahl observed that experimental worship emphasizing group dynamics was occurring 'in convents and monasteries, on church college and university campuses, on seminary campuses and at pastoral institutes and retreats'.[28] James White has commented with regard to Methodists: 'More venturesome congregations entered with gusto into what was called "experimentation". For the timid, an early service could try bal-

[27] 'Continuity and Change', p. 39.
[28] 'Secularity', p. 21.

loons and banners and leave the eleven o'clock service undisturbed.'[29]

Resistance to change was also found by Stark and Glock in their survey of religious beliefs during the 1960s. Unlike Carroll, who observed that a shift occurred with the generation born after World War II, Stark and Glock found a substantial difference in religious outlook between those over fifty and those under fifty. Those over fifty were significantly more likely to hold traditional beliefs and also more likely to attend church each week and to contribute financially to the church. The differences between the two sets of findings cannot be readily explained, but what is significant is that Carroll's study, as well as Stark and Glock's, found differing attitudes towards religious change, and both studies attributed the attitudinal differences to the cultural shift marked by World War II. Stark and Glock commented: 'World War II seems to mark a watershed between the older America of small town and rural living (or stable urban neighborhood), and the contemporary America of highly mobile, urban life and the development of a mass culture.'[30]

When Stark and Glock published their survey in 1968, they acknowledged that some liturgical experimentation was occurring, but claimed: 'There has been no substantial change in the offering of the sacraments, or of the character of the activities conducted at the congregational level.' They attributed this to institutional inertia and more specifically to the fact that supporters of a more traditional theological perspective remained in most congregations and were more active than more liberal laity. Clergy tended to be liberal, but they met resistance to change within their congregations. Wuthnow noted a similar gap between, on the one hand, less educated and more conservative laity, and, on the other hand, clergy and more educated laity who supported liberal social causes. By the end of the 1960s, there were noticeable declines in religious commitment and in church attendance among more educated, and generally younger, laity.[31]

[29] *Protestant Worship*, p. 168.

[30] *American Piety*, pp. 207–16; quotation from p. 207, n. 2.

[31] ibid., pp. 211–12; Wuthnow, *The Restructuring of American Religion*, pp. 160–4.

These studies do not provide empirical evidence of attitudes towards liturgical change. However, if we posit that theologically liberal laity and clergy would be most open to liturgical experimentation, then it is plausible that experimentation was accepted primarily by younger and more highly educated laity and by many clergy. It is likely that clergy provided leadership for innovations which were introduced, and that the audience receptive to these new ideas was found on college and university campuses and among other laity with at least some college education. There remained within the churches a strong traditional element, a core of people who were attached to more traditional worship and symbols and for whom those symbols continued to carry meaning. Despite this resistance to change, liturgical innovation encompassed not only congregational experimentation but also revision of liturgical texts.

The Process of Liturgical Revision
Although a primary goal of much of the liturgical experimentation during the 1960s was relevance, liturgy did not become totally detached from Christian tradition. For example, Robert Bellah observed that the juxtaposition of a traditional eucharistic liturgy with elements from the contemporary culture anchored that particular service in the Christian tradition while also making the eucharist a present reality. In so far as the traditional symbols functioned to call into question the contemporary cultural materials, Bellah found that the service did not become a mere validation of the culture of the 1960s.[32] Martin Marty argued that, despite the contemporary emphasis on the immediate present, if liturgy was Christian it would not lose altogether a sense of tradition. The reality of God made known in Jesus Christ is central to Christian liturgy and would not disappear entirely even if it was not as loudly proclaimed.[33]

However, the formulation of the Christian tradition was undergoing a fundamental change with the ascendancy of secularism. Marty and Massey Shepherd noted the decline of an ontological world-view influenced by Platonism. Shepherd

[32] *Beyond Belief*, pp. 212–15.
[33] 'The Context of Liturgy', p. 469.

this as a shift away from an understanding of faith as a series of propositions. Marty pointed in particular to e in belief in heaven and hell that was eroding consciousness of the cosmic dimension of worship. Both Shepherd and Marty saw a shift to a more existential theological perspective and the recovery of a biblical understanding of inaugurated eschatology. According to Marty, the changing world-view meant for the Church 'the renewal of the proclamation of eternal life in the fourth gospel's sense . . . more concerned with the meaning of Jesus Christ as the resurrection and the life, and of eternal life beginning to be a reality in the temporal sphere.' Shepherd described the contemporary theological shift in a similar manner:

> We live in a world of Becoming, and we do not yet know what we shall be. The transcendence of God is not a fixed entity, but the 'beyond' of our experience that draws us in uncharted but by no means capricious paths. Reality is in the ever-changing event and situation of the moment, and is defined in terms of relationships.

Marty and Shepherd pointed out that this radical change in world-view was having a significant impact on liturgy. Marty acknowledged that the tradition should be appropriated in forms suited to the contemporary situation, but criticized liturgical reform that focused solely on the temporal and immediate and cautioned that liturgy must also recognize realities beyond the contemporary world.[34]

The shift in world-view and in basic theological perspective was an important reason for liturgical revision. It was not sufficient for experimentation to take place in congregations. Texts developed for use in particular situations were rarely adequate for more general use, and many of the unofficial liturgical texts developed during the 1960s reflected the contemporary jargon of that decade and were highly introspective and verbose.

Yet churches did not undertake liturgical revision solely in response to contemporary cultural and theological shifts. In the Episcopal Church a series of Prayer Book Studies, presenting

[34] ibid., pp. 469–73; quotation from p. 470; Shepherd, 'The Dimension of Liturgical Change', pp. 251–3; quotation from p. 252.

proposed revisions of Prayer Book offices for study but not for worship, had been issued beginning in 1950 and led to an official revision process beginning in 1967. A factor in the production of the Lutheran *Book of Worship* was the desire for different Lutheran Churches in North America to share a common service book. Development of new worship materials for the United Methodist Church was approved after the 1968 merger of the Evangelical United Brethren Church with the Methodist Church. When the Presbyterian Church (USA) was formed during the early 1980s, a new worship book and hymnal were authorized. As churches developed new materials, their revisions influenced each other, and these were further influenced by the new liturgical materials issued after the Second Vatican Council.

These factors indicate internal institutional support for revision, one of the variables identified by Wuthnow as influencing cultural production. The institutional churches provided the necessary context for a process of revision to occur. Churches were willing to commit material resources to the production of new liturgical materials and to facilitate the use and evaluation of proposed materials.

The cultural context is evident when considering the potential audience for liturgical revision. The governing bodies of the various Protestant churches gave formal approval to the process of revision in their respective churches. In all likelihood, this receptivity to revision of liturgical texts was influenced by the same factors creating an audience for liturgical experimentation. Thus liturgical revision was in part the result of the cultural and social upheaval of the 1960s. If the factors influencing openness to religious change hold true for liturgical revision, then revision would have been supported most by clergy and by younger and more educated laity, although there is no empirical evidence to test this hypothesis.

In addition to institutional support and broader cultural factors, leadership for revision was provided by persons with expertise in worship and so drew upon the resources of contemporary liturgical and theological scholarship. This furnished the foundation in Christian tradition which prevented new texts from being primarily expressions of contemporary culture, that is, to use

Marty's language, bound to the 'here and now' with no cognizance of the 'there and then'.

The actual process of liturgical revision accorded with the premises of secular theology. In several Protestant denominations, the procedure was to present rites for trial use and evaluation, and then to modify those texts based upon responses from the larger church. Revision was not simply the production of texts by liturgical experts for uncritical use by congregations, but a process involving development of texts, evaluation, and further revision.[35] An underlying assumption of such a process is that texts are not fixed entities expressing static truths, but a means of communication with God and an expression of a community worshipping at a particular time and place. From the latter perspective, the responses of the worshipping community are essential to the development of new liturgical materials. This reflects the existential world-view described by Shepherd and Marty.

Also implicit in the invitation for congregations to evaluate proposed liturgical texts is an expectation that individuals will have the sophistication necessary to offer such critique. This correlates with theories of religious evolution which see as a key feature of modern religion a heightened self-awareness with respect to symbols. Contemporary Christians have some ability to reflect upon symbols and to distinguish between the symbols and the truths underlying those symbols. Doubtless this is not true of every contemporary Christian. But rising educational levels in all denominations may have brought about a larger population able to participate actively in a process of evaluation of proposed liturgical texts. Here the effects of the surrounding culture were indirect. The explosion of science and technology and the pressures of the Cold War led to significantly greater emphasis upon higher education and the provision of governmental resources to finance this education. More educated persons developed greater capacities to think critically, and this extended to critical thinking with regard to religious symbolism.

[35] See White, *Protestant Worship*, pp. 55, 77, 168–9; Charles P. Price, *Introducing the Draft Proposed Book: A Study of the Significance of the Draft Proposed Book of Common Prayer for the Doctrine, Discipline, and Worship of the Episcopal Church* (Church Hymnal Corporation, New York 1976), pp. 10–13.

Contemporary Liturgical Forms

Urban Holmes has argued that the modern self-awareness with regard to symbolism is evident in the revised prayer book of the Episcopal Church: 'The new prayer book has, consciously or unconsciously, come to emphasize that understanding of the Christian experience which one might describe as a post-critical apprehension of symbolic reality and life in the community.'[36] Holmes does not give specific examples of this post-critical awareness. However, many of the characteristics of the liturgical experimentation of the 1960s can be seen in the new liturgical books of the Episcopal Church and of other churches.

A key principle of modern liturgy is flexibility. Most contemporary liturgical books provide a variety of prayers and orders of service, rather than a single set form. The variety of liturgical forms and flexibility in their use implies that liturgy can and should be adapted to the circumstances of the worshipping community in a given time and place, rather than existing as a fixed entity largely separate from the realities of the world.

The language of the texts also relates to contemporary culture. Specific prayers acknowledge modern concerns, as for example a prayer in the *Lutheran Book of Worship* for 'Conservation of Natural Resources' and a petition in the Episcopal *Book of Common Prayer* for those who travel through outer space.[37] A significant development has been the use of inclusive language. The 1975 'Guidelines for Nonsexist Use of Language', issued by the National Council of Teachers of English, indicates a growing awareness of the bias inherent in the generic use of masculine nouns and pronouns. These concerns, arising from the contemporary culture, were taken up by the revisers of liturgical texts, as is apparent from a comparison of texts issued in the late 1960s with those produced only a few years later.[38]

[36] 'Education for Liturgy', p. 137.

[37] *Lutheran Book of Worship* (Augsburg Publishing House, Minneapolis 1978), p. 49; *The Book of Common Prayer* (Church Hymnal Corporation, New York 1979), p. 384.

[38] Compare Inter-Lutheran Commission on Worship, *Services: The Holy Communion*, Contemporary Worship 2 (Augsburg, Minneapolis 1970), with *Holy Baptism*, Contemporary Worship 7 (Augsburg, Minneapolis 1974); also Standing Liturgical Commission of the Episcopal Church, *Holy Baptism with the Laying-on-of-Hands*, Prayer Book Studies 18 (Church Pension Fund, New

The new liturgical forms have a much greater emphasis on action, including a renewed appreciation of the sacraments. In many places the weekly eucharist is normative. While this fulfils a goal of the Reformation and is often described as the recovery of the practice of the early Church, it also reflects the contemporary emphasis on involvement in worship, as Massey Shepherd observed: 'the sacramental actions, because they are symbolic forms of immediate, existential experience, are preferred to the steady round of the undramatic Daily Offices'.[39]

Along with this sacramental dimension, new liturgical forms encourage leadership by a number of liturgical ministers and participation by the entire congregation, rather than presenting liturgy as a performance by a professional cleric for a passive congregation. In recent years, some scholars have cautioned that the individualistic tendencies of contemporary culture have produced a climate in which worship is more a means of individual fulfilment than the action of a worshipping community. Liturgical revision has provided liturgy which invites corporate participation, but this ideal has not always been achieved.[40]

Thus contemporary liturgical revision is in many ways a product of socio-cultural changes since World War II. Robert Wuthnow asserts:

> In becoming more oriented to the self, in paying more explicit attention to symbolism, in developing a more flexible organizational style, and in nurturing specialized worship experiences American religion has become more complex, more internally differentiated, and thus more adaptable to a complex, differentiated society.[41]

York 1970), with *Holy Baptism, Together with A Form for Confirmation or the Laying-On of Hands by the Bishop with the Affirmation of Baptismal Vows*, Prayer Book Studies 26 (Church Hymnal Corporation, New York 1973).

[39] 'The Dimension of Liturgical Change', pp. 254–5.

[40] See M. Francis Mannion, 'Liturgy and the Present Crisis of Culture', and Mark Searle, 'Private Religion, Individualistic Society, and Common Worship', in Eleanor Bernstein (ed.), *Liturgy and Spirituality in Context: Perspectives on Prayer and Culture* (Liturgical Press, Collegeville 1990), pp. 1–46. For a more positive evaluation of subjectivism in late twentieth-century culture, see Michael B. Aune, 'Worship in an Age of Subjectivism Revisited', *Worship* 65 (1991), pp. 224–38.

[41] *The Restructuring of American Religion*, p. 305.

While liturgy is influenced by society and will continue to change as the society evolves, liturgy that remains truly Christian cannot be totally bound to current perceptions of reality. The new liturgical forms present the possibility of acknowledging the realities of the contemporary world and of God and invite Christians into communion with God and with one another. To the extent that liturgy evokes the healing and transforming power of God in the world, it proclaims the truth of God incarnate in Jesus Christ and offers hope amidst the sufferings and struggles of this world.

10

Liturgy and Technology

SUSAN WHITE

I have felt for His Wounds
    in nozzles and containers.
I have wondered for the automatic devices.
I have tested inane patterns
    without prejudice.
I have been on my guard
    not to condemn the unfamiliar.
For it is easy to miss Him
    at the turn of a civilization.[1]

In 'A, a, a, Domine Deus', the Welsh poet and engraver David Jones describes his own relentless search for God, and, in so doing, articulates the situation faced by the religious person in a technological society. Ultimately, however, Jones finds 'the glazed work unrefined and the terrible crystal a stage-paste'. The search for God among the 'nozzles' and 'automatic devices' of the modern world has taken him nowhere.[2]

Most observers of contemporary culture—not only poets, but also sociologists, ethicists, psychologists, and philosophers— comment upon the profound influence of technology and technological ways of thinking on late twentieth-century society. The technological matrix is described as our human 'habitat', as our

[1] David Jones, 'A, a, a, Domine Deus', which appeared in part in his *Epoch and Artist* (Faber & Faber, London 1959), p. 179, and was first published in its entirety in *Agenda* 5.1–3 (1967), p. 5.

[2] Another contemporary Welsh poet, R. S. Thomas, takes an alternative view of the possibility of meeting God while engaged in the quest for scientific truth. In his poem on Roger Bacon, Thomas says that Bacon 'dreamed on in curves and equations with the smell of saltpeter in his nostrils, and saw the hole in God's side that is the wound of knowledge and thrust in his hand and believed'. This poem is a part of his collection *Frequencies* (Macmillan, London 1978).

'environment'.³ 'Everyday life', writes the sociologist Peter Berger, 'in just about every one of its sectors is ongoingly bombarded, not only with material objects and processes derived from technological production, but with clusters of consciousness originating within the latter . . . [serving] as contributions to an overarching symbolic universe peculiar to modernity.'⁴ The result, in human terms, is what Berger has called 'the homeless mind'.

Of course the presence of technology itself is nothing new. Paul Tillich argues that technology, along with language, is a fundamental dimension of the human person in every age, one of the essential pre-conditions for our self-actualization.⁵ *Homo sapiens* is also *homo faber*, and questions surrounding the role of technology in human life are as old as philosophy itself.⁶ Indeed, the stories of Prometheus, Mondawmin, Eden, and Babel can be read as seeking to explicate this relationship in the language of myth and symbol.⁷ But what is new to Western society on the

³ On technology as 'habitat' see Gayle Ormiston (ed.), *From Artifact to Habitat: Studies in the Critical Engagement of Technology* (Associated University Presses, London 1990). On technology as 'environment' see 'Technology as an Environment' in Jacques Ellul, *The Technological Society* (Knopf, New York 1964), pp. 34–50. These ways of speaking of technology are very close to the way that late nineteenth-century observers spoke of 'evolution', which J. R. Illingworth described in *Lux Mundi* (London 1889) as the 'category of the age'.

⁴ P. L. Berger, B. Berger, and H. Kellner, *The Homeless Mind* (Vintage Books, New York 1973), p. 42.

⁵ Paul Tillich, *Systematic Theology*, vol. 3 (University of Chicago Press 1963), pp. 57, 259–60. Lewis Mumford argues that it is 'cultural work' (art, language, ritual) and not 'manual work' that is the distinctive mark of the human person, but that in previous ages the two were practically and philosophically joined. But for a critique of the concept of *homo faber*, see Lewis Mumford, *The Myth of the Machine*, 2 vols (Harcourt, Brace, & World, New York 1967–1970).

⁶ See for example Carl Mitcham, 'Three Ways of Being-With Technology', in Ormiston (ed.), *From Artifact to Habitat*, pp. 31–59.

⁷ Tillich claims that the exercise of free choice in the face of a myriad of technological possibilities is a primary source of human conflict (social, moral, and intellectual) in every age. 'The ambiguity of freedom and limitation in technical production is powerfully expressed in myths and legends. It underlies the biblical story of the tree of knowledge from which Adam eats against the will of the gods and in the Greek myth of Prometheus, who brings fire to men,

eve of the twenty-first century is the globalized, ideological pervasiveness of patterns of technical production, of technological devices and ways of thinking. 'Technology', says Jacques Ellul, 'is not content with *being,* or in our world, with being the *principal* or *determining factor.* Technology has become a system.'[8]

As a result, defining technology and the technological system, and isolating its essential characteristics, have been matters of serious concern both to sociologists and to philosophers of science for nearly thirty years. Although several major issues remain unresolved,[9] certain substantial points of agreement

---

also against their will. Perhaps the story of the Tower of Babel, telling of man's desire to be united under a symbol in which his own finitude is overcome and the divine sphere reached is nearest to our own situation. In all these cases, the result is both creative and destructive; and this remains the destiny of technical production in all periods. It opens up a road along which no limit can be seen, but it does so through a finite limited being' (*Systematic Theology*, vol. 3, p. 73).

[8] Jacques Ellul, *The Technological Society*, p. 35. Some recent work suggests that we have moved as a society into a post-industrial and post-technological world, one in which the more abstract forms of information processing are the dominant force: see for example David Harvey, *The Condition of Post-Modernity* (Blackwell, Oxford 1989). But for the most compelling and lively considerations of the discontinuity between pre- and post-industrial society, see Lynn White, Jr, 'The Virgin and the Dynamo Reconsidered', in *Machina ex Deo: Essays in the Dynamism of Western Culture* (MIT Press, Cambridge MA 1968). Lynn White is considered a pioneer in the history of technology as an academic discipline, and his many works are a rich mine of information and insight for the student of the interaction between religion and culture.

[9] One is the question of the relative 'autonomy' of technology, and the extent to which it can be spoken of as 'a thing'. Does technology have the necessary qualities of self-actualization and self-determination to enable us to 'reify technology and then attribute causal powers to it'? Many others look to the sense of technology as being 'out-of-control' and the threat that it might, under its own momentum, take over our lives against our human will. See Joseph C. Pitt, 'The Autonomy of Technology', in Paul T. Durbin (ed.), *Technology and Responsibility* (Reidel, Dordrecht 1987), pp. 99–114. (This question is, of course, not a new one. It is clearly what is being addressed by Mary Shelley in her 1818 novel *Frankenstein*, R. L. Stevenson in *Dr Jekyll and Mr Hyde* [1886] and H. G. Wells in *The Invisible Man* [1897].) A second set of unresolved questions revolves around the relationship between technology and utopianism. See Paul Ricoeur, 'Ideology and Utopia as Cultural Imagination', in D. M. Borchert and D. Stewart (eds), *Being Human in a Technological Age* (Ohio University Press, Athens 1979), pp. 73–88; and George Ovitt, Jr, *The Restoration of Perfection* (Rutgers University Press, New Brunswick 1986).

have been reached in this area. Most observers of modern industrial culture would agree that technology can be defined on at least three distinct, but interpenetrating, levels:

(i) The term technology refers to the artifacts resulting from a process of manufacture. This can be anything from a simple tool to a complex information-management system.[10] This definition refers, in computer terms, to 'hardware', to anything that by its existence extends the range of human capabilities beyond their natural limitations.

(ii) Technology can refer to the constellation of processes and structures by which such artifacts come into being. Assembly lines, automation, microprocessing, and robotics all fall under this definition, as well as the kinds of human techniques, skills, and knowledge needed to accomplish the tasks related to manufacture.

(iii) The term technology can refer to a larger set of attitudes and presuppositions which support and advance the technological enterprise. This is the conceptual framework which underlies the sense of a pervasive 'techno-culture', and we shall return to discuss the features of this technological world-view later in this essay.

Most often in ordinary discourse, the three separate definitions are taken together to refer to a socio-technical system in which hardware, technique, and a particular ideological frame of reference combine to aid in the pursuit of essentially pragmatic ends, generally associated with the augmentation of human capabilities.[11]

---

[10] There is the question of where the information technologies fit into this schema, and certainly some authors would suggest that information itself is a technological 'artifact'. See especially the writings of Marshall McLuhan.

[11] See Ormiston (ed.), *From Artifact to Habitat*, p. 15, for a slightly different set of definitions, and also Stephen J. Kline, 'Defining Technology', *Bulletin of Science, Technology and Society* 5:3 (1985), pp. 215–18. The definitions used in this present essay above are a distillation of these two approaches (which mainly attend to hardware) and add a definition implicit in the work of Jacques Ellul. Ellul's vision of a technological world-view and an autonomous technology are challenged by several authors: see n. 10 above, and also Lewis Wolpert, 'Technology is not Science', in his most recent collection of essays, *The Unnatural Nature of Science* (Faber & Faber, London 1992), pp. 25–35.

If technology, in all these senses of the word, is indeed the 'category of the age', what questions does this raise for the student of Christian liturgy? The first possibility, of course, is that it raises none at all. In Victor Turner's often-repeated definition, religious ritual consists of 'prescribed formal behaviour for occasions *not given over to technological routine*'.[12] Although there are certain flaws in this definition,[13] an inspection of liturgical textbooks, both past and present, would seem to suggest that technology (and, by extension, the technologized twentieth-century human person) does indeed fall outside the academic study of Christian worship.

If the 'modern technological person' is discussed at all, he or she tends to be discussed as a liturgical or ritual problem. Turner and others,[14] for example, speak about a debilitating fragmentation of experience in contemporary society, in which work, home, religion, leisure are compartmentalized rather than integrated. Many would subscribe, at least implicitly, to the idea that modern technological ways of thinking and behaving are unalterably opposed to the nature of the religious quest, and that the impact of technology is something to be fought against. And so one possible way of posing the question this raises for liturgists is: How can Christian ritual be so forged as to be an effective weapon in the battle against the forces of tech-

[12] Emphasis added. See for example Victor Turner, *The Forest of Symbols* (Cornell University Press, Ithaca 1967), p. 19; *From Ritual to Theatre* (Performing Arts Journal Publications, New York 1982), p. 79; and Victor Turner and Edith Turner, *Image and Pilgrimage* (Columbia University Press, New York 1978), p. 243.

[13] Ritologist Ronald Grimes has been especially rigorous in pointing out the flaws in Turner's definition. In *Beginnings in Ritual Studies* (University Press of America, Washington DC 1982) p. 54, he states that 'magical rites are occasions that refer to mystical powers in a technological manner, so ritual must not be definitionally separated from technology' and also that 'technological routine itself has a ritual quality which ought not be overlooked simply because it does not refer to divine beings'.

[14] See Turner, *From Ritual to Theatre*, p. 35: 'The clear division between work and leisure which modern industry has produced has affected all symbolic genres, from ritual to games and literature.' This is built upon and expanded by Tom Driver in his recent *The Magic of Ritual* (Harper & Row, San Francisco 1991), esp. pp. 230-6, and seems to be the underlying presumption of the work of Ronald Grimes.

nologized modernity?[15] Allied to this is the sense that the pervasiveness of a technological world-view has seriously eroded the ability of modern men and women to ritualize their religious experiences, and that the role of the liturgist is, in part, to 're-educate' a whole generation of Christian believers into more 'primitive' ways of being human.

But, for various reasons, not everyone will be content with this sort of analysis. For some it will seem excessively simplistic; for others, excessively negative. And in any case, most sociologists are agreed that it is impossible to turn back the clock, in order to create a psycho-social Garden of Eden:

> Contemporary society cannot divest itself of its technological structures *in toto*. . . . If we are 'stuck with' technology and bureaucracy we are also 'stuck with' those structures of consciousness that are intrinsic to those processes. Put differently, there are certain packages [of consciousness] that cannot be taken apart.[16]

Presuming that this is true, I would like to suggest that there are a least three more 'neutral' questions which can and should be addressed to the technological situation by those with interest in Christian worship, and that these three questions are integrally related to the three 'definitions' of technology we have offered above.

Thus the first is, in essence, a question of 'hardware': What have been the actual points of intersection between the history of technological change and the history of liturgical change? How has technology, its artifacts and its processes, been incorporated into and shifted the direction of liturgical development? To answer this kind of question, the liturgist must presuppose that Christian worship is shaped not only by ecclesiastical and theological forces, but also by forces operating in the larger social context of which it is a part. This kind of attention to the societal matrix has already had a profound effect on scholarly

[15] Mary Douglas, however, is among those few ritologists that see 'secularism' at work universally, and finds the same kind of fragmentation of experience (and concomitant difficulty in the ability to ritualize) both in industrialized societies and in the tribal societies on which she based her work. See *Natural Symbols* (Pantheon, New York 1973), preface.

[16] Berger et al., *The Homeless Mind*, p. 193.

approaches to the Bible, historical theology, and the history of Christianity,[17] and liturgical studies must surely also operate on this level.

The second question which technology addresses to liturgical studies correlates with our second definition of technology as a 'set of processes and structures' by which work is accomplished. In what ways have these sorts of technological processes affected the way in which liturgists do their work? Have we gradually made technological ideals and frames of reference integral to the liturgical enterprise?

This would seem to be a crucial time in the history of liturgics to ask this kind of question. Scholars in a number of the other disciplines which had their origins in the last century, including psychology, linguistics, and sociology, are beginning to look critically at the history of changes in the goals and methods of their own fields of endeavour. This sort historical self-analysis is now thought to be essential to the intellectual health and well-being of any scholarly community, and to the responsible advancement of a field of inquiry. Within the field of liturgical studies, there has already been some important recent work on the kinds of methodologies which were used in its formative period as an academic discipline.[18] Surely the next step in this process is to ask whether modern liturgiology is shaped as much by models derived from technology as nineteenth-century liturgiology was shaped by models derived from evolutionary theory and comparative anatomy.[19]

The final (and perhaps the most important) question posed by the pervasiveness of technology relates to the human person as a liturgical subject. Does the technological human being inter-

[17] See for example Wayne Meeks, *The First Urban Christians* (Yale University Press, New Haven 1983).

[18] Although the term liturgics is known as early as 1855 (John Ogilvie's Supplement of that year to his *The Imperial Dictionary, English, Technological, and Scientific* defines 'liturgics' as 'the doctrine or theory of liturgies'), by 1882 both Philip Schaff (in the *Encyclopedia of Religious Knowledge*) and William Blakie (*The Ministry of the Word*) can use it without further explanation. Slightly earlier is J. M. Neale, *Essays on Liturgiology* (London 1863).

[19] See especially Frederick Sommers West, 'Anton Baumstark's Comparative Liturgy in Intellectual Context' (Unpublished Ph.D. thesis, University of Notre Dame 1988).

act with worship and with the worshipping community in a particular fashion? Our third definition of technology speaks of a 'set of attitudes and presuppositions', or, in Berger's terms 'packages of consciousness', which are part of the framework within which the technological person operates. What happens when these packages are brought to the ritual act? If liturgical studies is in any sense a 'human science', as well as a historical and theological one, this issue must be tackled in a rigorous and intellectually respectable way.

For the reasons stated above, there has been the strong tendency in the past twenty-five years for liturgists to look to those working with tribal religion and among pre-literate communities for insights into the human ritual subject. The work of Victor Turner, Claude Lévi-Strauss, Arnold van Gennep, and Mary Douglas has had an enormous influence. There is in all of this, however, the underlying sense that if we could only strip away the layers of civilization and modernity we could get to the naked human subject.[20] But is this indeed the case? Liturgists operate within an academic theology in which the terms 'inculturation' and 'contextualization' have taken on enormous importance, and this has convinced not a few researchers that we must look very carefully at human ritual subjects as we find them, and not as we would wish them to be.

There is certainly insufficient space in this essay to answer any one of these questions adequately, let alone all of them.[21] But what I would like to do is to begin to suggest how the three questions posed by technology might be addressed by someone

[20] This echoes Max Weber's view that through the bureaucratization of so many aspects of life we have lost the 'personal and mystical' elements of our humanity. The question continues to be posed in philosophical discussions of the role of technology. As Daniel Yankelovich puts it: 'Can we be fully human in a society dominated by technology and impersonal institutions?' (His answer is a qualified 'Yes'.) See his 'Two Truths: The View from the Social Sciences', in Borchert and Stewart (eds), *Being Human in a Technological Age*, pp. 89–105. See also the title essay in Martin Heidegger, *The Question Concerning Technology and Other Essays* (Harper & Row, New York 1977), pp. 3–35.

[21] I am completing a longer study which attempts to look at these issues in greater depth: *Christian Worship in a Technological Society*, forthcoming from Abingdon Press, Nashville 1994.

whose primary concern is the study of Christian worship. In a sense, this volume of essays is intended as a piece of map-work. It is designed to take the current map of the liturgical territory and to superimpose upon it other maps of other territories — sociological or political or literary — and then to analyse the results. As we do this, we find that previously hidden contours in the terrain begin to emerge and old patterns of interpretation and analysis are called into question. And so with this in mind, the final sections of this essay will attempt to discover what hidden aspects of the liturgical landscape might be revealed by superimposing the technological map upon it.

Historical Intersections

It must be said at the outset that historians of technology have already made some very interesting efforts towards a correlation of liturgical and technological data, seeking to understand the degree to which changes in technology can be explained as responses to changing trends in Christian worship. Two important examples provide analyses of early-medieval farming technology and labour-management: Lynn White, Jr, and George Ovitt both look to monastic liturgical practice, and particularly to the recitation of the daily office, as the primary stimulus to developments in medieval farming technology and to what Ovitt calls the 'secularization of labor'.[22] They demonstrate that the expectation that religious communities would be economically self-sufficient simply could not be met by men and women who met regularly to say the office, and that this conflict (most often resolved in favour of the priority of reciting the office) engendered revolutionary changes in techniques for planting,

---

[22] See Ovitt, *The Restoration of Perfection*, ch. 5. 'The issue of manual labor was the first source of difficulty for the Cistercians, for they quickly discovered what earlier Benedictines had learned, that economic self-sufficiency was incompatible with the performance of the Divine Office' (ibid., p. 144). Lynn White, *Medieval Religion and Technology* (University of California Press, Berkeley 1978), is principally concerned with classical Benedictine monasticism, while Ovitt is analysing various monastic rules, with special attention to the twelfth-century Cistercians. Although they adopt slightly different stances on the intellectual grounding of technology, both White and Ovitt trace the roots of several modern technological trends to the interplay of *ora* and *labora* in the Middle Ages.

ploughing, and harvesting, and also provided the occasion for experiments with a division of labour and specialization.

The mutual influence of worship and technology has also aroused scholarly interest among sociologists of religion. Robert Bocock, for example, has studied the place of Christian ritual patterns in an industrialized society.[23] However, Bocock relies on a limited number of social analysts (mainly Durkheim and Marx) and leaves largely unanswered the question of what a technological society is and how its artifacts and processes actually relate to the liturgy. There has been an enormous amount of new research both in the history and philosophy of technology and in ritual studies since the publication of this book in 1974, and there is certainly a need for sociologists to take a second look at these questions with this material to hand.[24]

That liturgists have an significant contribution to make to the historical study of technology can be seen from the work of the Harvard professor David Landes. In his comprehensive survey of the history of timekeeping, Landes assesses the mutual influence between Christian liturgy and the development of increasingly precise methods of time measurement. He too is particularly interested in the monastic life of the eleventh to the thirteenth century, during which, he claims, the natural rhythms of solar time were replaced by the mechanical rhythms of clock-time, until, in the Cistercian houses in particular, clock-regulated liturgy and clock-regulated work functioned interdependently to create the 'well-tempered monastery'. Landes argues that 'the setting of prayer times by the clock [in this period] was no small matter. It represented the first step toward a liturgy independent of the natural cycle.'[25]

The call to relate the canonical hours more directly to the time of day, and thus to undercut the tendency of clergy to say

[23] *Ritual in Industrial Society: A Sociological Analysis of Ritualism in Modern England* (George Allen & Unwin, London 1974).

[24] Kieran Flanagan's recent *Liturgy and Sociology* (Macmillan, London 1991) does very little to meet that need, restricted as it is by its own relentless argument that only an archaic ritual structure (represented by a return to the Tridentine Roman Rite in Latin) will be able to turn aside the onslaught of modernity.

[25] *Revolution in Time* (Harvard University Press, Cambridge 1983), p. 60.

the offices at any convenient time without regard to its liturgical situation, has been an item on the agenda of the Liturgical Movement since its earliest days.[26] And it would be very reassuring to blame technology for the perennial difficulties we have had making sense of the daily office. But in this case the liturgist can provide a corrective to the desire of the historian of technology to attribute all social, intellectual, and religious change to a technological motivation. Already in the mid-eleventh century, Peter Damian was warning clergy of the dangers of reciting all the canonical hours in a single sitting.[27] And centuries before this, the division of the 150 psalms across the eight hours of prayer had seriously weakened the link between the content of devotion and the time of day. Certainly the work of Paul Bradshaw, William Storey, and Robert Taft on the history of the daily office (none of which appears in his bibliography) would have kept Professor Landes closer to the mark in his analysis.

But there is a case to be made for the impact of the technical capacity to 'pray by the clock' on Christian worship, even though it may not be that it represents the 'first step' in a liturgical life distanced from the rhythms of nature. In Western liturgy at least, the dominance of the clock as a determiner of liturgical time is felt everywhere, so that there is almost nothing that will elicit sharper comment from most church-goers than a service of public worship that 'runs over the hour'. And that dominance has grown with the increase of programmed 'God slots' on the radio and on television. It would seem that a healthy collaboration between liturgists and historians of technology in this area would go a long way in helping us to make sense of this, and to prove not only that the Golden Age of liturgical 'naturalism' may be further back than we suppose, but also that we are more deeply entrenched in the situation technology has made for us than we might have guessed.

One of the important things to notice at the beginning of any discussion of the intersection between Christian worship and

[26] For a classic critique of the monastic office as a pattern for daily prayer, see William G. Storey, 'The Liturgy of the Hours: Cathedral versus Monastery', in John Gallen (ed.), *Christians at Prayer* (University of Notre Dame Press 1977), pp. 61–82.

[27] Peter Damien, *Opusc.* XXXIV. 5.

technological 'hardware' is that there is a tendency, more pro-
nounced in certain ecclesial communities than in others, for
liturgy to be technologically regressive. Examples of this
tendency exist in abundance: the use of candles and torches, the
lighting of the New Fire with flint at the Easter Vigil, and the
pervasive preference of hand-worked over machine-worked
altarware, vestments, communion elements, and architectural
ornaments. One only has to listen to the rhetoric surrounding
the re-creation of a medieval stone-yard at the Cathedral of St
John the Divine in New York to see that antiquated artifacts
and crafting techniques have a positive value for many
Christians. The fact that these sorts of materials and processes
have often attracted various clusters of theological interpretation in no way absolves us from looking carefully at the question
of what it is, precisely, that gives retrogressive technology ritual
value as a part of what is broadly referred to as 'tradition'.[28]

But clearly there is also much liturgical ground to be gained
from looking at the more 'positive' points of contact between the
history of technological change and the history of Christian worship. We can analyse this contact in terms of several broad
classes of technological hardware. Agriculture technology,
engineering, print and information processing (including
timekeeping), biotechnology, and transportation all have
exercised influence on the shape of Christian worship and
Christian worshippers in various ways and at various times. And
as we try to develop an accurate account of the history of liturgical development, as we ask why certain liturgical shifts occurred,
or why they occurred at a particular time or place, the technological matrix needs to be considered alongside the theological, sociological, and political. We must even be willing to
acknowledge that in certain cases a given development in worship was more dependent on technology than on any other single
factor.

[28] There are, of course, certain groups within which advanced technology is
much appreciated. My colleague Michael Roberts has taken pains to point out
the 'quasi-sacramental' status of microphones, audio-amplifiers, and overhead
projectors among those of the more Evangelical and charismatic ecclesiastical
temperaments.

One example will suffice. Since 1876 every edition of the official ritual contained in *The Book of Discipline* of the Methodist Episcopal (later the United Methodist) Church has stipulated that only the 'pure and unfermented juice of the grape' be used at Communion, and for the past century the liturgical use of grape juice has been common among Baptists and Presbyterians, as well as among most of the other denominations which would define themselves as being broadly within the 'Free Churches'. The ideological roots of this practice lie deep within the history of the nineteenth-century temperance movement, but its practical roots can be traced to developments within biotechnology.

In his study of the origins of the grape-juice industry, William Chazanof tells the story of Dr Thomas E. Welch, a devout Methodist layperson, who worked towards the application of Louis Pasteur's milk sterilization process to fruit juices, with the clear intention of providing an unfermented grape product for use at Communion.[29] Fuelled by frustrated missionary zeal (he had offered himself for service on the mission field but was refused), Welch promoted his product widely within the Protestant churches as a way of communicating temperance principles within the communion service. Without the technological expertise which allowed the practical application of pasteurization to other food substances (itself spawned by the rise of bacteriology as a science in the 1860s[30]), this profound change in the liturgical life of a large segment of worldwide Protestantism could not have taken place.

Pasteur's germ theory of disease and the subsequent development of sterilization technology would have further impact on the practice of Communion, not only in the Free Churches, but across the denominational spectrum. Individual communion cups (first introduced in the last decade of the nineteenth century) and other devices for the hygienic distribution of the elements were developed during this period. In the 1934 Eugene

[29] *Welch's Grape Juice: From Cooperation to Cooperative* (Syracuse University Press 1977).

[30] For a helpful summary of Pasteur's work, see J. D. Bernal, *Science in History, volume 2: The Scientific and Industrial Revolutions*, 3rd edn (Watts, London 1965), and also the more recent study by Bruno Latour, *The Pasteurization of France* (Harvard University Press, Cambridge 1988).

McCoy Company church-goods catalogue (whose clientele were mainly Roman Catholics in the United States) an item called a 'hostainer' appears:

> An altar bread dispenser which is sanitary, rapid, and symbolic. No tweezers, spoons or fingers are used, simply slide the knob and one host drops into the ciborium. Hygienic and liturgically correct. Each: $30.00

These biotechnological issues continue to arise in the eucharistic life of the Christian churches, and especially as we confront the challenge of HIV infection and AIDS. And it may be again that specifically technological responses to this challenge will be shaping the liturgy of the future.[31]

Biotechnology is only one narrow band in the technological spectrum, and yet already from this briefest of glances we can begin to appreciate its influence on the theology and practice of Christian worship. There remain vast areas in the history of technology to be explored by liturgical scholars: the impact of printing on the sixteenth-century liturgical Reformation,[32] the mutual influence of medieval Gothic architectural and engineering principles and the multiplication of Masses, the relationship between the rise of experimental science and seventeenth-century Prayer Book revision, the impact of embalming on funeral rituals, the ways in which gas and electric lighting affected patterns of worship in the nineteenth century, and in the twentieth century the importance of mobility, climate control, pain control, life-support, and a host of things which shape our lives. The kind of conversation that I am now proposing between specialists in the various facets of liturgiology and historians of technology can only result in a more accurate map of the liturgical terrain.

[31] The Interfaith Group of the Terrence Higgins Trust and other organizations concerned with the religious and liturgical questions posed by HIV infections and AIDS are producing useful guidelines in this area.

[32] For a brief discussion of this, see Aidan Kavanagh, *On Liturgical Theology* (Pueblo, New York 1984), pp. 103–6. Perhaps more influential in this regard is modern information processing and the ability to produce and disseminate liturgical texts on an *ad hoc* basis.

Technologized Liturgiology

In the classic book on the psycho-social impact of technology, *The Homeless Mind*, the authors describe the hallmarks of technologized modernity. One of the principal elements in the technological 'cluster of consciousness' is a pervasive tendency towards bureaucratization. Bureaucracy is the principal mechanism by which a technologized society is transmitted to the individual, and by which it is managed and maintained. The 'homeless mind' presupposes that 'everything is organizable' and that bureaucratic forms can be applied 'in principle to just about any human phenomenon'.[33] 'Bureaucracy is not only orderly, but orderly in an imperialistic mode. There is a bureaucratic demiurge who views the universe as dumb chaos waiting to be brought into the redeeming order of bureaucratic administration.'[34]

It is worth noting in light of this analysis of the modern bureaucratized consciousness that the current volume of essays is offered in honour of someone who in many ways can be seen as the archetypal liturgical bureaucrat. A charter member of the Church of England Liturgical Commission, instrumental in the founding of the Joint Liturgical Group and the International Commission on English in the Liturgy, Ronald Jasper made his most important and lasting contributions to liturgiology in specifically bureaucratic contexts.[35] And there is little doubt that Jasper's experience of bureaucratic liturgiology is paralleled by his counterparts in almost every country in the world and across the denominational spectrum.[36]

[33] Berger et al., *The Homeless Mind*, p. 51. As early as 1915, the sociologist Robert Michels could refer to the trend towards bureaucratization as the 'iron law' of a modern society (*Political Parties: A Sociological Study of the Oligarchical Tendencies in Democracy*, New York).

[34] Berger et al., *The Homeless Mind*, p. 50.

[35] For his own description of what I have called the bureaucratization of the liturgy, see Ronald Jasper, *The Development of the Anglican Liturgy 1662–1980* (SPCK, London 1989).

[36] For the rapid rise of bureaucratic church structures in the twentieth century, see Robert Wuthnow, *The Restructuring of American Religion* (Princeton University Press 1988), pp. 23, 98–9; for similar developments in the Church of England, see Kenneth A. Thompson, *Bureaucracy and Church Reform, 1800-1965* (Clarendon Press, Oxford 1970).

Although since the establishment of the Congregation of Rites in 1588 there have always been groups which saw themselves as having general oversight in the production and implementation of service materials, the expansion and diversification of these groups in the past fifty years is remarkable. Since the middle of this century the proliferation of liturgical boards and agencies, commissions, congregations, and organized pressure groups corresponds to the bureaucratic tendencies in society at large. And this trend towards bureaucratization has spilled over into the liturgical lives not only of denominations but also (by a sort of ecclesiastical 'trickle-down' process) of congregations and individual worshippers as well:

> To the huge denominational bureaucracies that were erected earlier in the century have now been added dozens of highly institutionalized organizations oriented to special interest groups within denominations, to coordinating the complex relations among denominations, and to filling in the crevices with religious activities that denominations have not provided.[37]

Although there are other components to the technological 'cluster of consciousness' besides the bureaucratic, and other analyses of technologized modernity which do not lay such heavy emphasis on bureaucratic processes,[38] certainly the pervasiveness of bureaucratized liturgizing demands that we take a careful look at the specific ways in which it may shape the experience of worship for individuals and groups. A close inspection of the various characteristics of the bureaucratic system, and serious attention to the several messages which it sends, raises a number of important questions for late twentieth-century liturgists: How accurately do they describe the shape of the liturgical world as we know it? Is this what we intend? And (perhaps more to the point) is this what we *want*?

The first package of attributes pertains to the system and its output. Any bureaucracy tends towards the establishment of

[37] Wuthnow, *The Restructuring of American Religion*, p. 126.

[38] The work of the Cambridge sociologist Anthony Giddens, for example, in many ways presupposes a bureaucratized consciousness, but uses other categories to describe the impact of that consciousness on the individual self-in-society searching for meaning. See his *Modernity and Self-Identity: The Search for Meaning in the Late Modern Age* (Polity, Cambridge; Stanford University Press 1991).

arenas of competence, towards the compartmentalization of that competence, a reliance on proper procedure, orderliness, and predictability. 'Every bureaucracy must produce a system of categories into which everything within a certain jurisdiction can fit and into which everything can be handled.'[39] This is a system that, while it may not actively discourage creativity, at the very least aims at carefully managed creativity.

Because the system quickly becomes in some sense autonomous (there are, as we all know, certain bureaucracies which do nothing but operate *themselves*), they have a high degree of arbitrariness, since techniques and processes tend to become rigid and to be applied generally within pre-defined categories of necessity. At its best, a bureaucracy can deal efficiently with massive amounts of information and effectively channel the flow of demand. At its worst, the organization becomes simply a 'paper chase'.

But these attributes of a bureaucratic system have an immediate impact on the 'clientele' of that system. There is a strong impetus towards the anonymity of the client, since the bureaucracy tends towards 'reducing the concrete individual to a "case", a "number", or a member of a certain class, respectively, without significant remainder'.[40] People fall into abstract categories, and although the system is often disturbed by 'eruptions of concrete humanity',[41] on the whole the successful working of the operation depends on identifying and meeting the needs of the 'typical' client. Because of this, individual needs tend to be suppressed and depersonalization takes over. (It is this feature of the system that led J-P. Sartre to speak of the human spirit as a 'victim' of bureaucracy.[42])

The system attempts its radical depersonalization of the individual client in a number of ways. First, it imposes control upon the spontaneous expression of emotion,[43] and, indeed, one of

[39] Berger et al., *The Homeless Mind*, p. 50.

[40] Frederic L. Bender, 'The Alienation of Common Praxis', in Ormiston (ed.), *From Artifact to Habitat*, pp. 155–74.

[41] Berger et al., *The Homeless Mind*, p. 51.

[42] *Critique of Dialectical Reason*, ed. Jonathan Rée (NLB, London 1976), pp. 658–63. Sartre speaks here of bureaucracy as the 'total suppression of the human'.

[43] Berger et al., *The Homeless Mind*, pp. 57–8.

the functions of bureaucracy is to *assign* emotional states to its clients. The system allows only limited reciprocity. In other words, the feedback from client to bureaucracy is carefully managed (by, for example, the use of jargon), and this necessarily leads to relatively passive involvement on the part of the client. 'In short, bureaucracy transforms subjects (individuals as self-creative projects) into objects.'[44] Nevertheless, the basic expectation, on the part of both client and bureaucracy, is that the system is fair, and it is working for the general good of the clientele.

In his 1984 book *On Liturgical Theology*, Aidan Kavanagh suggests a number of difficulties in using 'authorized' liturgy imposed on worshippers from above (and presumably here he has in mind liturgical bureaucracy) as a normative source of theology.[45] But bureaucratic liturgiology clearly raises a number of related issues for contemporary liturgists. Does a highly compartmentalized system encourage sufficient cross-fertilization between, for example, liturgy and doctrine, liturgy and social issues, liturgy and religious education? Does a highly rigid and autonomous system allow for liturgical creativity to flourish? Does the restriction of feedback and the anonymity which the bureaucracy imposes on the clientele actively discourage community and individual 'ownership' of parochial liturgy? Can intentionally arbitrary systems take sufficient account of the wide variety of needs, emotions, desires, and anxieties that liturgical praxis is designed to meet? In short, are bureaucratic liturgical structures good for the public prayer of the Christian people?

Technological Consciousness meets Christian Liturgy

I have said that in one respect my mind has changed during the last twenty or thirty years. Up to the age of thirty, poetry of many kinds . . . gave me great pleasure, and even as a schoolboy I took intense delight in Shakespeare. But now for many years I cannot read a line of poetry: I have tried lately to read Shakespeare, and found it so intolerably dull that it nauseated me. I have also almost lost my taste for pictures or music. . . . My

[44] Bender, 'The Alienation of Common Praxis', p. 164.
[45] See especially chs 5 and 7.

> mind seems to have become a kind of machine for grinding general laws
> out of large collections of facts.[46]

This is Charles Darwin's lament: that his mind has become machine-like and that those faculties upon which 'the emotional part' of his nature depends have atrophied. The machine model —of society, of mind, of work, of the human person—has had a pervasive influence on Western consciousness since its beginnings in the scientific rationalism of the seventeenth and eighteenth centuries.[47] Although a 'machine-anthropology' is only one element within a whole constellation of attitudes, paradigms, and presuppositions which technology both binds together and legitimates, it has been a powerful one.[48] Karl Marx observed that the process of mechanized production creates not only an object fit for a particular human subject, but also creates the human subject itself, and Lewis Mumford took that one step further in his concept of the 'Megamachine', an amalgamation of persons and things which function together towards the efficient performance of given tasks. The more we look, the more we see the extent to which we ourselves have been and continue to be moulded to fit the world of technologi-

[46] Charles Darwin, 'Recollections of the Development of my Mind and Character', written in 1881 and printed in Francis Darwin (ed.), *Life and Letters of Charles Darwin* (London 1887).

[47] As we can detect in the Darwin quotation above, in some sense a physiological change must occur if a person would live comfortably in a technological society. See for example G. Claudin, *Paris* (Paris 1867), pp. 1–2: 'These [technological] discoveries bend our senses and our organs in such a way that causes us to believe that our physical and moral constitution is no longer in rapport with them. Science, as it were, proposes that we should enter into a new world that has not been made for us. We should like to venture into it; but it does not take us long to recognize that it requires a constitution that we lack and organs that we do not have' (cited in Wolfgang Schivelbusch, *The Railway Journey* (University of California Press, Berkeley 1977), p. 159). See also J. L. Casti, *Paradigms Lost: Images of Man in the Mirror of Science* (Morrow, New York 1989).

[48] Because of this ability to provide a cohesive and plausible world-view, technology is regarded by many social analysts as having taken on all of the salient features of religion. As one such observer says, 'the need for the sacred never, never subsides, but returns in a new religion, which in the twentieth century is science and technology' (David Lovekin, 'Technology and the Denial of Mystery', in Ormiston (ed.), *From Artifact to Habitat*, p. 89).

cal artifacts and processes, and the more we can see that the 'myth of the machine'[49] can stand as representative of the larger technological world-view.

Many recent commentators, however, suggest that the machine model is beginning to lose its influence, and that that loss of influence is one of the marks of post-modernity. They look to the rise of Green politics and theology, New Age religious movements, and a growing pessimism about the limits of technology as evidence of a shift in perception towards a more organic world-view. But this argument is by no means universally accepted, and even its supporters would agree that any such shift is in its very early stages, and that the 'myth of the machine' continues to retain much of its power in the corporate consciousness of the industrialized West. Whatever the current status of the 'myth of the machine', any liturgical analysis of the impact of technological thinking on those who worship will be incomplete without taking the mechanical paradigm into account. At the very least, it can provide a model for thinking about the way in which a given conceptual framework can influence the liturgical life of individuals and communities.

What specific issues does the 'myth of the machine' raise for liturgists as they reflect upon the ways in which contemporary men and women and children approach Christian ritual? How do people enmeshed (to a greater or lesser degree) in this particular context perceive the liturgical process in which they are engaging? Rather than looking at all of the various facets of the machine paradigm in attempting to answer these questions, it may be useful to isolate and to give attention to three particular features which have direct relevance in the study of Christian worship: the quest for elimination of 'play' (in the sense of increasingly small tolerances), componentiality, and a dependence on specialized knowledge.

In both simple and sophisticated machines, an elimination of play is considered essential to the smooth and efficient functioning of the device. In the early stages of the industrial age, it was

---

[49] In his important work of social analysis, *The Myth of the Machine* (cited above, n. 5), Lewis Mumford explores the impact of machine thinking on contemporary consciousness.

almost universally believed that one would eventually reduce
tolerances to nothing in all parts of a machine, and that perpetual motion (first proposed, it is thought, by Villard de Honnecourt in 1235) was feasible.[50] One eighteenth-century analyst
observed that 'whoever seeks from power more work than is
produced so far by our calculus or theory of mechanics, is in fact
seeking the *Perpetuum mobile* and will not find it. . . . He must
know what sort of theory is most important or in what manner
he can arrive at it, namely by avoidance or elimination of fric-
tion.'[51]

One important by-product of this quest for the elimination of
play is the notion of progressive perfectibility: the view that in
time and under the right circumstances one progresses towards a
machine (or a government, or a method of education, or a filing
system, or an opinion poll) perfectly suited to its task. Of course,
it might be argued that the liturgy, because it can to some extent
be categorized as an art-form, is therefore immune from this
sort of expectation of perfectibility. But there is ample evidence
that the ideal of progress has also made its mark on the arts. As
long ago as 1831, John Stuart Mill wrote in the *Westminster
Review*:

> It would be a pity that poetry should be an exception to the Great Law of
> progress that attains in human affairs; and it is not. The machinery of a
> poem is not less susceptible of improvement than the machinery of a cotton
> mill; nor is there any better reason why the one should retrograde from the
> days of Milton than the other from those of Arkwright.[52]

Not only the arts, but the natural world as well is seen to be
perfectible by the intervention of the machine. 'The cosmic free-

---

[50] See Friedrich Klemm, *A History of Western Technology* (George Allen &
Unwin, London; Scribner, New York 1959), pp. 88–93. De Honnecourt proposed a wheel fitted with weights and lodestones which had a myriad of sub-
sidiary uses, one of which is notably 'liturgical': 'In this fashion, one builds an
angel whose finger points always toward the sun. . . . In this fashion one makes
an eagle that always turns his head toward the deacon when he is reading the
Gospel.'

[51] Jacob Leupold, *Theatrum Machinarum hydraulicarum*, Leipzig 1725
(cited in Klemm, *A History of Western Technology*, p. 235).

[52] Cited in Lewis Mumford, *The Condition of Man* (Harcourt, Brace & Co.,
New York 1944), p. 305.

dom of the natural phenomenon', writes one late nineteenth-century enthusiast for the waterwheel, 'becomes transformed by the machine into an order and law that outside forces of an ordinary kind are unable to disrupt.'[53] And clearly this spills over into the expectation that the human person is also perfectible. Many observers have viewed the growth of such things as pop-psychology, astrology, alternative medicine, cryogenics, experimental genetics, and therapeutic approaches to religion as clear indications of the marketing power harnessed by the ideal of progressive human improvement in the late twentieth century.

The quest for the elimination of 'play' cannot be understood apart from the notion of 'componentiality', the idea that every system is made up of independent and self-contained units which, when brought into contact with other such units, form a working whole.[54] This paradigm applies equally to persons (as individual organisms or as elements within, for example, a social system or a work-force) as to complex machines, and can be contrasted to more organic models of organization. There is the strong tendency in this model for all components to be seen as of equal value, since each in its right place is necessary to the proper working of the system.

A direct result of both componentiality and the quest for the elimination of play is the increasing reliance on professional expertise. In a complex machine, there is the necessity that there be someone responsible for the individual specifications of each component part, in order that that part might be precisely suited to its task and that the whole machine might run smoothly. And to the extent that the machine model is applied to a given system or an activity, this perceived need for expertise is also present. Many have cited the medical profession as an example of specialized expertise run rampant,[55] but academic theology and the practice of religion are not far behind.

[53] Franz Reuleaux, *Theoretische Kinematik: Grundzuge einer Theorie des Machinenwesens* (Brunswick 1875), p. 234 (cited in Schivelbusch, *The Railway Journey*, pp. 169f.).

[54] See Berger et al., *The Homeless Mind*, pp. 32–3.

[55] For the relationship between the idea of the body as a machine and the growth and diversification of medical specialties, see Edwin Clarke and L. S. Jacyna, *Nineteenth-Century Origins of Neuroscientific Concepts* (University of California Press, Berkeley 1987).

One can begin to see that individuals who enter the liturgical 'system' with this kind of package of expectations will be making certain assumptions about the nature of their engagement with it. Certainly we have evidence that participants do in some ways apply the ideal of incremental perfectibility to the liturgy (either to the rites, to the experience of worshipping, or to themselves as worshippers). A pervasive sense that we are all engaged in a continuous process of professionalized 'tinkering' with liturgical texts and rites, and the high expectation by participants that they will gain emotional, psychological, and spiritual 'satisfaction' from the liturgy (along with a tendency to withdraw commitment if those expectations are not met), have been widely commented upon. And it also seems clear that the average worshipping congregation (as well as the average liturgist) has a fairly high expectation that the liturgy will have its expert practitioners.

In a recent paper delivered to the Anglican sub-group of the North American Academy of Liturgy, Leonel Mitchell describes what he calls 'the new rubricism' by which 'the breath of freedom and fresh air introduced by the revision of the liturgy is being quenched by the urge to get all the right choreography down on paper, so that we can all do it the same way'. As evidence, Mitchell cites the renewed popularity of liturgical manuals, such as Howard Galley's *The Ceremonies of the Eucharist*[56] and Byron D. Stuhlman's *The Prayer Book Rubrics Expanded*.[57] It can certainly be argued that these books presuppose the kind of mechanical model of the liturgy which we have been describing, a model in which each liturgical component can be isolated and each liturgical participant must have a clearly defined role and function in order for the liturgical 'machine' to work properly.

In the wider context, the quest for the elimination of play among independent ritual and textual and human components must be seen as a factor in the way worshippers approach the ongoing dialogue between liturgical absolutism on the one hand and liturgical relativism on the other. Although there have been several attempts since the Enlightenment to establish an organic

---

[56] Cowley Publications, Cambridge MA 1989.
[57] Church Hymnal Corporation, New York 1987.

view of the liturgy (expressed, for example, in the 1943 papal encyclical *Mystici Corporis*), they have largely failed to capture the popular imagination. The most recent calls for a more holistic model of the world and its contents (which many see as a direct response to the prevalence of technology) seem to have penetrated further, and are influential at least within certain sectors of theology as a discipline. Creation and liberation theologies and theories of social organization, for example, ask us to think seriously about what the mutual interdependence of all things might mean to our thinking:

> More than ever must the 'doors of perception' be cleansed through a critical animism that acknowledges the true social continuity of being, the relative immaturity and great tendency to err of our rational ego, the tempered maturity of the human capacity to marvel and to imagine — a critical animism that can transform those imaginings into humanized, cosmically rooted practices.[58]

Whether this ideal will penetrate the liturgical consciousness of Christian believers, and to what degree, we must wait to discover.[59]

Conclusion

All historians of the liturgy know the important writing of Romano Guardini, exemplified by his influential *The Spirit of the Liturgy*.[60] Fewer of them will be familiar with his later book *Das Ende de Neuzeit*,[61] in which he describes the intellectual and psychological legacy of the Enlightenment. Perhaps it was his liturgist's eye for the deeper meaning of things which allowed

---

[58] Eugene Rochberg-Halton, *Meaning and Modernity* (University of Chicago Press 1986), p. 277.

[59] As one example of a description of the liturgical enterprise which uses mechanical concepts, see paragraph 6 of 'Down to Earth Worship', the findings of the Third International Anglican Liturgical Consultation, York, England, 21–4 August 1989: 'The liturgy, *rightly constructed*, forms the People of God. . . . For a *Province or smaller unit* to be creative and to adapt a received worship tradition . . . it is greatly *dependent upon both the liturgical scholarship and expertise of its leaders and teachers*' (emphasis added). For the full text, see David Holeton (ed.), *Liturgical Inculturation in the Anglican Communion*, Alcuin/GROW Liturgical Study 15 (Grove Books, Nottingham 1990).

[60] English translation: Sheed & Ward, London 1930.

[61] Wurtzburg 1950.

Guardini to catch a glimpse of the world which technology was creating for us:

> All monsters of the wilderness, all horrors of darkness have reappeared. The human person again stands before the chaos; and all of this is so much more terrible, since the majority do not recognize it: after all, everywhere scientifically educated people are communicating with one another, machines are running smoothly, and bureaucracies are functioning.[62]

We have tried in this essay to make as neutral as possible an assessment of the ways in which technology has affected Christian worship, the Christian worshipper, and the academic and pastoral enterprise which seeks to understand them both. But this objectivity should not distract us from a serious look at the significant ways in which the technological matrix has deformed certain elements of belief and thought, elements which the traditional liturgy still takes for granted. Mystery, once the experience of that which was impenetrable and awesome, has become simply something to be uncovered, defined, and manipulated. Such important theo-liturgical concepts as time, judgement, death, retribution, and sin have been irrevocably altered within the human imagination, and the idea that there is a 'technological fix' to any problem is deeply embedded in our corporate consciousness. There is loose in the world a pervasive sense that it is technology which provides the legitimating myth for the choices made by individuals, communities, and nations.[63] Darwin's description of his own state of mind is a challenge too strong for us to ignore, and forces us to look into our own lives, as both liturgists and worshippers, for similar changes wrought by technology.

In the face of these massive questions, we might very well want technology and the world it creates simply to disappear. But that is not possible. Nor can we retreat into pious nostalgia or ecclesiastical isolationism. Unless we begin to look critically at the ways in which our own discipline is itself shaped by technological forces, and at the ways in which our liturgical history has been shaped by technological artifacts and processes, we will be ill-equipped to meet the challenges of ritualizing Christian

[62] ibid., p. 96.
[63] See Wuthnow, *The Restructuring of American Religion*, ch. 11: 'From Civil Religion to Technological Legitimacy'.

experience in the modern world. This kind of critical investigation is work which must be done quickly if Christianity is to be a home for the 'homeless mind' of the twenty-first century.

11

Liturgy and Theology

MAXWELL JOHNSON

In his conflict with Semi-Pelagianism over the necessity of divine grace throughout the entire process of human salvation, the monk Prosper of Aquitaine (c. 390–463), who was a product of Augustinian theology, argued that:

> in inviolable decrees of the blessed apostolic see, our holy fathers have cast down the pride of this pestiferous novelty and taught us to ascribe to the grace of Christ the very beginnings of good will, the growth of noble efforts, and the perseverance in them to the end. In addition, let us look at the sacred testimony of priestly intercessions which have been transmitted from the apostles and which are uniformly celebrated throughout the world and in every catholic church; so that the law of prayer may establish a law for belief [*ut legem credendi lex statuat supplicandi*]. For when the presidents of the holy congregations perform their duties, they plead the cause of the human race before the divine clemency and, joined by the sighs of the whole church, they beg and pray that grace may be given to unbelievers; that idolaters may be freed from the errors of their impiety; that the Jews may have the veil removed from their hearts and that the light of truth may shine on them; that heretics may recover through acceptance of the catholic faith; that schismatics may receive afresh the spirit of charity; that the lapsed may be granted the remedy of penitence; and finally that the catechumens may be brought to the sacrament of regeneration and have the court of the heavenly mercy opened to them.[1]

Although Prosper's argument on the basis of the *lex orandi* is an addition to one based on the teaching of the apostolic see, liturgical theologians have tended to latch on to this principle as the primary one for discerning a principal source for the Church's faith and theology. How is liturgy a 'source' for theology? What is the relationship between the Church's prayer and its faith and doctrinal formulations? How does liturgy shape believing?

[1] *Capitula Coelestini* 8 (Migne, *Patrologia Latina* 51, 205–12). English translation from Geoffrey Wainwright, *Doxology* (Epworth Press, London; Oxford University Press, New York 1980), pp. 225–6.

The answers to the above questions are not easy. In fact, the answers given to them—as well as the precise interpretation and methodological weight of Prosper's principle—vary from one theologian to another. The definitions of liturgy and theology and the presence or absence of a verb in the use of Prosper's phrase are important keys in attempting to answer the question of the precise relationship between liturgy and theology in the writings of various theologians. Does the theologian supply a verb (*lex orandi lex est credendi*), omit the verb in favour of the principle's popular shorthand formulation (*lex orandi, lex credendi*), or keep the verb as it appears in Prosper's own text (*ut legem credendi lex statuat supplicandi*)?

In order to illustrate both the complexity of this problem and the lack of consensus in liturgical theology today, this essay focuses on the relation between liturgy and theology in three contemporary and highly influential liturgical theologians from three different Christian traditions: Alexander Schmemann (Russian Orthodox), Geoffrey Wainwright (British Methodist), and Aidan Kavanagh (Roman Catholic). All three subscribe to Prosper's phrase as a fitting methodological principle. But all three offer different definitions of liturgy and theology. All three use different verbs (or no verb) in their appropriation of Prosper's principle. And, consequently, all three provide different understandings of the relationship between *lex orandi* and *lex credendi*.

Alexander Schmemann: *lex orandi lex 'est' credendi*
The late Alexander Schmemann devoted a number of his writings to the question of the relationship between liturgy and theology.[2] According to him, neither 'liturgical theology' as a

---

[2] See his *Introduction to Liturgical Theology*, 2nd edn (St Vladimir's Seminary Press, Crestwood NY 1975); *For the Life of the World* (St Vladimir's Seminary Press, Crestwood, NY 1973); 'Liturgical Theology, Theology of Liturgy, and Liturgical Reform', *St Vladimir's Theological Quarterly* (1969), pp. 217–24; and 'Liturgy and Theology', *The Greek Orthodox Theological Review* 17 (1972), pp. 86–100. Thomas Fisch has recently edited a collection of Schmemann's essays on this topic in *Liturgy and Tradition: Theological Reflections of Alexander Schmemann* (St Vladimir's Seminary Press, Crestwood NY 1990).

sub-discipline within the broader theological curriculum nor the attempt to develop a 'theology of liturgy' from which one might deduce the correct norms to which a programme of liturgical reform must conform are adequate approaches to this question. Rather, theology as the 'orderly and consistent presentation, explication and defense of the Church's faith' must be rooted in the very experience of the faith itself, an experience which is 'given and received in the Church's *leitourgia* — in her *lex orandi*'.[3] In other words, for Schmemann the *lex orandi* 'is' (*est*) the Church's *lex credendi*, and the theological task is ultimately an interpretative and descriptive process which attempts 'to grasp the "theology" as revealed in and through liturgy'.[4] He maintains that if theology is

> the attempt to express Truth itself, to find words adequate to the mind and experience of the Church, then it must of necessity have its source where the faith, the mind, and the experience of the Church have their living focus and expression, where faith in both essential meanings of that word, as Truth revealed and given, and as Truth accepted and 'lived,' has its *epiphany*, and that is precisely the function of the 'leitourgia.'[5]

There is therefore no need for specific kinds of theology called either 'liturgical theology' or 'theology of liturgy'. Although theology should not be reduced to liturgy, all Christian theology should somehow be 'liturgical', in that it has 'its ultimate term of reference in the faith of the Church, as manifested and communicated in the liturgy'.[6]

But what is it in liturgy that makes the liturgical experience this 'epiphany' of the Church's faith in such a way that it is the ultimate source for theological reflection and discourse? For Schmemann it is not a particular liturgy with its given texts, rubrics, ritual acts, and interpretations that does this. It is, rather, what he calls the liturgical *Ordo*, the basic underlying structure and theology of liturgy enshrined, even hidden, within the various Byzantine *ordines* and *typica*. It is 'the unchanging principle, the living norm or "logos" of worship as a whole,

---

[3] 'Liturgy and Theology', pp. 89–90.
[4] 'Liturgical Theology, Theology of Liturgy, and Liturgical Reform', p. 218.
[5] ibid., p. 219.
[6] 'Liturgy and Theology', p. 95.

within what is accidental and temporary'.[7] And the unchanging principle, norm, or 'logos' presented by this *Ordo*, having apostolic and Judeo-Christian origins, is a particular understanding and revelation of the co-relation of a normative eschatology, cosmology, and ecclesiology which are manifested in the very core of the Church's liturgical act and experience, especially in the eucharist (a manifestation of the eternal kingdom of God) celebrated by the Church within time. Indeed, the principle of the *Ordo* is the 'co-relation and conjunction of the Eucharist with the liturgy of time in which we recognize the fundamental structure of the Church's prayer, as having existed from the very beginning in her "rule of prayer" '.[8] Thus, within the *lex orandi* of the early Church there was, in his opinion, an 'organic . . . self-evident connection and interdependence of the Lord's Day, the Eucharist, and the Ecclesia (the coming together of the faithful as "church")',[9] manifesting an eschatological, ecclesial, and cosmological vision. He continues:

> It is clear that on the one hand, this connection still exists *liturgically*, but it is equally clear that on the other hand, it is neither understood nor experienced in the way it was understood and experienced in the early Church. Why? Because a certain theology and a certain piety shaped by that theology, by imposing their own categories and their own approach changed our understanding of the liturgy and our experience of it.[10]

Since this organic connection between world, Church, and kingdom 'still exists liturgically', it is within the liturgy above all that

> the Church is *informed* of her cosmical and eschatological vocation, *receives* the power to fulfill it and thus truly *becomes* 'what she is'—the sacrament, in Christ, of the Kingdom. In this sense the liturgy is indeed 'means of grace' . . . in the all-embracing meaning as means of always making the Church what she is—a realm of grace, of communion with God, of new knowledge and new life. The liturgy of the Church is cosmical and eschatological because the Church is cosmical and eschatological; but the Church would not have been cosmical and eschatological had she not been given, as the very source and constitution of her life and faith, the *experience*

---

[7] *Introduction to Liturgical Theology*, p. 32.
[8] ibid., p. 70.
[9] 'Liturgical Theology, Theology of Liturgy, and Liturgical Reform', p. 219.
[10] ibid., pp. 219–20.

of the new creation, the experience and *vision* of the Kingdom which is to come. And this is precisely the 'leitourgia' of the Church's cult, the function which makes it the source and indeed the very *possibility* of theology.[11]

Because the Church's *lex orandi* is the Church's true *lex credendi*, the task of theology is merely to explicate, explain, and defend this liturgically received vision and experience. Although Schmemann nowhere says this, he seems to imply that theology —if not a 'reduction' to liturgy—is, nevertheless, synonymous with catechesis or mystagogy, that is, an explanation of the vision and experience mediated in and by the liturgy.

Thus, one does not seek a 'reform' of the liturgy. Rather, the liturgy is allowed to remain as it is, while the critical task of the theologian is to articulate and make clear the unchanging apostolic theological principle of the *Ordo* contained and expressed therein. Schmemann's theological model, therefore, is much closer to preaching than it is to lecturing, more at home in the patristic pulpit than in the medieval or modern theological academy.

Schmemann's overall concern, of course, was more with theology itself than it was with liturgy. What he sought was the reintegration of liturgy, theology, and piety within his own Eastern Orthodox tradition, a tradition in which he saw theology as having become captive to (Western) scholastic categories cut-off from the living liturgical tradition, and in which the essential eschatological, cosmological, and ecclesiological vision and principle of the liturgical structure or *Ordo* had been obscured (from the time of Constantine onwards) in favour of an increasingly 'mysteriological piety'. Though well aware of the historic and current problems in Eastern liturgy, Schmemann saw the solution not in changing the liturgy, but in restoring both theology and piety to their original and organic connection with the *lex orandi* itself. What needed changing was not the liturgy, but a theology and piety divorced from the unchanging (but often hidden) principle of the Church's fundamental and constitutive 'rule of prayer'. With those bent on reforming the Orthodox liturgy Schmemann claimed that

11 'Liturgy and Theology', p. 92.

no meaningful discussion . . . is possible because . . . any interest in precisely the *meaning* of the liturgy as a whole, of the 'lex orandi' in its relationship to 'lex credendi' is absent, because the liturgy is viewed as an end in itself and not as the 'epiphany' of the Church's faith, of her experience in Christ of herself, the World and the Kingdom.[12]

The way in which Prosper's principle is appropriated in the approach of Alexander Schmemann is clear. It is within the liturgy itself, at least within what Schmemann identified as the unchanging principle of the liturgy, that the Church's faith is revealed and expressed and so becomes the 'source' for theological reflection and discourse, even if that discourse is limited to the explanation, explication, and defence of that 'liturgical' vision.

This is a strong argument. Indeed, *lex orandi lex est credendi* reminds us that what the Church believes, teaches, and confesses will certainly be reflected and expressed within its worship. Consequently (and this is true not simply for Eastern Orthodoxy), if one wants to understand a particular religious tradition one must not only read its theological texts but experience and consciously study its worship, a fact which seems so obvious that it should make the study of liturgy a required part of every academic curriculum of theological or religious studies.

It is also true, however, that Schmemann's theological interpretation of the unchanging eschatological, cosmological, and ecclesiological principle of the *lex orandi* is precisely that, a *theological* interpretation. And, whether one agrees with this intepretation or not, the fact remains that this, ultimately, is Schmemann's own interpretation and vision of what the liturgy is, reveals, and what its role should be in theological reflection and discourse — a vision supported in large part[13] by the now outdated work of both C. W. Dugmore[14] on the normative character of Jewish synagogue worship for early Christian worship and Gregory Dix[15] on the so-called primitive and universal 'shape' of the liturgy and the post-Constantinian decline and

---

[12] 'Liturgical Theology, Theology of Liturgy, and Liturgical Reform', p. 222.

[13] See *Introduction to Liturgical Theology*, pp. 40–71.

[14] *The Influence of the Synagogue upon the Divine Office* (Oxford University Press 1944).

[15] *The Shape of the Liturgy* (Dacre Press, Westminster 1945).

shift from an eschatological to a historical focus. In other words, in spite of his own reluctance to offer a 'theology of liturgy', it is precisely a theology of liturgy that Schmemann provides, an elucidation of the 'correct' theological vision, norms, and principles which not only govern the liturgical celebration but function as the sources for theology itself.

If this is a correct reading of Schmemann's approach, then his hesitation to embrace a programme of reform of Orthodox liturgy does not appear as a logical corollary. To this Western Christian at least, it would seem that if Schmemann is right in noting that the underlying, unchanging, and fundamental principle of the *Ordo* has been so obscured by a scholastic theology and concomitant mysteriological piety such that it has changed not only the understanding but also the 'experience' of liturgy, then the recovery of this principle might indeed provide the basis of a liturgical reform which would allow the Church's true *lex orandi* to function in a clearer fashion as 'source' for both theology and piety. In other words, could it not be said that not only should the organic connection of theology and piety with liturgy be rediscovered, but that the liturgy itself should also be reformed today according to the true *lex orandi*, so that whatever gets in the way of and obscures this principle in the liturgical act itself is suppressed? Contrary to the romantic and popular myth of the unchanging Christian East, Eastern Christian liturgy has changed, can change, and is being changed today in various ways. Byzantine liturgical history teaches us that.[16] What Schmemann offers, however, in spite of his protests to the contrary, is a theological vision which might provide some substance and rationale for guiding such a programme of reform and renewal among those in the Christian East who find it desirable and necessary.

Geoffrey Wainwright: *lex orandi, lex credendi*

In the last two chapters of the second part of his now classic systematic theological study *Doxology*, Geoffrey Wainwright pre-

---

[16] See Robert Taft, 'How Liturgies Grow: The Evolution of the Byzantine Divine Liturgy', in idem, *Beyond East and West: Problems in Liturgical Understanding* (Pastoral Press, Washington DC 1984), pp. 167–92; and *The Byzantine Liturgy: A Short History* (Liturgical Press, Collegeville 1992).

sents both a critical study of the relation between *lex orandi* and *lex credendi* and a brief survey of the use of this formula in the history of doctrine. If *lex orandi lex 'est' credendi* is the key to Schmemann's approach, it is the absence of a verb altogether which characterizes Wainwright's appropriation and use of Prosper's principle. For Wainwright it is clear in this context that by *lex orandi* he means the liturgy primarily as liturgical 'text' or 'feast' and by *lex credendi* he means faith or believing primarily as 'doctrine' or 'dogma'. He says that

> the Latin tag *lex orandi, lex credendi* may be construed in two ways. The more usual way makes the rule of prayer a norm for belief: what is prayed indicates what may and must be believed. But from the grammatical point of view it is equally possible to reverse subject and predicate and so take the tag as meaning that the rule of faith is the norm for prayer: what must be believed governs what may and should be prayed.[17]

Wainwright notes further that in the history of Christian doctrine the *lex orandi* has played a more normative role within the Roman Catholic tradition than it has within Protestantism. While particular doctrines have certainly shaped liturgy and liturgical practices in various historical periods within Roman Catholicism,[18] it is particularly in Protestantism that the *lex credendi* has exercised almost absolute control over liturgical life:

> Roman Catholicism characteristically appeals to existing liturgical practice for proof in matters of doctrine. There *lex orandi, lex credendi* is most readily taken to make the (descriptive) pattern of prayer a (prescriptive) norm for belief, so that what is prayed indicates what may and must be believed. Protestantism characteristically emphasizes the primacy of doctrine over the liturgy. The phrase *lex orandi, lex credendi* is not well known among Protestants, but they would most easily take the dogmatic norm of belief as setting a rule for prayer, so that what must be believed governs what may and should be prayed.[19]

As an ecumenically minded and orientated Protestant theologian, however, Wainwright attempts to take seriously the

[17] *Doxology* (Epworth Press, London; Oxford University Press, New York 1980), p. 218.

[18] See ibid., pp. 259–63.

[19] ibid., p. 252.

historically authoritative character of the *lex orandi* in shaping doctrine. In support of this, at least in the patristic period, he draws attention to Ignatius of Antioch's equation of the Docetists' abstinence from the eucharist with a denial on their part of the reality of Christ's incarnation; Tertullian and Irenaeus invoking Christian sacramental practice against the Gnostic devaluation of matter; the arguments of Athanasius and Basil for the divinity of the Holy Spirit based on the baptismal formula against the Pneumatomachian denial of the Spirit's divinity; Basil of Caesarea's dispute with those same Pneumatomachians on the proper interpretation of both the uncoordinate and co-ordinate forms of the trinitarian doxology; the witness of liturgical practice supporting the clause 'with the Father and the Son he [i.e., the Holy Spirit] is worshipped and glorified' in the third article of the Creed of Nicea-Constantinople; and, among other possible examples from this period, Ambrose interpreting the interrogative form of the baptismal formula in use at Milan as teaching orthodox trinitarian doctrine.[20] In all of these cases it is the liturgy which has shaped doctrine, the *lex orandi* which has established the *lex credendi*, and not the other way around.

However, because Wainwright is concerned about 'worship getting out of hand'[21] and about the mutual and conjunctive interplay between worship and doctrine, he offers further both a particular definition of liturgy in relation to doctrine and a number of theological criteria or tests for determining whether or not a liturgically originated doctrine is consistent with that definition. 'Worship . . . is a source of doctrine', he writes, 'in so far as it is the place in which God makes himself known to humanity in a saving encounter. The human words and acts used in worship are a doctrinal locus in so far as either God makes them the vehicle of his self-communication or they are fitting responses to God's presence and action.'[22] And the criteria he suggests are three tests of origin, spread, and ethical correspondence. Each of these calls for additional comment.

---

[20] ibid., pp. 228–9, 232–4; 'The Praise of God in the Theological Reflection of the Church', *Interpretation* 39 (1985), p. 42.

[21] 'The Praise of God', p. 42.

[22] *Doxology*, pp. 242–3.

The test of origins

According to Wainwright, the more that ideas and practices can be traced back to Jesus himself, the more authoritative weight they are to be given. However, since this is extremely difficult —if not impossible—to determine, it is the post-Easter Church 'which must be credited with an authority of historical origination second only to Jesus himself'.[23] And since Jesus and this post-Easter Church have as their primitive witness the writings of the New Testament, the test of origins is whether a particular liturgical text or practice conforms to that of the primitive Church as it is reflected in the canonical New Testament. The canon of scripture, therefore, is the primary criterion to be applied in determing whether a given liturgical text or practice is authoritative for doctrine, and 'Protestants in dialogue with Catholics must not give up their insistence on the need for a scriptural test to be applied to Christian worship and doctrine, however difficult the application may be'.[24]

The test of spread in time and space

Conformity to scripture is not the only criterion for determining the authority of the *lex orandi*. 'Theology draws, too,' he writes, 'on the Tradition of the Church, in which certain elements or periods impress themselves as more authentic and hence serve as standards.'[25] By this he means that 'the closer a liturgical item comes to the universality of the vincentian *quod semper, quod ubique, quod ab omnibus*, the greater will be its importance as a doctrinal locus'. Indeed, 'it is hard to believe that any practice approaching universality in the Christian tradition should be so far removed from the divine truth as to lack suitability as a source of doctrine'.[26] Therefore, both scripture and the 'universal' Christian doctrinal tradition (i.e., primarily the golden age of the patristic writers and the great ecumenical councils of the fourth and fifth centuries) appear to function as criteria in a complementary fashion.

[23] ibid., p. 243.
[24] ibid., p. 242.
[25] 'The Praise of God', p. 44.
[26] *Doxology*, p. 243.

But having said this, Wainwright is quick to point out exceptions to the applicability of this Vincentian canon. While the practice of infant baptism, for example, may correspond to this canon, the fact that many have questioned its appropriateness throughout Christian history and others have even abandoned it altogether not only calls into question Augustine's use of it 'as "proof" for his doctrine of original sin' but also advocates the doctrinal significance of 'repentance, faith and personal commitment' to God in relation to baptism. Similarly, Wainwright sees further exceptions to this canon in that traditional Protestant rejections of both the sacrificial nature of the eucharist and the cult of the Virgin Mary seriously call into question the claim of their universal acceptance in the Church.[27]

It is within the Marian cult and the related Marian dogma of the Roman Catholic tradition, in particular, where Wainwright especially emphasizes the need for a necessary conjunctive linkage between *lex orandi* and *lex credendi*. As one example of this, the dogma of the immaculate conception of Mary can be considered. According to Wainwright, the argument of Pius IX in *Ineffabilis Deus* that the establishment of the feast and of propers for the Conception of the Virgin by previous popes constituted the *lex orandi* and was itself evidence for the dogma's traditional acceptance is actually 'a new *lex orandi* . . . seen by Pius to have been deliberately introduced by his papal predecessors in order to promote . . . a particular doctrine'.[28] It is at this point that Wainwright suggests that Protestants, accustomed as they are to the normative character of the *lex credendi* over the *lex orandi*, might well ask 'why the Roman magisterium did not curtail, rather than sanction and even encourage, popular devotion [to the Virgin Mary] when it took an aberrant turn'.[29]

To call such a process an 'aberrant turn', however, says more about Wainwright's own theological position than it does about the *lex orandi* principle itself. In fact, it makes one wonder whether Wainwright's use of the principle is not ultimately a specific apologetic for Protestant doctrine alone. That is, Wain-

27 ibid., p. 244.
28 ibid., p. 238.
29 ibid., p. 240.

wright allows the *lex orandi* to function as a source for the *lex credendi* only if it supports those dogmas with which he finds himself in doctrinal agreement. But a Roman Catholic historian of doctrine might surely respond by noting that (a) both popular and liturgical devotion to Mary is at least as old as the third- or fourth-century Greek prayer *Sub tuum praesidium*, which contains the phrase 'holy Mary, Mother of God'; (b) the earliest datable Marian feast—'Mary the Mother of God' on 15 August —is already included in the fifth-century Armenian Lectionary reflecting (presumably) the fourth-century Jerusalem liturgy; (c) the doctrinal title *Theotokos*, officially defined at Ephesus in 431, is shaped precisely by the popular liturgical practice which invoked her under that title; (d) Mary is commemorated in the *Communicantes* of the Roman eucharistic prayer from at least the fifth century; and (e) by the seventh century Rome had already instituted a feast of Mary on 1 January and adopted the earlier Eastern Marian feasts of 2 February, 25 March, 15 August, and 8 September.[30]

Whether a dogma of the immaculate conception of Mary can or should be deduced from the *lex orandi* is, of course, a debatable topic. But, in a general sense, the existence of a Marian *lex orandi* shaping a Marian *lex credendi* within the Christian tradition would certainly seem to fit the test of the Vincentian canon, at least within a universal patristic and pre-Reformation context in both the East and the West. Moreover, current ecumenical discussion of the principal Roman Catholic dogmas of Mary's immaculate conception and assumption may yet find a way to make possible an even more 'universal' acceptance of their theological intent. The Anglican theologian John Macquarrie writes:

> I believe that these two dogmas, when purged of mythological elements, can be interpreted as implications of more central Christian teaching. Theologically, of course, their significance does not lie in anything they say about the private biography of Mary but as pointing to moments in the life of the community of faith, for here . . . there is an intimate parallel between Mary and the Church.[31]

[30] See P. Jounel, 'The Veneration of Mary', in A.-G. Martimort (ed.), *The Church at Prayer*, vol 4 (Liturgical Press, Collegeville 1986), pp. 130ff.

[31] *Principles of Christian Theology*, 2nd edn (Charles Scribner's Sons, New York 1977), p. 397.

To cite but one example of these implications, Macquarrie suggests elsewhere that the dogma of the immaculate conception may in fact parallel the *sola gratia* principle of the Reformation tradition.[32] Even in the case of the ecumenical Church today, therefore, the *lex orandi*, in so far as it concerns the Marian cult, may yet serve as a source for shaping faith and doctrine in those issues which currently serve as dogmatic symbols of division.

The test of ethical correspondence

While recognizing that there is no clear one-to-one relationship between liturgy and ethics, Wainwright claims that 'a liturgical practice which is matched with some directness by holiness of life makes a weighty claim to be treated as source of doctrine; and any link that could be traced between a liturgical practice and moral turpitude would to that extent disqualify the liturgical practice as a source of doctrine'.[33] But this is a difficult test to apply to either liturgical practice or doctrine, and Wainwright does not offer any concrete examples. Liturgical acts that promote or serve merely to bless the *status quo* of political and economic systems, racism, or sexism might surely fall into this category. Yet, as he himself notes, 'in so far as the sacraments, or any form of worship, fail to produce appropriate fruit in the lives of the participants, the failure is due to a lack or refusal on the human side of the encounter with God'.[34] In other words, while a particular liturgical text, practice, or feast may be ethically inappropriate, generally speaking, unethical behaviour is more often the result of the (mis)appropriation, (mis)use, or (mis)understanding of the text, practice, or feast on the part of the worshipping community. Instead of a clear test to be applied to the liturgy in relation to doctrine in general, this criterion of ethical correspondence seems to be a call for an ongoing prophetic critique of the liturgy in order to draw out and underscore its ethical implications.

However, one might apply this test of ethical correspondence to what Wainwright cited above as the other Roman Catholic

---

[32] See *Mary for All Christians* (Eerdmans, Grand Rapids 1990), p. 75.

[33] *Doxology*, p. 245.

[34] ibid., p. 403.

example of a liturgical practice — generally lacking in Protestantism — from which doctrinal conclusions have been made: the sacrificial eucharist. In spite of his noting this as lacking universal acceptance, and so presumably failing the test of the Vincentian canon, the fact of the matter is this: although a sacrificial understanding of the eucharist may not be explicitly formulated in scripture (the first test), the history of Christian eucharistic celebration, anaphoral texts, and interpretation from the late first-century *Didache* up to (but not including) Luther's *Formula Missae* of 1523 certainly understands the eucharist in sacrificial terms and categories. If anything meets the problematic criterion of the Vincentian canon, at least up to the Reformation period, certainly a sacrificial understanding of the eucharist does. Again, therefore, Wainwright's overall Protestant theological orientation receives more weight than the *lex orandi* principle itself. Nevertheless, it is Wainwright himself who argues for the possibility of an ecumenical theological interpretation of eucharistic sacrifice:

> Could not the contentious notion 'we offer Christ' paradoxically be seen as antipelagian? It could be an acknowledgement that we have nothing else to offer. . . . To say 'we offer Christ' may then become a bold way of acknowledging the transforming presence and work of Christ within us. Again, paradoxically, it could thus be the very opposite of pelagianism.[35]

But does a sacrificial theory of the eucharist issue in a particular ethic or holiness of life? While a *do-ut-des* approach to religious ritual is always a danger, a community which is formed by such a sacrificial understanding may well perceive that its life of ministry and service in and to the world is to be one of sacrificial self-offering in union with Christ, into whose own pattern of self-offering, celebrated and actualized in the eucharist, they have been and are to be conformed. A sacrificial eucharist, therefore, may indeed meet Wainwright's criterion of ethical correspondence and so function, according to his own definition, as an authoritative source of dogma.

The use and appropriation of Prosper's principle in Wainwright's approach is also clear. But the role he assigns to the *lex*

[35] *Doxology*, pp. 272–3.

orandi in the development of doctrine is a very limited one. Although he calls for the mutual or conjunctive interplay of both *lex orandi* and *lex credendi*, it is clear that his overall preference is for the *lex credendi* as the dominant of the two principles. Even the above three tests or criteria are theological doctrinal tests, not specifically liturgical ones.[36] Like Schmemann, Wainwright's primary concern is with theology more than it is with liturgy. And, while he claims that reflective theology 'can and should draw on the experience of the church in worship for its reflection' rather than relegating such experience to 'practical theology', it is clear that this plays a secondary role to other theological tasks. That is, theology 'has the task of reflectively expounding the worship of the church in order to facilitate an intelligent participation in it', but its task also includes 'the responsibility, where necessary, of criticizing particular acts of worship and the formulations and practices of the liturgy'.[37] In other words, it might be said that what Wainwright ultimately offers is not a liturgical theology but a particular (Protestant) theology of liturgy or theological approach to the liturgy, in which it is not the *lex orandi* but the *lex credendi* that has the final authoritative say in the worship, doctrine, and life of the Church, even if all three of these are to have the doxological praise of God as their goal.

Aidan Kavanagh: *Ut legem credendi lex statuat supplicandi*

In distinction from both Schmemann and Wainwright, it is precisely Prosper's use of the third-person subjunctive form of the Latin verb *statuo* which serves as the methodological key in Aidan Kavanagh's approach to the relationship between liturgy and theology. In direct response to Wainwright, Kavanagh says that *lex orandi, lex credendi* can only become what Wainwright calls a Latin 'tag' in modern usage

> when the two laws are allowed to float free from each other by the removal of the verb which originally united them. That verb was *statuat*, as in *lex supplicandi legem statuat credendi*: The law of worshiping founds the law of

---

[36] On this, see David Power's review of Wainwright's *Doxology* in *Worship* 55 (1981), p. 64.

[37] Wainwright, 'The Praise of God', pp. 43–4.

believing. So long, I think, as the verb stays in the sentence it is not possible to reverse subject and predicate any more than one can reverse the members of the statement: the foundation supports the house. Having said that, one cannot really say that the house supports the foundation. . . . Similarly, I think, one cannot first say that the *lex orandi* or *supplicandi* founds or constitutes the *lex credendi*, and then add that, of course, the latter also founds and constitutes the former. The verb blocks this. The old maxim means what it says.[38]

It is this understanding of the constituting function of the *lex orandi* for the *lex credendi* which characterizes the major section of his recent book, *On Liturgical Theology*.[39]

Instead of looking at liturgy either as a 'text' (i.e., a *locus theologicus* for the drawing out of specific doctrinal conclusions) or as an *Ordo* in which the Church's faith and vision of reality make their 'epiphany' so as to be expounded theologically, Kavanagh is concerned with the foundational character for all theology of the liturgical *act* itself:

> If theology as a whole is critical reflection upon the communion between God and our race, the peculiarly graced representative and servant of the cosmic order created by God and restored in Christ, then scrutiny of the precise point at which this communion is most overtly deliberated upon and celebrated by us under God's judgment and in God's presence would seem to be crucial to the whole enterprise.[40]

According to Kavanagh, it is the liturgical act which founds the faith of the Church and makes theological reflection possible. This is because, in his opinion, believing is consequent to the constitutive function of the liturgical act:

> Belief is always consequent upon encounter with the Source of the grace of faith. Therefore Christians do not worship because they believe. They believe because the One in whose gift faith lies is regularly met in the act of communal worship—not because the assembly conjures up God, but because the initiative lies with the God who has promised to be there always. The *lex credendi* is thus subordinated to the *lex supplicandi* because both standards exist and function only within the worshipping assembly's own subordination of itself to its ever-present Judge, Savior, and unifying Spirit.[41]

[38] 'Response: Primary Theology and Liturgical Act', *Worship* 57 (1983), p. 324.

[39] Pueblo, New York 1984. See especially pp. 73–150.

[40] ibid., p. 78.

[41] ibid., pp. 91–2.

And what occurs in a liturgical act, in this encounter with the One regularly met in the act of communal worship, is the beginning of a continual Hegelian dialectic of thesis, antithesis, and synthesis worked out within the worshipping community. In a liturgical act a given community (thesis) is, in his words, 'brought to the brink of chaos', i.e., changed by this liturgical encounter with God in word and sacrament (antithesis). It then goes away to 'reflectively adjust' to this change (synthesis) until the next liturgical encounter when the process begins all over again. 'It is the *adjustment* which is theological in all this,' he writes. 'I hold that it is theology being born, theology in the first instance. It was what tradition has called *theologia prima.*'[42]

The distinction between *theologia prima* and *theologia secunda* is, of course, an extremely important one for Kavanagh. If *theologia prima* is 'theology being born' in the worshipping community's reflective adjustment to its experience of and encounter with God in the liturgical act, *theologia secunda* is second order (systematic) theological study done by the professionally trained academic theologian, even within that subdiscipline called 'liturgical theology'. It is the primacy of this *theologia prima* that Kavanagh advocates in and for the overall theological task. For, according to him,

> the liturgical dialectic of encounter, change, and adjustment to change amounts to a reflective *and* lived theology which is native to all the members of the faithful assembly. This is *theologia* which is constant, regular, and inevitable as these people encounter God in worship and adjust to the changes God visits upon them. The liturgical assembly is thus a theological corporation and each of its members a theologian. . . . Mrs. Murphy and her pastor are primary theologians whose discourse in faith is carried on . . . in the vastly complex vocabulary of experiences had, prayers said, sights seen, smells smelled, words said and heard and responded to, emotions controlled and released, sins committed and repented, children born and loved ones buried, and in many other ways. . . . [Their] vocabulary is not precise, concise, or scientific. It is symbolic, aesthetic, and sapiential. . . . Nowhere else can that primary body of perceived data be read so well as in the living tradition of Christian worship.[43]

It is thus this encounter between God and the world, an encounter enacted in the rite of the liturgical assembly, about

---

42 ibid., pp. 74, 76.
43 ibid., pp. 146–7.

which *theologia secunda* 'forms propositions'.[44] From this primary theological act of liturgy 'other acts of secondary theology take their rise within that life of right worship (*orthodoxia*) we call the liturgical assembly, the community of faith, the Church'.[45] *Lex orandi*, therefore, constitutes, establishes, or founds *lex credendi*. Prosper's principle cannot be accurately construed in any other way.

Because it is the liturgical act and experience of the assembly which is primary, it is from the critical reflective adjustment to this act and experience that, in Kavanagh's opinion, the Church develops its canonical norms. These are: (1) the canon of holy scripture, which regulates what should be read and heard, and thereby 'keeps the assembly locked into the fundamental relationship that gives it is unique character . . . , namely, its relationship to the presence in its midst of the living God'; (2) the canon of baptismal faith, that is, the trinitarian-baptismal creeds, which 'distill the substance of revealed Gospel into baptismal form' and so 'keep the assembly's worship firmly rooted in relationship to a divine Presence which is . . . communitarian and personal'; (3) the canon of eucharistic faith, contained in the eucharistic prayers, which 'distill the substance of revealed Gospel and its baptismal creeds into strictly euchological forms of thanksgiving and petition within the corporate person of him whose Gospel is in motion for the life of the world'; and (4) the collection of canon laws, 'which regulate the daily living and the due processes of assemblies of Christians in conformity with the foregoing canons of scripture, creed, and prayer'.[46] These various canons are not the result of *theologia secunda*, not the result of an imposed or legislated doctrinal control from the outside, but the fundamental way in which the liturgical assembly as a social group comes to govern its liturgy and its life so that the liturgical encounter with the Source of the grace of faith remains, indeed, primary for its faith and life.

As is the case with both Schmemann and Wainwright, Kavanagh's use and appropriation of Prosper's principle is quite

[44] ibid., p. 145.
[45] ibid., p. 96.
[46] ibid., pp. 141–2.

clear. His firm insistence on the use of the proper verb, however, makes it serve a quite different function than it does in either Schmemann or Wainwright. If both of them are primarily concerned with theology, Kavanagh's overriding concern is with liturgy. Thus he attempts to present what might truly be called a *liturgical* theology. By focusing not on liturgical 'text' or 'principles' but on the foundational character of the liturgical act itself, Kavanagh has provided a great service for liturgiologists and theologians alike. It is the liturgical act which must be studied and analysed—by whatever methodological disciplines —because it is the first and ongoing act and experience by which Christians encounter the gospel in their midst. The primacy of the liturgical act, event, and experience therefore must be kept primary, and theological attention must be given to the symbolic, mythical, and ritual language of this event, as this is the primary 'theological' language of the liturgical community's 'experience'.

Kavanagh's approach, however, is not without its problems. The first of these may be called the lack of evaluative criteria. As Geoffrey Wainwright notes in a review of Kavanagh's book,

> it needs to be asked, by what criteria a particular pattern or act of worship is to be discerned as truly Christian. How do we know that when 'something vastly mysterious' transpires (p. 76), it is an effect of the Holy Trinity? How do we know that an 'experience of near chaos' (pp. 73–75) is a tryst with the God of Jesus Christ? How do we know that 'the flow of liturgical worship,' 'like the current of a mighty river' (p. 87), is in fact borne along by the Holy Spirit?[47]

In other words, the ongoing dialogue between 'Mrs. Murphy and her pastor' may well be an imprecise, unconcise, and non-scientific *theologia prima* conversation formed by years of experiencing a variety of liturgical acts and events, but there would seem to be a need for some kind of criterion in determining whether or not either of them has adequately and accurately perceived the meaning of those acts. Is there not at least the possibility in their conversation not only of different interpretations but of 'wrong' interpretations (held and expressed by either one), shaped not by *the* gospel but by some other gospel, value,

[47] *Worship* 61 (1987), pp. 183–4.

or religious orientation? After all, both Mrs Murphy and her pastor could be imprecise, unconcise, and non-scientific heretics.

A second, but closely related, problem is this. Although the liturgical act and experience may always be primary in shaping the faith of the community, has there ever been a liturgical act, since the Last Supper itself, which has not also been the result of, and hence shaped by, what Kavanagh calls *theologia secunda*? Indeed, the very liturgical act and canons by which the assembly seeks to govern its worship and life are also the result, at least in part, of second-order theological reflection on the part of the teaching authority in the Church. While it may be that the liturgical experience of the community is what gives birth to the various forms of liturgy and its canonical norms in its continual reflective adjustment to the encounter with God in the first place, the history of liturgy demonstrates that the liturgy itself, and hence the content of a particular liturgical *act*, which certainly includes the *texts* read and performed, is also shaped and 'constituted' by secondary theology. Thus, the distinction between *theologia prima* and *secunda*, writes the Anglican liturgiologist Paul Bradshaw,

> can be used only with caution. While it may be true that liturgical rites may on occasion manifest the immediate and intuitive turning of human beings toward God, and so may offer a different perspective from that of the academic theologian, yet equally both in the past and in the present liturgical texts and rubrics are often themselves the products of *theologia secunda*, compositions deliberately intended to reflect some previously articulated doctrinal position.[48]

Finally, focusing on the liturgical act and experience as the saving encounter with the Source of the grace of faith and claiming that Christians 'believe because the One in whose gift faith lies is regularly met in the act of communal worship' runs the risk of isolating and absolutizing the liturgical act in relation to other possible encounters with this One who is the Source. Kavanagh does not mean, of course, that the liturgy 'produces' faith or that the liturgy is some kind of Pelagian guarantee that those worshipping will automatically receive faith. Rather, it is

[48] 'The Reshaping of Liturgical Studies', *Anglican Theological Review* 72 (1990), p. 482.

the Church's *lex supplicandi* which nourishes, strengthens, clarifies, and perhaps brings to expression a developing faith.[49] Nevertheless, the danger of this kind of language may be, ultimately, to bind the proclamation and hearing of the Word to its liturgical forms. And, for that matter, if it is *not* the liturgical act which Kavanagh intends as primary for both faith and theology, then it becomes very difficult to understand how the liturgical act can be *theologia prima* at all. Thus, one is led to ask whether there is not something else which is even more primary than this liturgical act, some kind of *lex credendi* perhaps which comes to expression in, is continually nourished by, but, nevertheless, in some fundamental primordial way 'constitutes' the *lex orandi*? And might not this 'something else' be the living address of the Word of God spoken and responded to in faith, which is indeed present in, experienced by, and celebrated in the liturgical act, but in no way bound to that act but bound instead to the Spirit of God?

Conclusion

Vatican II's Constitution on the Sacred Liturgy says that the liturgy is both 'fount' or source and 'summit' of the Church's life. That there exists in general an intimate relationship between liturgy and theology, that the prayer of the Church is related to its faith and doctrine, and that what the Church does in liturgy shapes what it believes all seem self-evident. But beyond this general statement that liturgy and theology are companions, the precise nature of that relationship is allusive and obscure. The meaning of that relationship, as the above survey of our three liturgical theologians has demonstrated, depends more on the particular interpretation and weight given to it in an individual theologian's approach. Consequently, the three variations of the *lex orandi* principle tell us more about the particular theologies of Schmemann, Wainwright, and Kavanagh than they do about whatever meaning and weight Prosper of Aquitaine may have originally intended by the enunciation of this principle.

Nevertheless, it is fair to ask which (if any) of them is the closest to the usage of Prosper himself. In this regard, Kavanagh says that

[49] *On Liturgical Theology*, p. 99.

> *Lex supplicandi* is something much more specific than the broad and fuzzy notion of the 'practice of the Church'. . . . It is a law of supplicatory prayer —not prayer or worship in general, but of prayer which petitions God for the whole range of human needs in specific, a law of euchological petition. This is the nub of the reason why the *lex supplicandi* founds and constitutes the *lex credendi* and is therefore primary for Christian theology. The way Christians believe is, somehow, constituted and supported by how Christians petition God for their human needs in worship.[50]

But is this what Prosper actually implies? As noted at the beginning of this essay, Prosper's use of this principle is another argument against Semi-Pelagianism made by him *in addition to* one based on the 'inviolable decrees of the blessed apostolic see'. Furthermore, it seems quite clear that what gives the *lex orandi* any authority whatsoever in this context is that: (1) this 'sacred testimony of priestly intercessions' has been, in Prosper's opinion, 'transmitted from the apostles' themselves; and (2) it is 'uniformly celebrated throughout the world and in every catholic church'. Since this is the case, the *lex supplicandi* also can be said to 'constitute' the *lex credendi*, not in isolation but because it conforms to the traditional and biblical *doctrinal* teaching of the Church. In other words, Prosper's argument is a doctrinal one which uses liturgical evidence in addition to other factors because that liturgical evidence is consistent with those other sources.[51] It would be extremely difficult not to see the parallel here with Wainwright's criteria of both the canon of scripture and conformity to the *quod semper, quod ubique, and quod ab omnibus* of Vincent of Lerins. Indeed, both Prosper and Wainwright are concerned principally with orthodoxy (understood correctly not as 'right worship' but as 'right belief'[52]). In spite of the absence of a verb, therefore, it is the overall *approach* of

[50] *On Liturgical Theology*, p. 134.

[51] On the original doctrinal use and meaning of this phrase in Prosper of Aquitaine, see the important essay by Paul de Clerk, ' "Lex orandi – Lex credendi". Sens origenel et avatars historique d'un adage équivoque', *Questions liturgiques* 59 (1978), pp. 193–212; English translation by Thomas Winger forthcoming in *Studia Liturgica* 24 (1994).

[52] In spite of recent popular attempts to argue the contrary, 'orthodoxy' means 'right belief'. It does not come from *orthodoxologia*, 'right worship' or 'right glory', but from *orthodoxeo*. See G. W. H. Lampe, *A Patristic Greek Lexicon* (Clarendon Press, Oxford 1965), p. 971. It is thus a doctrinal, not a liturgical-doxological word.

Wainwright which most closely approximates that of Prosper himself.

This does not, however, make Wainwright's Protestant doctrinal conclusions or his implied insistence on the supremacy of the *lex credendi* over the *lex orandi* correct. After all, liturgy does shape, found, or constitute the faith, believing, and doctrinal teaching of the Church. It did not do this only in the so-called golden age of the fourth- and fifth-century patristic period, but it has done so throughout history and continues to do so today, especially in a contemporary context of ecumenical liturgical renewal and reform. Nevertheless, both principles must be allowed to function complementarily in the pursuit and articulation of doctrinal truth. While Wainwright certainly intends this to happen, his focus on the superiority of the *lex credendi* over the *lex orandi* actually inhibits their complementarity in favour of a particular theological and doctrinal orientation to which the *lex orandi* must conform, just as Kavanagh's insistence on the constituting superiority of the *lex orandi* does the same in an opposite manner and Schmemann's equation of the two actually, if not intentionally, reduces theology to a doctrinal explication and defence of an irreformable liturgy.

The Jesuit theologian Edward Kilmartin, concerned like Wainwright with the relation between liturgy and doctrine, offers a much more balanced approach to this question, an approach which holds *lex orandi* in dialectic tension with *lex credendi*. According to Kilmartin, to focus on either the *lex orandi* or the *lex credendi* to the exclusion of the other threatens to obscure the unique value of two different kinds of expression of faith:

> The slogan 'law of prayer—law of belief' leaves in suspense which magnitude might be the subject, and which the predicate, in particular instances. Consequently, it seems legitimate to state the axiom in this way: *the law of prayer is the law of belief, and vice versa.* . . . On the one hand, the law of prayer implies a comprehensive, and, in some measure a pre-reflective, perception of the life of faith. On the other hand, the law of belief must be introduced because the question of the value of a particular liturgical tradition requires the employment of theoretical discourse. One must reckon with the limits of the liturgy as lived practice of the faith. History has taught us that forms of liturgical prayer and ritual activity, however orthodox, often had to be dropped or changed to avoid heretical misunder-

standing. Moreover, in new historical and cultural situations, the question of the correspondence between the community's understanding of Christian truth, and its expression in the liturgy and that of the authentic whole tradition, must continually be placed. To respond responsibly to this problem, other sources of theology must be introduced along with the liturgical-practical grounding of the knowledge of faith.[53]

All three variations of the one principle of Prosper of Aquitaine summarized in this essay find their echo in Kilmartin's synthetic statement. The law of praying *is* the law of believing (Schmemann) and the law of praying *constitutes* the law of believing, providing a kind of *theologia prima*, 'prereflective perception of the life of faith' (Kavanagh). But, just as importantly, the law of believing cannot be allowed to function in isolation from other legitimate theological principles without distorting the theological quest for and articulation of truth (Wainwright). Therefore, whether any verb, even Prosper's own verb of choice, is used or not in particular formulations of the *lex orandi* principle, both the *lex orandi* and the *lex credendi* must and do function together in the development of doctrine and in the theological reflection, discourse, and self-interpretation of the Church catholic.

[53] *Christian Liturgy I. Theology* (Sheed & Ward, Kansas City 1988), p. 97.